JACOBITES

of
LOWLAND SCOTLAND
ENGLAND, IRELAND, FRANCE
and SPAIN

1745

Frances McDonnell

CLEARFIELD

Copyright © 2000 by Frances McDonnell
All Rights Reserved.

Printed for
Clearfield Company, Inc. by
Genealogical Publishing Co., Inc.
Baltimore, Maryland
2000

International Standard Book Number: 0-8063-4999-9

Made in the United States of America

INTRODUCTION

The reign of the House of Stuart came to an end in 1689 when the unpopular, pro-Catholic monarch James VII of Scotland, II of England, fled from London to France. In exile in Rome and Paris, adherents to the cause of restoration, known as Jacobites, worked to recover for the Stuarts the two thrones. Before the 1745 rebellion there were two previous, unsuccessful attempts by the House of Stuart to regain the throne of Great Britain, in 1715 and 1719. Bonnie Prince Charlie's equally unsuccessful bid was the third and last occasion an attempt was made to wrest the throne from the House of Hanover.

The rebellion of 1745 is almost always referred to as if a particularly Highland affair. While the emphasis of interest has concentrated on the Highland Jacobites, there was a significant minority from south of the Highland line. These included men from the Scottish Lowlands, northern England, Ireland, France and a few from Spain. This book identifies these men whose contribution has been generally overlooked.

In the Scottish Lowlands, there remained a lingering sympathy for the House of Stuart. Records show that the majority of Lowland recruits came from the capital and its surrounds, forming Roy Stuarts Edinburgh Regiment.

The Manchester Regiment comprised men recruited from the north of England. It marched from Manchester to Derby, and back to Carlisle, where it formed part of the unfortunate garrison which surrendered to Cumberland. The men of the Regiment were then subjected to a particularly bloody Hanovarian revenge. Nearly all the officers and sergeants were hanged and the others transported to the American Colonies. Its career was brief, and against the optimistic expectations of the campaign's leaders, it was the sole military contribution of England to the Jacobite cause.

The support offered by the Catholic French Court to the Jacobite cause came about through a traditional rivalry between England and France, and a leaning towards the co-religionist House of Stuart. In effect, very few French military units actually landed on Scottish soil, most being captured at sea. These units in the pay of France included a substantial number of volunteers from Irish and Scottish Regiments. After capture, those of French origin were treated as prisoners of war and for the most part sent back to France.

Frances McDonnell
St Andrews, 2000

Jacobites of Lowland Scotland, England, Ireland, France and Spain

1745

References

CQS	Cumberland Quarter Sessions
JAB	Jacobites of Aberdeen and Banff
MR	Muster Roll of Prince Charles Edward Stuart's Army
NAS.GD	National Archives of Scotland: Gifts and Deposits
PRO.SP	Public Record Office: State Papers
PRO.CO	Public Record Office: Colonial Office
PRO.T1	Public Record Office: Treasury
RH	Register House
SHS	Scottish History Society, Prisoners of the '45.
SRO.GD	Scottish Record Office: Gifts and Deposits
SRO.JC	Scottish Record Office: Justiciary Court
SRO.RH	Scottish Record Office: Register House
SRO.CH	Scottish Record Office: Church Records

JACOBITES OF LOWLAND SCOTLAND ENGLAND, IRELAND, FRANCE and SPAIN

1745

ABBOT, JOSEPH, conveyed from Penrith to Brough, Westmoreland in the company of 19 other Jacobites. *CQS.354.*

ABBOT, ROBERT, conveyed from Penrith to Brough, Westmoreland in the company of 19 other Jacobites. *CQS.354.*

ACARD, PIERRE, French Service. From France. Taken at sea, imprisoned Berwick on Tweed. Discharged. *SHS.2.4.*

ADAM or ADAMS, ROBERT, labourer from Stirling, aged 18, captured at Carlisle and imprisoned there and in York Castle. Transported 24 March 1747 or 5 May 1747 from Liverpool to Leeward Islands in *Veteran*, arriving Martinique June 1747, captured at Carlisle. *SHS.2.4, PRO.SP36.102.*

AIKMAN, JOHN, porter from Leith, Midlothian. Assisted in rifling the Old Stage Coach lofts of their horses provisions

provisions and carried them to the rebels whom he likeways assisted in driving their waggons, etc. Now about Leith. Evidence from John Balfour in Leith, stage coach master. *SHS.8.244, SHS.8.340.*

AITKEN, WILLIAM, aged 20, impost waiter from Edinburgh, Midlothian. Accompanied Lord Elcho as his servant in the rebellion. Tansported 24 February 1747 from Liverpool to Virginia in *Gildart,* arriving Port North Potomac, Maryland, 5 August 1747. *PRO.T1.328, MR50, SHS.7, SHS.8.244, SHS.8.260.*

AITKENHEAD, JOHN, younger of Jaw, Slamanan parish, Stirling. Carried arms in the rebel Life Guards and was active in robbing the country of horses. Now lurking. *SHS.8.264.*

AITKIN, WILLIAM, servant to Lord Elcho, from Fife. Accompanied his said master in the Rebellion. Whereabouts not known. *SHS.8.260.*

AITON, ANDREW, resident of Crail, Fife. Joined the rebels before Preston battle and carried arms. Was in the rebellion 1715. Said to be dead. *SHS.8.62.*

AITON, WILLIAM, resident of Crail, Fife. Enticed out the above Andrew, his brother, furnished him, Earl of Kelly etc with arms and spoke disrespectfully of his Majesty. At home. Evidence from John Black and Thomas Taylor, shoemakers in Crail. *SHS.8.62, SHS.8.352.*

ALCHEARE, PIERRE, Bulkeley's French Service. Taken at sea 30 November 1745, imprisoned Berwick, Hull February 1746. Discharged. *SHS.2.6.*

ALEXANDER, WILLIAM, from Glasgow. Roy Stuart's (Edinburgh) Regiment. Imprisoned Dalkeith 3 October

1745, Edinburgh Castle, Edinburgh 15 January 1746, Carlisle 8 August 1746. "A common Highlander." No further reference to him. He does not appear on the transportation lists. *SHS.2.7, MR206.*

ALLAN, ALEXANDER, aged 24, shoemaker from Edinburgh. Duke of Perth's Regiment. Imprisoned 22 November 1745 Dalkeith, 22 November 1745, Edinburgh Tolbooth 8 August 1746, Carlisle. Transported 24 February 1747. *SHS.2.6, MR69.*

ALLAN, CHARLES, aged 19, cooper's servant from Leith. Son of Hary Allan in Leith. Donald Macleod reported that he had behaved exceedingly well in his distress when on board ship, although he was himself ill. He is said to have "worn a white cockade." Mons. Carpentier tried to claim him as a soldier of the French Royal Scots. Evidence from Henry Morison, William Gibson, George Calder and James Boyle, Excise Officers. *SHS.8.340, SHS.2.8.*

ALLAN, JAMES, merchant from Edinburgh, Midlothian. Carried arms in the pretender's son's Life Guards. Whereabouts not known. Evidence from George Porteous, Excise Officer. *SHS.8.244, SHS.8.338.*

ALLAN, JOHN, wright and glazier, Alloa. Joined the rebels about the time of Preston battle, was made Sergeant of Artillary and continued with them till dispersed. Whereabouts not known. *SHS.8.146.*

ALLAN, JOHN, aged 19, labourer, Manchester Regiment. He gave evidence against the officers of his regiment at their trial. Transported 1747. *MR.196.*

ALLAN, JOHN, wright from Alloa. Evidence from Anthony Newby excise officer at Stirling and William and James Davidson, elders in Alloa. *SHS.8.348.*

ALLEN, CHARLES, aged 19, from Leith. Cooper's servant, son of Harry Allen. Bore arms, wore a white cockade and went into England with the rebels. *BMHS.30.74, SHS.8.244.*

ALLEN, WILLIAM, glover from Leith. Grant's Regiment. Imprisoned 20 December 1745 Carlisle. Taken at Capture of Carlisle. No further reference to him. *SHS.2.10.*

ALVES or ALVIS, ANDREW, apprentice writer from Edinburgh. Imprisoned Edinburgh 16 September 1745, Edinburgh Tolbooth. Released under General Pardon, 1747. Committed on 16 September 1745, being the day before the rebels entered Edinburgh, for having that day brought a messge to Archibald Stewart, then Provost of Edinburgh, from the person called the Duke of Perth, then with the rebel army, importing threatenings against the town in case of refusing entrance to the rebels. The prisoner says he occasionally met with the rebels in their way from Linlithgow to Edinburgh, and thought it was his duty to relate to the Lord Provost what had been told him. The Hon James Leslie was present when the above message was delivered, and heard Alves acknowledge that he had also seen the Pretender's son. *SHS.2.10.*

ANANDALE, JOHN, shoemaker from Arbroath, Forfar. Carried arms as a volunteer in the rebel army. Whereabouts not known. *SHS.8.244.*

ANCRUM, JAMES, from Bo'Ness, Linlithgowshire. Salt overseer to the Duke of Hamilton at Bonhard pans. On suspicion. It was said that he "assisted in taking and carrying off two Dragoon horses out of Kinneil Park for the Rebels use." Tried at Carlisle, he was found guilty and sentenced to death but was reprieved and sentenced to be transported, but died in prison November 1748. Imprisoned in Blackness Castle, Canongate 7 August 1746, Carlisle August 1746, Lancaster and Liverpool. *SHS.2.10, SHS.8.264, SHS.8.381.*

ANDERSON, GEORGE, junior, tanner from Haddington. Joined the rebels when they went from England, got a Captain's commission, and was with them till the end. Killed or lurking. *SHS.8.132.*

ANDERSON, JOHN, Bulkeley's French Service. Taken at sea 30 November 1745, imprisoned Berwick, Hull February 1746. Discharged. *SHS.2.12.*

ANDERSON, JOHN, journeyman sadler from Haddington. Voluntarily joined the rebels when they went to England. Whereabouts not known. *SHS.8.132.*

ANDERSON, JOHN, wright from Seton, joined the rebel army after Preston and continued with them till after Culloden battle. Fled this country. *SHS.8.132.*

ANDERSON, ROBERT, younger of Whitburgh, Haddington. Was one of the rebel gentleman Quartermasters, joined them before Preston battle and conducted them to attack the King's army there the night before the battle, and continued with them all along till dispersed. Now lurking in the country. *SHS.8.132.*

ANDERSON, ROBERT, brewer from Carnock, St Ninians parish, Stirlingshire. Wore a white Cockade and carried arms in the service of the rebels and assisted in robbing the country. At home. Evidence from Alexander Bow and George McVie, smiths in Carnock and Patrick Robertson, merchant in Elphingston. *SHS.8.54, SHS.8.316.*

ANDERSON, ROBERT, Stirling. May have been the Stirling brewer who "wore a white cockade and carried arms," or Robert Anderson, younger of Whitburgh, one of the "general quartermasters." Imprisoned in Newgate 7 May 1747, his disposal is unknown. *SHS.2.12.*

ANDREW, JOHN, Manchester Regiment. From Lancashire. Died? *MR.196.*

ANGUS, ROBERT, salt watchman from West Pans, Haddington. Acted as salt officer and uplifted the salt duty for behoof of the rebels. Continues a watchman. *SHS.8.132.*

ANTONIO, DON BENITO, Spanish Service. Imprisoned at sea in *Prince Charles*, Berwick on Tweed. Discharged. *SHS.2.14.*

ARBUTHNOT, Sir JOHN, Captain, Lord John Drummond's French Royal Scots Cavalry. Banker in Paris, French officer. Sir John Arbuthnot was the son of Robert Arbuthnot and newphew of the celebrated Court physician Dr John Arbuthnot, who was on the King's side at Killiecrankie and had to leave the country. He went to Rouen and became a merchant there and in Paris. His son John became a French Knight and was in the French army. Sir John was pardoned on condition of transportation. Imprisoned 30 December 1745 Carlisle, London. Taken at Carlisle. Pardoned on condition of transportation to America, February 1746. Transported 1747. *MR.61, SHS.2.14.*

ARMSTRONG, ANGUS, Ogilvy's Regiment, aged 24 from Nithsdale, tailor, Edinburgh. Imprisoned in Inverness and Tilbury Fort. Nothing further is known of him. *SHS.2.16.*

AUCHENLECK, ANDREW, of Cunnachie, Monymeal parish, Fife. Joined the rebels and carried arms from after the battle of Preston till dispersed. Was in 1715 rebellion. Whereabouts not known. *SHS.8.62.*

AULD, JOHN, aged 14 from Falkirk, Stirlingshire, drummer, Kilmarnock's Horse. "A boy of 14; confesses that he acted as a drummer to Kilmarnock's Horse, but was forced thereto by his stepfather." Imprisoned Stirling 23 April 1726, Edinburgh, Carlisle 8 August 1746. Transported 1747. *SHS.2.16, MR43.*

BAAD, WILLIAM, brewer and maltster from Letham, Airth parish, Stirlingshire. Assisted the rebels as a guide, carried their arms and secured boats for them to pass the Forth. At home. Evidence from James Rae, barber in Airth and Alexander Archibald, shoemaker there. *SHS.8.54, SHS.8.316.*

BAGGOT, JOHN, Major, commanded Murray of Broughton's Hussars. Imprisoned Culloden, Inverness, London. Pardoned on condition of banishment, 2 July 1747. A Franco-Irishman. He commanded the body of Hussars, 50 strong, raised in Edinburgh, of which Murray of Broughton was titular colonel. This unit was later called Baggot's Hussars. At Culloden he was wounded rather badly and was treated subsequently as a prisoner of war. *SHS.2.18.*

BAGGOT, MARK (or MATTHEW), Captain (Adjutant), Fitzjames' Horse, French Service. Taken at Culloden. Discharged. *MR38.*

BAGGOT, THOMAS, Captain, Fitzjames' French Service. Imprisoned Inverness, Marshalsea. Discharged. *SHS.2.18.*

BAGGOT, WILLIAM, Captain, Fitzjames's Horse, French Service. Taken at Culloden. Discharged. *MR38*.

BAGONE, HENRY, Clare's French Service. Taken at sea 28 November 1745, imprisoned Berwick February 1746, Hull. Discharged. *SHS.2.18*.

BAILLIE, ALEXANDER, Captain, Lord John Drummond's French Service. Captured at sea on *Esperance* 25 November 1745 on way to Montrose. Imprisoned Deal, HM Smack *Caroline* Grenwich 2 December 1746, Marshalsea. Pardoned on condition of perpetual banishment 2 July 1747. He was transferred to the custom house smack *Caroline*. *SHS.2.18*.

BAIN, DONALD, labourer from Dunrobin. Carried arms in the rebel army. Whereabouts not known. *SHS.8.244*.

BAIN McINTOSH, ROY. Evidence from John Chapman junr, Excise Officer and Ensign, Jonathan McKay of the Sutherland Militia. *SHS.8.342*.

BAIN, WILLIAM, innkeeper, Fountainbridge, St Cuthbert's Parish, Midlothian. Carried arms in the rebel army and was very active in oppressing the country by seizing horses, etc. Whereabouts not known. *SHS.8.244*.

BAIRD or BEARD, WILLIAM, Sergeant, aged 25, collier from Falkirk, imprisoned in Stirling 23 April 1746 and Carlisle 8 August 1746. "Coal hewer to Kilmarnock." He was tried at Carlisle 19-16 September 1746 and sentenced to death, though he claimed that he had surrendered under Cumberland's order. He was reprieved and ordered to be transported, but was pardoned on condition of enlisting. *SHS.2.20, SHS.8.264*.

BALD, JAMES, Manchester Regiment. Labourer aged 21 from Wigan. Imprisoned Carlisle, Lancaster Castle. "A papist." Nothing more is known of his disposal. *SHS.2.20, MR.196.*

BALDER, DONALD, French Picquets. Imprisoned Stirling Castle 16 December 1746. "Deserted from the rebel service." Discharged. *SHS.2.20, MR136.*

BALFOUR, ALEXANDER, farmer from Collinburgh, Kilconquar, Fife. Assisted the rebels and transported a card load of arms from Collinsburgh to Falkland for their use. Now at home. Evidence from Thomas Bogle, surgeon and Bessie Thom, spinster in Colinsburgh. *SHS.8.260, SHS.8.344.*

BALFOUR, HENRY, from Dunboag, Fife. Furnished one David Weems a rebel with a horse. At home. *SHS.8.62.*

BALFOUR, WILLIAM, surgeon from Aberdour, Fife. Joined the rebels and went into England with them. Whereabouts not known. *SHS.8.260.*

BALL, THOMAS, Manchester Regiment. From Lancashire. Taken at capture of Carlisle, 30 December 1745. No further reference to his disposal. Died? *MR.196, SHS.2.22.*

BALLEY, LOUIS, French Service. Taken at sea, imprisoned Berwick February 1746, Hull. *SHS.2.22.*

BANKS, ALEXANDER, weaver in Bonnington Mills, Leith, Midlothian. Carried arms as a volunteer in the rebel army. Whereabouts not known. *SHS.8.246.*

BAPTISTE or BATICE, JEAN, Berwick's French Service. Taken at sea, Berwick on Tweed. Discharged. *SHS.2.22.*

BARCLAY, ALEXANDER, bleacher from Blaeboe, Kemback parish, Fife. Carried arms in the service of the rebels and for them collected the revenue in Angus. In Cupar, Fife. *SHS.8.62.*

BARDGETT, EDWARD, conveyed from Penrith to Brough, Westmoreland in the company of 19 other Jacobites. *CQS.354.*

BARN, JAMES, a French officer, French Service. Imprisoned 1 February 1746, Stirling 13 February 1746. Discharged. This man was probably sent to Berwick before being exchanged as a prisoner of war. *SHS.2.24, MR135.*

BARNAVAL or BARNWELL, BASIL, Lieutenant, French Royal Scots. Imprisoned 23 April 1746, *Prince Charles* (late *Hazard*), HMS *Sheerness*, Berwick. Pardoned on condition of perpetual banishment 2 July 1747. *SHS.2.24, MR38.*

BARNAVAL or BARNWELL, JOHN, French Service. Imprisoned Marshalsea. *SHS.2.36.*

BARNAVALL, ... Lieutenant, Fitzjames Horse, French Service. Taken at sea 21 February 1746, *Charite*, imprisoned London. Pardoned on condition of perpetual banishment 2 July 1747. *SHS.2.24.*

BARNAVALL, GEORGE, Lieutenant, Berwick's French Service. Taken at sea *Louis XV,* 28 November 1745, Edinburgh Castle 26 December 1745, Berwick February 1746, Hull. Pardoned on condition of perpetual banishment 2 July 1747. *SHS.2.26.*

BARNAVALS or BARNWELL, EDWARD, Lieutenant, Berwick's French Service. Imprisoned 24 March 1746

Prince Charles (late *Hazard*), HMS *Sheerness*, Berwick. Pardoned on condition of perpetual banishment 2 July 1747. *SHS.2.26.*

BARNAVALS or BARNWELL, WILLIAM, Lieutenant, Berwick's French Service. Imprisoned 24 March 1746 *Prince Charles* (late *Hazard*), HMS *Sheerness*, Berwick. Pardoned on condition of perpetual banishment 2 July 1747. *SHS.2.26.*

BARNEVAL, ROBERT, French Service. Pardoned conditionally on going abroad permanently 20 October 1748. This is the only reference to this man that has been discovered. *SHS.2.26.*

BARNETT, GEORGE, Berwick's French Service. Imprisoned at sea 28 November 1745, Berwick February 1746, Hull. Discharged. *SHS.2.26.*

BARNIE, JOHN, servant to Earl of Kelly, Kelly House, Carnbee, Fife. Carried arms with the rebels as servant to his said master. Serving David Aitkin Tenent in Camela and parish of Carnbee. *SHS.8.62.*

BARRY, DAVID, Bulkeley's French Service. Imprisoned at sea 28 November 1745, Berwick February 1746, Hull. Discharged. *SHS.2.26.*

BARRY, LEWIS, Bulkeley's French Service. Taken at sea 28 November 1745, imprisoned Berwick, Hull. *SHS.2.28.*

BARRY, RICHARD, Bulkeley's French Service. Taken at sea 28 November 1745, imprisoned Berwick, Hull. *SHS.2.28.*

BARTLETT, JOHN, Manchester Regiment, cordwainer from Kellough, Co Down, Ireland. Imprisoned Carlisle; Chester Castle, York. Pleaded guilty at his trial 8

October, and was sentenced to death, but reprieved and pardoned conditionally on enlistment, 22 July 1748. *MR.196, SHS.2.28.*

BARTON, LEWIS, Manchester Regiment, from Lancashire. Taken at the capture of Carlisle 30 December 1745, also imprisoned Lancaster Castle. Tried at Carlisle 19 September 1746 but recommended to mercy by a jury. Tranported 1747. *MR.196, SHS.2.29.*

BARTON, THOMAS, Sergeant, Manchester Regiment, yeoman from Heskett, Cumberland. Imprisoned at Morpeth 30 July 1746, Morpeth, Carlisle. He was tried at Carlisle 19 September 1746. He was charged with "having carried letters from the rebels to the magistrates of Carlisle requiring the town to be surrendered." The letters were not produced, and the judges refused to accept parole evidence. Consequently he was acquitted. *SHS.2.28, MR196.*

BATEMAN, KATHERINE, Keppoch's Regiment. From Belfast. Imprisoned Carlisle, Chester Castle. Released. *SHS.2.30.*

BAXTER, DAVID, from Cupar, Fife, Duke of Perth's Regiment, imprisoned 1746 prison ship *Pamela*, Tilbury. Weaver in Murray of Niviland's factory in Crieff. *SHS.2.30.*

BAYNE, EDMUND, Englishman. Taken at capture of Carlisle 30 December 1745. Was tried at Carlisle 19 September 1746 and acquitted. *SHS.2.22.*

BAYNE, JOHN, servant to Murray of Broughton, Tweedale. Had a command in the rebel Hussars and was very active in seizing horses etc for their use. Now lurking about Edinburgh. Evidence from William Bennet, Excise

Officer and William Younger in Linton in Tweedale. Joined the rebels at the very beginning and has been most active in their service. *SHS.8.338, SHS.8.84.*

BEAN, PETER, Roy Stewart's (Edinburgh) Regiment. From Aberdeen. Taken at Carlisle. Died? *MR206.*

BEATT, DAVID, merchant from Leith, Midlothian. Carried arms in the Pretender's son's Life Guards. Whereabouts not known. Evidence from Henry Morison, William Gibson, George Calder and James Boyle, Excise Officers. *SHS.8.246, SHS.8.340.*

BECKETT, THOMAS, French Service. Taken at sea, imprisoned Berwick. Died in prison 1746. *SHS.2.28.*

BELL, JOSEPH, conveyed from Penrith to Brough, Westmoreland in the company of 19 other Jacobites. *CQS.354.*

BELL, PETER, Life Guards, from Glasgow. "Joined in the Rebel Life Guards at Glasgow on their retreat, influenced by his mother." Evidence from Matthew Wilson, maltman, and William Brownlee, innkeeper, both in Glasgow. *SHS.2.32, SHS.8.274, SHS.8.346.*

BELL, THOMAS, conveyed from Penrith to Brough, Westmoreland in the company of 19 other Jacobites. *CQS.354.*

BELL, WILLIAM, Manchester Regiment, aged 46, from Berwickshire. Imprisoned 30 December 1745 Carlisle, York Castle. Bookseller. Taken at capture of Carlisle. Transported 8 May 1747 to Antigua, or from Liverpool to Leeward Islands in *Veteran*, arriving Martinique June 1747. *SHS.2.32, PRO.SP36.102, MR.196.*

BENDLETON, JOHN, Manchester Regiment. Imprisoned Carlisle, Lancaster Castle. Does not appear to have been transported. May have died. *MR.196, SHS.2.34.*

BERRIE, JOHN, extraordinary salt watchman from Prestonpans. Acted as salt watchman for the rebels while in this country. Now at home. *SHS.8.132.*

BERRY, JOHN, from Hereford, servant to Mr Vaughan. Imprisoned Chester Castle, London. Discharged. "He was a soldier in Col Murray's, taken at Prestonpans." He gave evidence against several prisoners. *SHS.2.34.*

BERT, JACOB, Bulkeley's French Service. Taken at sea 28 November 1745, imprisoned Berwick, Hull. Discharged. *SHS.2.34.*

BERWICK or BERSWICK, JOHN, Lieutenant, Manchester Regiment. Linen draper from Manchester. Imprisoned 30 December 1745 Carlisle, London (Southward). Hanged Kennington Common 30 July 1746. Was known in the Prince's army as "the duke." Was captured at the surrender of Carlisle. Tried and sentenced to death 16 July 1746. *MR.195, SHS.1.147, SHS.2.34.*

BETAGH, WILLIAM, Major Fitzjames' Horse. Taken at sea 21 February 1746 *Bourbon*, imprisoned Berwick, London (Marshalsea). Pardoned on condition of perpetual banishment 2 July 1747. He appealed for release in February 1748. *SHS.2.34.*

BETTS, JOHN, Ensign, Manchester Regiment, from Lancashire. Imprisoned 30 December 1745 Carlisle, London, Clerkenwell Prison. Escaped July 1746. He appears to have escaped before or during his trial. *MR.195, SHS.2.34.*

BIBBY, HENRY, aged 22, Manchester Regiment. Weaver from Wigan. Taken at the capture of Carlisle 30 December 1745. Imprisoned in Carlisle and Lancaster Castle. Transported to Antigua 8 May 1747. *MR.196, SHS.2.34.*

BIGG, JAMES, Lord Lewis Gordon's Regiment. From Newark. Taken at the capture of Carlisle, 30 December 1745, and imprisoned Carlisle and Lincoln Castle. Died in captivity. *SHS.2.34.*

BINNING, WILLIAM, labourer from Newbottle, Midlothian, imprisoned 2 February 1746 Bristo, 5 February 1746 Edinburgh Tolbooth. Carrying baggage. Released under General Pardon 1747. *SHS.2.34.*

BIRMINGHAM, THOMAS, Lieutenant, Clare's French Service. Imprisoned 24 March 1746 *Prince Charles* (late *Hazard*), HMS *Sheerness*, Berwick, London. Pardoned on condition of perpetual banishment 2 July 1747. *SHS.2.36.*

BISSET, ROBERT, Lord Kilmarnock's Troop, brickmaker from Leith, Midlothian, imprisoned 2 May 1746 Perth, 10 August 1746 Canongate, Carlisle. May have been the Leith brickmaker who "joined the rebels at Dalkeith and carried arms" and was in Leith Prison. Nothing more is known about him. Evidence from Henry Morison, William Gibson, George Calder and James Boyle, Excise Officers. *SHS.2.36, SHS.8.340, SHS.8.246.*

BLACK, JAMES, from Edinburgh, imprisoned Perth 6 February 1746. On suspicion. Servant to James Stewart of Goodtrees. Arrested by order of Lord Albemarle. No evidence against him. Discharged on bail 8 May 1746. *SHS.2.36.*

BLACK, THOMAS, glazier from Mussleburgh. Was sergeant in the rebel artillary and with them during the whole rebellion. Killed or absconding. *SHS.8.132.*

BLAIR, LEWIS, from Edinburgh, imprisoned 29 April 1746 Dundee, discharged 12 August 1746. Falconer. "On suspicion of treason." *SHS.2.38.*

BLAW, CHARLES, son to Castlehill, Culross. Came over with Lord John Drummond and joined the rebels now at Stirling. Evidence from John Rolland and Robert Geddes, bailies in Culross and John Halkerston, town clerk there. Imprisoned 25 February 1746 Perth, 12 May 1746 Stirling, 20 March 1746-7 Edinburgh Castle. "2nd son to Castle Hill." His father John had been apprehended in June 1745 and imprisoned in England. Charles Blaw landed from France with Lord John Drummond's force at Montrose in the autumn of 1745 and joined the Prince in Stirling. He took part in the battle of Falkirk. He was shown as "a French prisoner" in the Jail return of Edinburgh. Discharged. It is probably this man's father who is referred to in the Mercury of 25 September 1745: "The same day (19 September), John Bleau of Castlehill, Esq, was committed to Newgate, after long examination, by the Marquis of Tweeddale, his Majesty's principal Secretary of State for the Kingdom of Scotland. *SHS.8.146, SHS.8.348, SHS.8.378, SHS.2.38, MR.62.*

BLEAU, or BLAW or BLAIR of Castle Hill, JOHN (sometimes styled GEORGE), aged 53 from Castlehill, Culross, Fife, imprisoned 5 June 1745 Canongate, 5 June 1745 Edinburgh Tolbooth, 18 June 1745 Sent to London, Newgate Prison. Along with Sir Hector Maclean he was apprenhended in Edinburgh by George Durie of Grange on 5 June 1745 on suspicion of intention to raise the highlands. He was put in Edinburgh Tolbooth on information by George Durie of Grange, by order of the

Lord Advocate, and was thence taken to London on 18 June. The reason for his apprehension was no doubt the fact that early in 1745 he had been sent over to France by the Duke of Perth to inform the Prince of the state of affairs in Scotland. When he got to London he was placed in irons in Newgate, and he remained without trial in prison for one and a half years, when he was released on bail on 28 February 1745. He was in London until 18 November and then returned to Scotland. His later life ended in a tragedy. On 4 September 1767 he murdered one William Cairs, was tried and hanged, probably on 30 October at Stirling. *SHS.2.38.*

BLONDEN, JOHN, Clare's French Service. Taken at sea 28 November 1745, imprisoned Berwick February 1746, Hull. *SHS.2.38.*

BLOOD, ANDREW, Captain, Manchester Regiment, from Yorkshire. Taken at capture of Carlisle. Imprisoned Carlisle 30 December 1945, and Southwark (London). Tried on 18 July and pleaded guilty and executed 30 July 1746 at Kennington Common. *MR.195, SHS.1.147, SHS.2.40.*

BOAK, JOHN, conveyed from Penrith to Brough, Westmoreland in the company of 19 other Jacobites. *CQS.354.*

BOCIK, JAMES, resident of St Andrews, Fife. Drank the Pretender's health and influenced John Dewar to engage in rebellion. At home. *SHS.8.62.*

BODIN, CHARLES, French Officer, Artillery, French Service. Imprisoned 17 April 1746 Inverness. Discharged. *SHS.2.40, MR135.*

BOES, JOSEPH, Lord John Drummond's Regiment, from Westmeath, Ireland. Imprisoned June 1746 Moidart, 4 April 1747 Glasgow, 4 March 1747 Edinburgh. Discharged. "In the French Picquets. Deserted from the rebels a few days before the battle of Culloden, and surrendered to Col Campbell in June 1746. Deserted in Edinburgh on way to Berwick. *SHS.2.40, MR137.*

BOES, WILLIAM, French Service "Ruthe's Regiment" from Westmeath, Ireland. Imprisoned June 1746 Moidart, 4 February 1747 Glasgow, 4 March 1747. Discharged 4 March 1747. "In the French Picquets. Deserted a few days before the battle of Culloden and surrendered to Col Campbell in June 1746. *SHS.2.40, MR137.*

BOLD, THOMAS, Manchester Regiment, aged 21, labourer from Wigan. Imprisoned Carlisle and Lancaster. Transported to Antigua 8 May 1747. *MR.196, SHS.2.40.*

BOLTON, THOMAS, Manchester Regiment. From Warrington. Taken after the capture of Carlisle, imprisoned 30 December 1745 Carlisle, Lancaster Castle. Died? *MR.196, SHS.2.40.*

BONAR or BONNER, WILLIAM, French Service. Captured on *Soleil,* imprisoned Marshalsea. Discharged. *SHS.2.40.*

BONCOEUR, JACQUES, Berwick's French Service. Imprisoned Berwick on Tweed. Discharged. *SHS.2.40.*

BONE, JOSEPH, French Service. Captured on *Soleil* 25 November 1745, imprisoned London (Marshalsea). Discharged. Taken at sea in the *Soleil* privateer. *SHS.2.40.*

BOOTH, WILLIAM, French Service. Pardoned conditionally on permanent banishment 3 July 1747. *SHS.2.42.*

BORNER, JACOB, Berwick's French Service. Imprisoned Berwick on Tweed. Discharged. *SHS.2.42.*

BOSTON, THOMAS, Pitsligo's Horse, from Preston. Imprisoned 30 December 1745, Carlisle. Taken at capture of Carlisle. No further reference to him. *SHS.2.42.*

BOSWALD, THOMAS, writer in Edinburgh, Midlothian. Carried arms in the Pretender's son's Life Guards. Whereabouts not known. *SHS.8.244.*

BOSWELL, DAVID, merchant from Dubbieside, Markinch, Fife. Joined the rebels and carried arms in Lord Pitsligo's Regiment. Now lurking. Evidence from James and William Wall Walker and David Goodsir, all in Leven. *SHS.8.260, SHS.8.344.*

BOUGLASS, ALEXANDER, miln wright from Haddington. Was with the rebels the most part of the time they were in this country, but deserted them when they went to England. Now at home. *SHS.8.132.*

BOULION, JOSEPH, French Officer. Imprisoned Inverness, London (Marshalsea). Discharged. *SHS.2.42, MR135.*

BOURE, JOHN, Duke of Perth's Regiment, tailor from Culross. Imprisoned 25 February 1746 Perth, 10 August 1746 Canongate, Carlisle. Discharged. There is no further reference to his disposal. *SHS.2.42.*

BOURGOGNE, PIERRE, Lally's French Service. Imprisoned 30 December 1745 Carlisle, Marshalsea. Discharged. Taken at fall of Carlisle. *SHS.2.42.*

BOUSTON, GEORGE, Manchester Regiment. "Taken in actual rebellion." There is no further reference to him. Died? *MR.196, SHS.2.42.*

BOWER, BARTHOLEMEW, precentor to the non jurant meeting, Haddington. Carried messages and commissions for the rebels and publicly insulted the well affected to the government. Now at home. *SHS.8.132.*

BOWER, JOHN, tailor from Glasgow, imprisoned Pathfoot 1 May 1746 and Stirling Castle. Transported 20 March 1747, or 24 February 1747 from Liverpool to Virginia in *Gildart*, arriving Port North Potomac, Maryland 5 August 1747. *SHS.2.44, PRO.T1.328.*

BOWIE, JOHN, journeyman tailor, Canongatehead, Edinburgh, Midlothian. Carried arms in the rebel army. Whereabouts not known. Evidence from Robert Ramsay, tailor in St Mary's Wind, Edinburgh. *SHS.8.244, SHS.8.338.*

BOY, JAN, Fitzjames' Horse, French Service. From France. Taken at Culloden. *MR38.*

BOYD, CHARLES, Mr, second son to Kilmarnock, Callander House, Linlithgow. Acted as Captain in the Pretender's son's Life Guards. Now lurking. *SHS.8.264.*

BOYD, GEORGE, servant to Charles Boyd, Callander House, Linlithgow, Lord Kilmarnock's Life Guards, imprisoned in Carlisle and York. Servant of Lord Kilmarnock for many years. Was tried at York, pleaded guilty, and was sentenced to death. He was reprieved conditionally on enlisting in Boscawen's Force 22 July 1748. *SHS.2.46, SHS.8.264, SHS.8.381.*

BOYER, ALEXANDER, from Ayrshire, servant in Dundee. Imprisoned in Inverness Aug 1746 and Tilbury Fort. There is no further reference to him. *SHS.2.46.*

BOYER, JOHN, jail in Whitehaven. *CQS.359.*

BOYSTONE, HENRY, tailor from Staffordshire. Imprisoned 1 February 1746 Stirling, 7 February 1746 Stirling. Released under General Pardon, 1747. *SHS.2.46.*

BRADEN, JOSEPH, French Artillery, Merchant from Philipsville, Flanders. Imprisoned 30 December 1745 Carlisle, Chester. Discharged. Taken at capture of town. *SHS.2.46.*

BRADLEY, PETER, Duke of Perth's Regiment. Aged 30, weaver from Monaghan, Ireland. Imprisoned Carlisle, Lancaster Castle. Transported 21 February 1747. *SHS.2.46.*

BRADSHAW, JAMES, Captain, Manchester Regiment, later of Elcho's Troop of Life Guards. Imprisoned 16 April 1746 Culloden, Inverness, London (Southwark). "Gentleman, otherwise Warehouseman, otherwise Chapman." In business in the check trade. Joined the Prince 29 November 1745, and was first appointed Captain of the Manchester Regiment, and thence, after a quarrel with Col Townley, was transferred to the Prince's Life Guards. He was taken prisoner after Culloden and suffered much from brutal ill-treatment, especially in the ship *Jane of Leith* which took many prisoners to London. He pleaded not guilty. Sentenced to death, July 1746, and executed 28 November 1746 at Kennington Common. *MR.195, SHS.2.46.*

BRADSHAW, WILLIAM, Ensign, Manchester Regiment. Taken at capture of Carlisle. Imprisoned 30 December

1745 Carlisle. There is no further reference to him. *MR.195, SHS.2.46.*

BRADY, MICHAEL, Sergeant, Manchester Regiment. Irish. Imprisoned at Stafford, York Castle. He deserted the regiment when it returned from Derby to Manchester. He was convicted at York on 2 October 1746 and sentenced to death. Executed in York, 8 November 1746. *MR.195, SHS.1.147, SHS.2.46.*

BRAITHWAITE, JAMES, Manchester Regiment. Saddler, from Penrith, Cumberland. Imprisoned Carlise and Newcastle. Was tried at Carlisle and acquitted. *MR.196, SHS.2.48.*

BRAND, JAMES, Major, Baggot's Hussars, aged 30, watchmaker from Canongate, Edinburgh. Son of Alexander Brand, watchmaker, Edinburgh. He "Commanded a party of rebel hussars and assisted in levying the Cess at Selkirk." At his trial on 9 September 1746 he asked to be transported in lieu of the death penalty, but this was refused. He was executed 18 October 1746 in Carlisle. Evidence from George Porteous, Excise Officer and James Miller, writer in Selkirk. *SHS.2.48, SHS.8.244, SHS.8.338.*

BRAYNE, EDMUND, Manchester Regiment. From Lancashire. Taken at capture of Carlisle. Imprisoned 30 December 1745 Carlisle. No further reference to him. Died? *MR.196, SHS.2.48.*

BREAK, JOHN, merchant in Edinburgh. Carried arms at the battle of Preston and wore a white cockade. Now at home. Evidence from James Murray, Tailor in Cannongate. *SHS.8.338, SHS.8.244.*

BRENAN, EDWARD, Clare's French Service. Imprisoned at sea 28 November 1745, Berwick, February 1746, Hull. Discharged. *SHS.2.48.*

BRENAN, WILLIAM, Captain, Fitzjames' Horse, Merchant from London and Paris. Imprisoned 28 April 1746, Saltcoats 28 April 1746, Irvine 6 March 1747, Berwick. Discharged 23 November 1747. *MR38, SHS.2.48.*

BRERES, ROBERT, Joiner from Ellel, Lancaster. Imprisoned Lancaster, Chester Castle. "Was imprisoned in Lancaster for enlisting men for the Pretender," and thence sent to Chester to await trial. There is no record of his disposal. *SHS.2.48.*

BREWER, GEORGE, Manchester Regiment. Imprisoned York Castle. "Taken in actual rebellion." Northing is known of his disposal. *SHS.2.50.*

BRINDLE, MATTHEW, Manchester Regiment. From Lancashire. Imprisoned 30 December 1745 Carlisle, Lancaster Castle. Taken at capture of Carlisle. Nothing more is known about him. *MR.196, SHS.2.50.*

BRINOU, PIERRE, Clare's French Service. Imprisoned at sea, 28 November 1745, Berwick February 1746, Hull. Discharged. *SHS.2.50.*

BRISCARE or BRISCOE, MATTHEW, Clare's French Service. Imprisoned at sea 28 November 1745, Berwick February 1746, Hull. Discharged. *SHS.2.50.*

BRITTOUGH or BRITTER or BRATTER, WILLIAM, Ensign, Manchester Regiment. Imprisoned London. Lawyer's clerk from Manchester, son of an Exciseman. Tried at Southward; convicted, but reprieved. Was one of a party of prisoners who assaulted the prison staff. Transported 21 July 1748. *SHS.2.50*.

BRODIE, DAVID, chaplain to Lady Blantyre, Leadington. Said to have carried arms in the rebel service at the battle of Preston. Supposed at home. *SHS.8.134*.

BRODIE, WALTER, shoemaker from Blance, Haddington. Joined the rebel army and gave information upon the neighbourhood of concealed arms. Whereabout not known. *SHS8.134*.

BRODIE, WILLIAM, gunsmith from Canongate, Edinburgh, Midlothian. Beat up and recruited men and levied money in the country for the rebel service. Now lurking in town. Evidence from Ninian Trotter, George Robertson and Francis Pringle, Excise Officers. *SHS.8.338, SHS.8.244*.

BROMLEY, ANNE, Perth's Regiment, from Newcastle. Imprisoned Carlisle, Chester Castle. Discharged. *SHS.2.50*.

BROUSDOUN, JOHN, interpreter, French Service. From Flanders. Imprisoned 30 December 1745, Carlisle. Discharged. Taken at fall of Carlisle. *SHS.2.50, MR135*.

BROWER, GEORGE, Manchester Regiment. Died? *MR.196*.

BROWN, ANDREW, baillie of the regality, Dalkeith. Did conjunctly with James Elphinston levy upwards of £50 of Excise which was paid to the rebels except a small balance which remains in the Clerks hands, but was compelled under pain of military execution. Dead. *SHS.8.134*.

BROWN, DAVID, resident of St Andrews, Fife. Carried arms in the rebel service under the Earl of Kelly. Lurking in Fife. *SHS.8.62*.

BROWN, FRANCIS, Manchester Regiment. Aged 27, husbandman from Lancashire. Taken at capture of Carlisle. Imprisoned 30 December 1745 Carlisle, Lancaster Castle. Transported to Antigua 8 May 1747. *MR.196, SHS.2.52.*

BROWN, GAVIN, of Bishoptoun, Millhead, Nithsdale. Attended the Pretender's son at Dumfries with a white cockade and gave him what assistance he could. *SHS.8.142.*

BROWN or BROWNE, IGNATIUS MICHAEL, Captain, Lally's Regiment, French Service. Imprisoned *Prince Charles* (late *Hazard*), 24 March 1746, Tongue 24 March 1746, HMS Sheerness, Berwick, London. Pardoned on condition of perpetual banishment, 2 July 1747. A French Irishman, Chevalier de St Louis, of Lally's Regiment, who came over with the French envoy in October 1745, and was appointed colonel by the Prince. He was left in Carlisle when the Jacobite army retired north, but managed to escape at the surrender, and rejoined the Prince. After the battle of Falkirk he was sent to France to inform Louis XV of the victory. He returned in command of some fresh French troops to Scotland, in March 1746, in the *Hazard*, later known as *Prince Charles*, which was driven ashore at Tongue by four warships, with its passengers and crew; was taken prisoner by Lord Reay and his militia and sent to London as a French prisoner of war. *SHS.2.52.*

BROWN, JOHN, vintner from Leith, Midlothian. With a party of rebels took a horse from Thomas Mill at Leith. Now at home. Evidence from Thomas Miln, mason, Powderhall, Edinburgh. *SHS.8.246, SHS.8.340.*

BROWN, JOHN, from Westminster. Imprisoned 18 May 1746 Stirling Castle. The Stirling Jail return has an entry against him that he was in "Brigadier Skelton's Regiment, Major Ransford's Company." This indicates that he was a deserter from the Army. He was probably handed over to the military authorities. *SHS.2.54.*

BROWN, RICHARD, Manchester Regiment. Carpenter from Lancashire. Imprisoned 30 December 1745 Carlisle, Lancaster Castle. Pardoned on condition of enlistment 22 July 1748. Taken at capture of Carlisle. Tried at Carlisle 19 September and sentenced to death, and pardoned on condition of enlistment. *MR.196, SHS.2.54.*

BROWN, THOMAS, Clare's French Service. Taken at sea 28 November 1745, imprisoned Berwick February 1746, Hull. Discharged. *SHS.2.54.*

BROWN, WILLIAM, salt officer from Prestonpans. Acted first as Officer and then as collector of the salt duty under the rebels but absconded on their going for England. Prisoner. *SHS.8.132.*

BROWN, WILLIAM, from Prestonpans, Duke of Perth's Regiment, imprisoned in Haddington, discharged 9 September 1746. This may have been William Brown, Salt officer, Prestonpans, who "acted first as an officer and then as collector of Salt duty under the rebels, but absconded on their going for England." He was then taken prisoner. *SHS.2.54.*

BROWNLIE or BROWN, ALEXANDER, Artillery. Aged 20, watchmaker from Edinburgh. Imprisoned 30 December 1745 Carlisle, York Castle, and Lincoln Castle. Taken at fall of Carlisle, transported to Antigua 8 May 1747, or 8 May 1747 from Liverpool to Leeward Islands on *Veteran*, arriving Martinique June 1747. Parent, Archibald Brownlie. *SHS.2.54, MR132, PRO.SP36.102.*

BRUCE, HENRY, Mr, of Clackmannan. Joined the rebels at Edinburgh and was made an officer in their army. Whereabouts not known. Evidence from William and Alexander Anderson, James Dempster, John Ferguson, Robert Lindsay, William McViccar, William Steen and Robert Wilson, all residents in Clackmannan. *SHS.8.146, SHS.8.348.*

BRUCE, JAMES, gentleman from Clackmannan, Elcho's Life Guards, imprisoned in Edinburgh Castle. "Taken in actual rebellion." Taken prisoner at Leith in February 1747 trying to escape from the country. Perhaps this was Mr James Bruce, Gentleman, Clackmannan, who joined the Prince's Life Guards in Edinburgh. His further disposal cannot be traced. Evidence from William and Alexander Anderson, James Dempster, John Ferguson, Robert Lindsay, William McViccar, William Steen and Robert Wilson, all residents in Clackmannan. Condition of Mansion House, habitable. Rental £100. *SHS.2.56, SHS.8.146, SHS.8.348.*

BRUCE, JOHN, Vintner from Leith, Midlothian. Went into the rebellion and carried arms. Whereabouts not known. Evidence from the neighbourhood and Henry Morison, Excise Officer. *SHS.8.246, SHS.8.340.*

BRUILEZ or BRUELY, or BRULAY, IAN or JEAN, from Lorraine, France. Soldier, Lord John Drummond's Regiment, French Royal Scots Cavalry. Taken 7 February 1746. Imprisoned 7 February 1746 Stirling Castle, Canongate, Edinburgh Tolbooth, 15 July 1746. Discharged 1747. *MR.62.*

BRUMBLY, ….., Duke of Perth's Regiment. From Essex. Imprisoned 30 December 1745, Carlisle. Taken at capitulation of Carlisle. No further reference to him. *SHS.2.58.*

BRYMER, ALEXANDER, baker from Leith, Midlothian. Forced out his son to go into the rebellion. Now at home. Evidence from all his neighbourhood. *SHS.8.246, SHS.8.340.*

BRYMER, ROBERT, baker, son to Alexander Brymer, Leith, Midlothian. Carried arms in the rebellion, but forced by his father. Whereabouts not known. Evidence from all his neighbourhood. *SHS.8.246, SHS.8.340.*

BUCHARD, PATRICK, smith, from Benvie. Carried arms in the rebel army. Whereabouts not known. Evidence from John Chapman and George Porteous, Excise Officers. *SHS.8.244, SHS.8.342.*

BUCKLON or BOKILION, MARTIN, Berwick's French Service. Imprisoned Berwick on Tweed. Discharged. *SHS.2.60.*

BUDET, JEAN, Berwick's French Service. Imprisoned Berwick on Tweed. Discharged. *SHS.2.60.*

BUIST, JAMES, from Fife, imprisoned Perth 24 February 1746 and Stirling Castle. He was probably a deserted, as the Perth Jail return says he "belonged to General StClair's Regiment, Captain Scots Company." In that case he was probably handed over to the military authorities. *SHS.2.62.*

BURKE, JOHN, Captain, Clare's French Service. Aged 45, from France. Imprisoned Inverness, *Wallsgrave*, Tilbury, London, Marshalsea. Discharged. He gave evidence for defence of Nicholas Glascoe. *SHS.2.62, MR135.*

BURKE, MICHAEL, Lieutenant, Dillon's French Service. Imprisoned Inverness, Marshalsea. Discharged. *SHS.2.62, MR135.*

BURKE or BURCK, RICHARD, Captain, Dillon's French Service. Aged 40 from Artois, France. Imprisoned at sea, Berwick February 1746, Hull June 1746, *Dolphin* Tilbury, London, Marshalsea. *SHS.2.62, MR135.*

BURN, JOHN, Manchester Regiment. Aged 24, servant, from Northumberland. Imprisoned Carlisle, Lancaster Castle. *MR.196, SHS.2.62.*

BURN, JOHN, Manchester Regiment. Aged 22 from Northumberland. Taken at capture of Carlisle. Imprisoned 30 December 1745 Carlisle, York Castle. Transported 21 February 1747. *MR.196.*

BURNE, ... Cornet, Fitzjames' Horse. From France. Imprisoned *Charite* London, Marshalsea. Taken at sea. Discharged. *SHS.2.62.*

BURNETT, JOHN, of Campfield, Kincardine, Captain of Artillery, Captain Colonel Grant's. Imprisoned 30 December 1745 Carlisle, London, Southwark. Pardoned and banished on 21 July 1748 on condition of never returning. He is said "to have belonged to the artillery company at Woolwich." He said he was forced out by Glenbucket. He commanded the Carlisle Castle artillery. He fired the first cannon at the English army from Carlisle. He was taken prisoner at Carlisle on the surrender of the town, December 1745. He was sent to London, tried and convicted, but reprieved. Judge Burnett wrote to the Duke of Newcastle in his favour on 1 June 1747. He was pardoned in July 1748 and banished on condition of his not returning to the country. *SHS.2.64.*

BURTHEY, MARY, from Hamilton, Lanarkshire, Perth's Regiment. Imprisoned in Carlisle and Chester Castle. Discharged. *SHS.2.64.*

BURTON, JOHN Dr. Imprisoned 30 November 1745 York, 30 November 1745 York Castle, 11 March 1746 London. Released 25 March 1747. An entusiastic Jacobite he was made prisoner on suspicion of having crossed England with the intention of kissing the Prince's hand. On arriving in London he was sent to a messenger's house and remained in his custody until 25 March 1747, when he was released. The Attorney-General had reported on 15 July 1746 that there was not enough evidence to prosecute him. *SHS.2.64.*

BUTLER, ..., Lieutenant, Fitzjames' Horse French Service. Taken at sea 21 February 1746 *Charite*, imprisoned Berwick, London, Marshalsea. ?Pardoned conditionally on perpetual banishment 20 October 1748. This may have been the Thomas Butler who was pardoned 20 October 1748. *SHS.2.66.*

BYRNE, GARRAT, French Service. Pardoned conditionally on perpetual banishment 20 October 1748. No other reference to this man has been traced. *SHS.2.66.*

BYRNE or BYREN, JAMES, Captain, French Service. From France. Imprisoned Berwick, Edinburgh Castle. "Says he is a native of France and came over to Scotland as a Captain in the French Picquets." This may have been the Lieutenant Byren who was in the Berwick prison in July 1746, and was probably captured along with several others in the French Service in the *Prince Charles* by HMS *Sheerness*. *SHS.2.66.*

BYRN, PATRICK, Lieutenant Bulkeley's French Service. From France. Taken at sea 25 November 1745, imprisoned Berwick February 1746, Hull. Discharged. *SHS.2.66.*

CADDEL, ROBERT, gunsmith from Doune, Stirlingshire. Evidence from John Christy, multerer in Doune Miln, John Mitchel, merchant there, Alexander Campbell, gunsmith there, James Kemp, innkeeper there and James and William Taylors both innkeepers there. *SHS.8.318.*

CADDEL, THOMAS, senior, gunsmith from Doune, Stirlingshire. Evidence from John Christy, multerer in Doune, and Allan Stewart, vintner in Doune. *SHS.8.318.*

CADDEL, THOMAS, junior, gunsmith from Doune, Stirlingshire. Evidence from John Christy, Multerer in the Mill there, and Alexander Campbell, gunsmith in Doune. *SHS.8.318.*

CAIRNS, JAMES, extraordinary salt watchman from Prestonpans. Acted as salt officer and collector for the rebels during their stay in this country. At home. *SHS.8.134.*

CAIRNS, JOHN, merchant from Edinburgh, Midlothian. Carried arms as a volunteer in the rebel army. Whereabouts not known. *SHS.8.246.*

CALBREATH, JAMES, son of William Calbreath, Miller, Pows Mill, St Ninians parish, Stirlingshire. Carried arms with the rebels at Falkirk. Lurking. *SHS.8.54.*

CALLAGHAN, ……., Captain, Irish Piquets. Killed at Perth. , *MR135.*

CALLANDER, EDWARD, journeyman goldsmith from Edinburgh, Midlothian. Carried arms as Lieutenant in the rebel army. Whereabouts not known. Evidence from

George Porteous and John Smith, Excise Officers. *SHS.8.246, SHS.8.338.*

CALLANDER, JAMES, late Deacon of the Bakers, Innerkeithing. Joined the rebels at Edinburgh but sickened and left them before the battle of Falkirk. Left the country. Evidence from William Roxburgh, John Kirkcaldie and Adam Turnbull, all bailies in Kirkcaldy. *SHS.8.146, SHS.8.348.*

CAMBIEN, ANGLE, Berwick's French Service. From France. Taken at sea, imprisoned Berwick on Tweed. Discharged. *SHS.2.66.*

CAMERON, ……., of Loc. Was a Colonel in the rebel army during the whole rebellion. Whereabouts not known. *SHS.8.246.*

CAMERON, DANIEL, coachman to Countess of Kincardine, Dunfermline. Carried arms at Preston battle in the rebel army, after that returned to his service, but was very active in carrying messages for the rebels. Whereabouts not known. Evidence from William Wilson, town clerk of Dunfermline, John Pearson, wright in Torry and Andrew Glen, excise officer in Torryburn. *SHS.8.146, SHS.8.248.*

CAMERON, DANIEL, French Service, from France. Taken at sea; Berwick. Discharged. *SHS.2.74.*

CAMERON, LACHLAN, French Service, from France. Taken at sea 25 November 1745, *Soleil*, imprisoned Deal, Customs Smack *Caroline*, Marshalsea. Discharged. Was an officer in French service. Captured at sea in the Soleil privateer making for Scotland. *SHS.2.84.*

CAMERON, PETER, Vintner from Edinburgh. Imprisoned on suspicion 6 February 1747 Edinburgh Castle. Released June 1747. *SHS.2.86.*

CAMERON, ROBERT, Captain Rooth's (French Service). Imprisoned 25 November 1745 *Esperance* (late *Soleil*) brought into Deal, Deal, Customs Smack *Caroline* Greenwich, Marshalsea. Captured at sea on the way to Montrose. Pardoned on condition of perpetual banishment 3 July 1747. *SHS.2.86.*

CAMERON, SAMUEL, 2nd Lieutenant, Lord John Drummond's Regiment. Imprisoned Iesperancel 25 November 1745, Deal, Customs Smack, *Caroline* Greenwich, Marshalsea. Pardoned on condition of perpetual banishment 3 July 1747. Brother of Alexander Cameron of Glenevis. Captured at sea. This man became a spy and informer against Jacobite prisoners. Dr Archibald Cameron, in his last statement, dated 6 June 1753, speaks of himas "the basest of their spies" and as one of his "accusers." When Mrs Cameron went over to France he was, according to Bishop Forbes, tried by a court-martial and imprisoned and banished. *SHS.2.86.*

CAMPBELL, ..., of Tornagrew, Ensign, Roy Stewart's (Edinburgh) Regiment. ?Killed at Culloden. *MR205.*

CAMPBELL, ALEXANDER, (Inverness), Berwick's Regiment, Irish Piquets. Taken at Culloden. *MR137.*

CAMPBELL, ARCHIBALD, publican from Falkirk, "A common fellow, for treasonable practices." Imprisoned 3 November 1745 Falkirk, Stirling Castle, 13.2.1746 Leith, released under General Pardon, 1747. *SHS.2.88.*

CAMPBELL, CHARLES, Lieutenant, Roy Stewart's (Edinburgh) Regiment. Excise Officer. Taken, turned King's Evidence and was discharged. *MR205.*

CAMPBELL, DUNCAN, in jail in Whitehaven. *CQS.359.*

CAMPBELL (alias BRUCE), JAMES, Gentleman from Clackmannan, imprisoned on suspicion of treason 22 January 1746/7 on board a ship in Leith roads, 24 January 1746/7 Edinburgh Castle, 8 August 1746 Carlisle. He was arrested in a ship trying to leave the country. Nothing is known of his fate. He may have died in Carlisle. *SHS.2.94.*

CAMPBELL, JOHN, Captain, Roy Stewart's (Edinburgh) Regiment. Aged 35, of Kinloch. Taken. *MR205.*

CAMPBELL, MARTHA, Perth's Regiment, from Hexham. Imprisoned Chester Castle. Released. Taken at Carlisle. *SHS.2.96.*

CAMPBELL, WILLIAM, Roy Stewart's (Edinburgh) Regiment. Aged 21, weaver from Grantully, Perthshire. Taken at Carlisle. Transported 5 May 1747 from Liverpool to Leeward Islands in *Veteran*, arriving Martinique June 1747. *SHS.2.98, MR206, PRO.SP36.102.*

CANE, JOHN, Roy Stewart's (Edinburgh) Regiment. Writer, Edinburgh, Clerk to Stores. Taken and transported. *MR206.*

CARMICHAEL, JAMES, servant from Leith. He accompanied Rev Robert Forbes from Leith, in an attempt to join the Prince when he landed. Both of them, with five others, were arrested at St Ninians on 7 Sept 1745 and confined in Stirling Castle until 7 February 1746, when they were roped together and sent to Edinburgh Castle. This roping was carried out by order of Lord Albemarle. He was released 29 May 1746. *SHS.2.98.*

CARPENTIER, FRANCOIS, Lally's French Service. From Dieppe, France. Imprisoned 30 December 1745 Carlisle, Marshalsea. Discharged. Taken at capture of Carlisle. *SHS.2.102.*

CARPENTIER, JOSEPH, Clare's French Service. Taken at sea 28 November 1745, imprisoned Berwick, February 1746 Hull, Marshalsea. Discharged. *SHS.2.102.*

CARRUTHERS, WILLIAM, servant to Kirkconnal, Kirkcudbright Stewartry. Attended his master in the rebellion but left them in England. Now in Kirkconnal. *SHS.8.142.*

CARROLL, PATRICK, Berwick's French Service. Taken at sea 27 November 1745, imprisoned Berwick February 1746, Hull, Marshalsea. Discharged. *SHS.2.102.*

CASEY or CASSIE, ANDREW, from Traquair, Tweeddale, Borders, Elcho's Life Guards, imprisoned Inverness June 1746, prison ship *Jane of Leith*, Tilbury, died June 1746. *SHS.2.104, SHS.8.376, SHS.8.84.*

CASTILOVO, EDMUND, Bulkeley's French Service. Taken at sea 28 November 1745, imprisoned Berwick February 1746, Hull, Marshalsea. *SHS.2.104.*

CELLARS, CHARLES, Roy Stewart's (Edinburgh) Regiment. From Perth. Taken and escaped. *MR206.*

CHABRILLARD, GUILLAUME, French Royal Scots, French Service. Taken at sea, imprisoned Berwick on Tweed. Discharged. *SHS.2.106.*

CHADDOCK, JAMES, Manchester Regiment. From Wigan. Imprisoned 30 December 1745 Carlisle. Pardoned on condition of enlistment 22 July 1746. Taken at capture of Carlisle. Tried at Carlisle September 1746 and sentenced to death, but reprieved and pardoned on condition of enlistment. *MR.196, SHS.2.106.*

CHADDOCK or CHADWICK, THOMAS, Lieutenant, Manchester Regiment. Tallow Chandler from Staffordshire. Imprisoned 30 December 1745 Carlisle, London, Southwark. Shown in Southwark Jail returns as "gentleman, otherwise tallow chandler." Taken at Capture of Carlisle. Tried and convicted 16 July 1746, executed at Kennington Common on 30 July 1746. *MR.195, SHS.1.147.*

CHADLY, THOMAS, Manchester Regiment, from Preston. Imprisoned 30 December 1745 Carlisle. Taken at capture of Carlisle. There is no further reference to him. *SHS.2.106, MR196.*

CHALME, JACQUES, Berwick's French Service. From France. Imprisoned Perth, Canongate, Berwick. Discharged. *SHS.2.106.*

CHALMERS, or CHAMBERS, CHARLES, Elcho's Life Guards, aged 30, merchant from Edinburgh. Imprisoned 25 April 1746 Perth, April 1746 Montrose, Inverness, *James and* Mary Medway. Transported 31 March 1747 from London to Barbados in *Frere. SHS.2.106, BMHS.30.75.*

CHALMERS, JOHN, Dillon's French Service, Irish Piquets. "A common man" from Kinneil. Imprisoned 20 May 1746 Arbroath, Carlisle. Transported 21 March 1747. *SHS.2.108, MR137.*

CHAMPION, NICOLAS, French Service. Imprisoned Marshalsea. Discharged. *SHS.2.110.*

CHAPE or CHAPP, JAMES, Roy Stewart's (Edinburgh) Regiment. Aged 21, blacksmith from St Marnock's Kirk, Banff. Transported 24 February 1747 from Liverpool in *Gildart*, arriving Port North Potomac, Maryland 5 August 1747. *SHS.2.110, MR206, PRO.T1.328.*

CHAPMAN, MATTHEW, Berwick's French Service, from France. Imprisoned at sea 28 November 1745, Berwick February 1746, Hull, Marshalsea. Discharged. *SHS.2.110.*

CHARNLEY, THOMAS, Manchester Regiment, aged 19, weaver from Walton. Imprisoned 30 December 1745 Carlisle, Lancaster Castle. Transported to Antigua 8 May 1747. Taken at surrender of Carlisle. *SHS.2.112.*

CHARRACH, DAVID, Roy Stuart's Regiment. From Lancashire. Imprisoned 30 December 1745 Carlisle, Lancaster Castle. Taken at capture of Carlisle. He probably died, as his name does not appear in the transportation lists. *SHS.2.112, MR206.*

CHEISLEY, JOHN, Manchester Regiment. Taken, and transported 1747. *MR196.*

CHERSLEY, JOHN, Manchester Regiment. Imprisoned 30 December 1745 Carlisle. Transported to Antigua 8 May 1747. SHS.2.112.

CHESTERFIELD, JOHN, Manchester Regiment, from Lancashire. Imprisoned 30 December 1745 Carlisle, Lancaster Castle. Transported 21 February 1747. Taken at capture of Carlisle. *SHS.2.112, MR196.*

CHISHOLM, DONALD, soldier, French Royal Scots Cavalry. Aged 23, from Inverness-shire. Taken, turned Kings Evidence and was discharged. *MR.62.*

CHRYSTIE, ALEXANDER, servant, South Ferry, Fife. Carried arms in the rebel service and was active in robbing the country of arms. Whereabouts not known. *SHS.8.64.*

CLARK, HENRY, gentleman from Canongate, Midlothian. Carried arms in the rebel army and robbed Mr Scot's house. Now a prisoner in Carlisle. Evidence from Ninian Trotter, George Robertson and Francis Pringle, Excise Officers. When arraigned at Carlisle he pleaded guilty, and was sentenced to death, but died in prison before 14 November 1746. *SHS.8.379, SHS.8.246, SHS.8.338.*

CLARK or CLARKE or CLARGUE, PATRICK, Captain, Berwick's French Service. Imprisoned 17 April 1746 Inverness. Pardoned on condition of perpetual banishment 3 July 1747. *SHS.2.116, MR135.*

CLARK, ROBERT, from Leith, imprisoned 7 September 1745 St Ninians, 7 September 1745 Stirling Castle, 4 February 1746 Edinburgh Castle, released 29 May 1746. He was one of the party which accompanied the Rev Robert Forbes on his journey north to join the Prince when he landed. Captured in St Ninians, the party was sent first to Stirling and then to Edinburgh Castle. *SHS.2.118.*

CLARK, SAMUEL, blacksmith from Carlisle. Imprisoned Carlisle. "No further proceedings recorded". As he did not plead at the trial he must either have been released or died. *SHS.2.118.*

CLARKE, DONALD, soldier, French Royal Scots Cavalry. Aged 38, from Argyllshire. Taken. Died? *MR.62.*

CLAVERING, EDMUND (EDWARD), Manchester Regiment, from Northumberland. Imprisoned Carlisle, York Castle. Executed at York, 1 November 1746. "One of the party of rebels that went to plunder Lord Lonsdale's seat at Lowther Hall." "Taken in actual rebellion." Pleaded guilty at his trial on 1 October and was sentenced to death. *SHS.1.148, SHS.2.118, MR196.*

CLAVERING or HAMILTON, ELIZABETH. Imprisoned Carlisle, York, The Ship *Veteran.* Transported from Liverpool to Antigua 8 May 1747, arriving Martinique June 1747. From Banff, wife of Edmund Clavering. "Brown, thin, a sempstress." She petitioned for release. *SHS.2.118.*

CLELAND, GEORGE, shipmaster, Pittenweem, Fife. This being a Magistrate in his abode, disuaded the traders from allowing officers of the Revenue to survey or pay them their duties. He attended the rebels collecting and used his authority for them. At home. Evidence from Janet Todie, victualer in Pittenweem and Janet Mason, wife of William Thomson, brewer there. *SHS.8.64, SHS.8.352.*

CLELAND, ROBERT, merchant, Crail, Fife. Magistrate in his abode, disuaded the traders from allowing officers of the Revenue to survey or pay them their duties. Evidence from John Ross, excise officer and the town council. *SHS.8.64, SHS.8.352.*

CLELLAND, JOHN, from Linlithgow, gunner, Artillery, imprisoned 30 December 1745 Carlisle, York Castle. Taken at capture of Carlisle. He probably died, as he was neither released nor transported. *SHS.2.118.*

CLERK, ... soldier, Lord John Drummond's Regiment, French Royal Scots Cavalry. From France. "Carried north by the Duke's army." Taken 18 February 1746. Discharged. *MR.62.*

CLERK, LAURENCE, Fitzjames Horse, French Service. Surrendered May 1746. *MR38.*

CLOSS or CLOSE, JAMES, soldier, Lord John Drummond's French Royal Scots Cavalry. Imprisoned 1 February 1746 Stirling, 7 February 1746 Stirling Castle, 13 February 1746 Leith, 25 June 1746 Edinburgh Jail, Canongate. From Ireland, (deserter, Bragg's Regiment). Deserted and surrendered. Discharged 2 March 1747. "Declares he was a soldier in Bragg's Regiment in Flanders, that he was taken prisoner by a French Hussar and enlisted with them, and came over to Scotland with the French picquets and delivered himself up to General Blakeney after the battle of Falkirk, 22 November 1746. *MR.62, SHS.2.118.*

COCHRAN, WILLIAM, of Ferguslie, Paisley, Renfrewshire. Joined and went along with the rebels and continued till the last. Now lurking. Worth £100 per annum. Evidence from William Pollock, writer, Hugh Montgovery, ferrier, and James King, smith, all in Renfrew. *SHS.8.292, SHS.8.326.*

COCKBURN, JAMES, stocking weaver from Glasgow, imprisoned Tower of London. While in prison he wrote to his children saying, "Should it please God I be taken to himself I leave you two of my stocking frames. Let me entreat you to imitate your grandfather in his valuable talents of honesty and probity, for this truth will always be found the best policy." It is not known what became of him. *SHS.2.120.*

COLEMAN, AUSTIN, Manchester Regiment, weaver from Treimlin, Co Mayo, Ireland. Imprisoned Carlisle, Chester Castle. He turned King's Evidence against Colonel

Townley at his trial and many other officers, and was pardoned, 15 July 1746. *SHS.2.120, MR196.*

COLIENO, PIERRE, 2nd Captain, Spanish Ship. Imprisoned 17 April 1746 Inverness. Discharged. Probably discharged as prisoner of war. *SHS.2.120, MR135.*

COLLIN or CULLIN, JOHN, Berwick's French Service, from France. Taken at sea, Berwick. Discharged. *SHS.2.120.*

COLLINGWOOD, LAWRENCE, Manchester Regiment, from Northumberland. Imprisoned 30 December 1745 Carlisle, Lancaster Castle. Taken at capture of Carlisle. His disposal is unknown. *SHS.2.120, MR196.*

COLLINGWOOD, THOMAS, Manchester Regiment, yeoman from Carlisle. Imprisoned 30 December 1745 Morpeth and Carlisle. Acquitted September 1746. Captured at the surrender of Carlisle on 19 September 1746(?) Was tried at Carlisle and acquitted. It was stated that this was due to Mr Cuthbertson, town clerk of Newcastle, "suppressing, or at least not producing the prisoners examination." *SHS.2.120, MR196.*

COLQUHOUN, DUNCAN, Lieutenant, Lord John Drummond's French Royal Scots Cavalry. Deserter from Paul's Regiment. Taken at Culloden 17 April 1746, executed (hanged) 28 April 1746. *MR.61, SHS.2.122.*

COLQUHOUNE, CHARLES, wright from Pleasance, St Cuthbert's parish, Edinburgh, Midlothian. Carried arms in the rebel army. Was steward in the Pretender's son's Cellars and a commissary for his army. Now lurking at home. Evidence from David Morison, brewer and John Davidson, wright in the Abbey. *SHS.8.246, SHS.8.338.*

COMERFORD, NICHOLAS, Captain, Bulkeley's French Service, from France. Imprisoned Culloden, Inverness. Discharged. *SHS.2.122, MR135.*

COMERIE, JOHN, Captain, Roy Stewart's (Edinburgh) Regiment. From Braes of Atholl. Taken at Carlisle. Died in prison. *MR205.*

COMRY, WILLIAM, steward to Earl of Murray, Duniebrisle. Joined the rebels when first at Perth, and continued with them till dispersed. Whereabouts not known. Evidence from William Roxburgh, John Kirkcaldie and Adam Turnbull, all bailies in Kirkcaldy. *SHS.8.146, SHS.8.348.*

CONGLETON, JOHN, surgeon from Edinburgh, Midlothian. Carried arms as a volunteer in the rebel army. Whereabouts not known. *SHS.8.246.*

CONNEL or CONELL, MORRIES or MAURICE, Clare's Regiment, French Service. From France. Imprisoned 26 November 1745 off Montrose, December 1745 Edinburgh Castle, Royal Infirmary 25 June 1746, Canongate 15 July 1746, Edinburgh Jail from Canongate Jail. Discharged. "Confesses he is a soldier of Clare's French Regiment and came over with them to Scotland. *SHS.2.122.*

CONNELL, ANDREW, Corporal, Berwick's French Service. From France. Taken at sea, imprisoned Berwick. Discharged. *SHS.2.122.*

CONNOLLY, WILLIAM, Duke of Perth's Regiment, from Londonderry. Imprisoned 30 December 1745 Carlisle, Chester Castle, York Castle. Executed York 1 November 1746. Deserter Scots Fusiliers. Taken at capture of Carlisle. At his trial it was stated that he had formerly been in the Scots Fusiliers, and that at Prestonpans he had "advised to kill the redcoats, especially of Lee's regiment, because they would know him again," and also that he had killed an English soldier. He was convicted and executed. *SHS.2.124.*

CONNOR, ANNE, Strickland's Regiment, from Longreat, Galway. Imprisoned Carlisle, Chester Castle. Discharged. *SHS.2.124.*

CONNOR, DENNIS, Clare's French Service. Imprisoned at sea 28 November 1745, Berwick February 1746, Hull, Marshalsea. Discharged. *SHS.2.124.*

CONNOR, JOHN, Duke of Perth's Regiment, stonecutter from Longhart, Galway. Imprisoned 30 December 1745 Carlisle, Chester Castle, London. Discharged. Was servant to Col. Strickland in Carlisle. Taken at capture of town. Turned King's Evidence. *SHS.2.124.*

CONWAY, JAMES (JOSEPH), Captain, Calre's French Service. Imprisoned *Louis XV* 28 November 1745, Edinburgh Castle 26 December 1745, Berwick February 1746, Hull, Marshalsea. Discharged. Captured at sea. *SHS.2.124.*

CONWAY, MATTHEW, Clare's French Service. Imprisoned at sea, 28 November 1745, Berwick February 1746, Hull, Marshalsea. Discharged. *SHS.2.126.*

COOK, HUMPHRY, blacksmith from Derby, Manchester Regiment. *MR196.*

COOK, JOHN, French Service, from England. Imprisoned Carlisle. Transported. He asked not to be sent back to France, and was transported. *SHS.2.126.*

COOK, RICHARD, soldier, Lord John Drummond's Regiment, French Royal Scots Cavalry. From Dumfries. Delivered up to Colonel Howard 6 August 1746. "Confesses that he deserted from Lieutenant General Thomas Howard's Regiment in Flanders and enlisted in Drummond's French regiment and came over with it to Scotland. He was probably hanged as a deserter in Inverness. *MR.62, SHS.2.126.*

COOK, THOMAS, French Picquets. Imprisoned 16 December 1745 Stirling Castle. Pardoned on condition of perpetual banishment 3 July 1747. Deserted from rebel service. *SHS.2.12, MR137.*

COOKE, ..., Brigadier General, French Service. Imprisoned at sea 21 February 1746, *Bourbon*, Marshalsea. Discharged 1747. Taken at sea. *SHS.2.126.*

COOKE, ..., Captain, Fitzjames Regiment. Imprisoned *Charite*, Marshalsea. Discharged 1747. Taken at sea 21 February 1746. *SHS.2.126.*

COOKE, WILLIAM, Manchester Regiment, from Lancashire. Imprisoned 30 December 1745 Carlisle, Lancaster Castle. Pardoned on condition of enlistment 22 July 1748. Taken at capture of Carlisle. Tried at Carlisle 19 September 1746 and sentenced to death, but pardoned on condition of enlistment. *SHS.2.126, MR196.*

COOPER, ANDREW, servant to a Cooper in Leith, Midlothian. Wore a white cockade, carried arms and went to England with the rebels. Whereabouts not known. Evidence from William Gibson, Henry Morrison, George Calder and James McDuff, Excise Officers. *SHS.8.246, SHS.8.340.*

COOPER, ANDREW, son to David Cooper, Gardener, Canongate, Edinburgh, Midlothian. Carried arms in the rebel army. Now lurking at home. *SHS.8.246.*

COOPER, WILLIAM, Manchester Regiment, from Lancashire. Imprisoned 30 December 1745 Carlisle, Lancaster Castle. Taken at capture of Carlisle. No further reference to him. *SHS.2.126.*

COPPACK or COPPOCH, THOMAS, Rev, Chaplain, Manchester Regiment. Brasenose College, Oxford. Imprisoned Carlisle, Chester Castle, Lancaster Castle, Carlisle. Executed at Carlisle, 18 October 1746. An English clergyman; son of John Coppoch, a Manchester tailor. He joined the Prince at Manchester, was appointed chaplain to the Jacobite Manchester Regiment, and was promised the Bishopric of Carlisle. In his speech before his execution he said his crime was "for taking up arms to restore the royal and illustrious house of Stewart," and complained of brutal treatment he had suffered at the hands of Lord Mark Ker's dragoons when taken prisoner from Carlisle to Lancaster. *MR.195, SHS.1.148, SHS.2.128.*

COPPOCH, JOHN, Manchester Regiment. Tailor from Manchester. Imprisoned 30 December 1745 Carlisle, Lancaster Castle. Pardoned on condition of enlistment 22 July 1748. Brother of the Rev Thomas Copoch. Taken at capture of Carlisle 19/26 September 1746 and sentenced to death, but recommended to mercy by the jury. He was pardoned on condition of enlistment. *SHS.2.128, MR196.*

CORDIER, GUILLEUME, soldier, Lord John Drummond's French Royal Scots Cavalry. Frenchman. Imprisoned Perth 18 February 1746 "taken north by the Duke's army." Discharged. *MR.62, SHS.2.128.*

CORSER, ARCHIBALD, weaver from Fisheraw, Haddington. Joined the rebels, went with them to England and deserted them on their retreat from thence. Lurking. *SHS.8.134.*

COTTAM or COTTON, JOHN, Manchester Regiment, aged 17, labourer from Clifton, Lancashire. Imprisoned 30 December 1745 Carlisle, Lancaster Castle. Transported to Antigua 8 May 1747. "A sprightly lad." Taken at capture of Carlisle. *SHS.2.128, MR196.*

COUPAR, ANDREW, son to David Coupar, yr, Cannongate. Evidence from James Easson, Excise Officer and Cromwell Easson, shoemaker, Edinburgh. *SHS.8.338.*

COUGLEY, MICHAEL, from Ireland. Imprisoned 27 April 1746 Saltcoats, 27 April 1746 Irvine. "Handed over to military authorities" 27 February 1747. Soldier "of Col. De Promet's Regiment." This man was probably in the French service, in which case he would have been released in due course; or he may have been a deserter and dealt with accordingly. *SHS.2.130.*

COURTNEY, JOHN, Berwick's French Service. Imprisoned at sea 28 November 1745, Berwick February 1746, Hull. Discharged. *SHS.2.130.*

COUTTS, ALEXANDER, a goldsmith's servant, Leith, Edinburgh, Midlothian. Carried arms in the rebel army. Whereabouts not known. Evidence from Robert Gordon and Robert Low, goldsmiths in Edinburgh. *SHS.8.246, SHS.8.338.*

COVELIER, FRANCOIS, from France. Imprisoned Canongate. Discharged. *SHS.2.130.*

CRAGG or CRAIG, THOMAS, Manchester Regiment. From Manchester. Imprisoned 30 December 1745 Carlisle. Released. Taken at capture of Carlisle. Turned King's Evidence against Captain Fletcher and many other prisoners at his trial on 16 July 1746. *SHS.2.132, MR196.*

CRAICH, FRANCIS, brewer and merchant, Clackmannan. Combined with the rebels at Edinburgh and Clackmannan, gave them information of arms concealed and of horses which they took, aided in oppressing the country by causing them provide victuals etc, and assisted in collecting the Excise upon a Sabbath Day. Caused the Excise Officer be apprehended and imprisoned for three days, publicly insulted the well-affected and aided and assisted the rebels several other ways too tedious here to relate. Now at home. Evidence from Alexander Anderson, James Dempster, Johnathan Donaldson, John Ferguson and many other inhabitants in Clackmannan. *SHS.8.146, SHS.8.348.*

CRAMP, THOMAS, Lord Lewis Gordon's Regiment. From Wigan. Imprisoned 30 December 1745 Carlisle, Lancaster Castle. Taken at capture of Carlisle. No further reference to him. *SHS.2.132.*

CRAW, ANDREW, Mr, living at Netherie, Midlothian. Carried arms in the Pretender's son's Life Guards. Whereabouts not known. *SHS.8.246.*

CRAWFORD, ELIZABETH, merchant, Anstruther Wester, Fife. Drank the Pretender's son's health, attended him at Edinburgh and sent a barrel of gunpowder to his use. At home. Evidence from George Brown and Kathleen Reid, both servants to the said Elizabeth Crawford and John Brown, town treasurer in Anstruther Wester. *SHS.8.64, SHS.8.352.*

CRAWFORD, HENRY, portioner of Crail, Fife. Furnished the rebels with money and welcomed them to town, advised them to secure the Excise Officers and their books, was in the rebellion and knighted by the Pretender 1715 yet has a pension of 55 lib. per annum from the Trustees for Improvement of Manufacturers. At home. Evidence from Alexander Oliphant and John Brown, brewers in Crail. *SHS.8.62, SHS.8.352.*

CREAGIE or CREAGU, JAMES, French Service. Pardoned on condition of permanent banishment 2 July 1747. *SHS.2.132.*

CRIBB, DAVID, Roy Stewart's (Edinburgh) Regiment. Aged 48, from Angus. Taken. Died? *MR206.*

CRICHTON or CRIGHTON, JAMES, Glenbucket's Regiment. Aged 25, mason from Edinburgh. Imprisoned 30 December 1745 Carlisle, York Castle. Pardoned on condition of enlistment 22 July 1748. Taken at capture of Carlisle. Pleaded guilty at his trial on 2 October 1746, was sentenced to death but reprieved, and pardoned on condition of enlistment. *SHS.2.134.*

CRIGHTON, ROBERT, salt watchman, Cockenzie. Acted as salt officer and collector for the rebels during their stay in this country. In Prestonpans. *SHS.8.134.*

CRISTOFF, JOHN, French Service. Imprisoned at sea *Soleil* 25 November 1745, Marshalsea. Discharged. A Swiss in French service. Taken at sea on the way to Scotland in the *Soleil* privateer. *SHS.2.134.*

CRONINE, CORNELIUS, Clare's French Service. Taken at sea 28 November 1745 *Soleil*, imprisoned Berwick February 1746, Hull. Discharged. *SHS.2.136.*

CROOKSHANKS, CHARLES, extr. salt watchman from Cockenzie. Acted as salt watchman under the rebels during their abode in this country. At home. *SHS.8.134.*

CROMBIE, PATRICK, workman from Haddington. Joined the rebels soon after Preston battle and gave information of persons well affected to the government. Whereabouts not known. *SHS.8.134.*

CROSBIE, JOHN, Surgeon in French Service. Aged 30 from Westmeath. Imprisoned 11 May 1746 Perth, 12 May 1746 Stirling Castle, Carlisle. Transported 21 February 1747. He is shown in the Carlisle List as a French Doctor. His name appears on the transportation lists, but he was probably exchanged as a prisoner of war. *SHS.2.136, MR135.*

CROSBIE, ROBERT, Captain, Lally's French Service. From Westmeath, Ireland. Imprisoned 1 July 1746 Perth. Executed 17 September 1746. Was tried at Perth by court-martial as a deserter from Skelton's Regiment in the British Army in Flanders and sentenced to death. His execution was carried out with difficulty. The Perth hangman ran away, the Stirling hangman dropped dead when called upon; eventually a fellow-prisoner carried it out. *SHS.2.138.*

CROSBY, WILLIAM, Manchester Regiment. Weaver from Ballycrydaff, Meath, Ireland. Imprisoned 30 December 1745 Carlisle, Chester Castle. Transported July 1748. Taken at capture of Carlisle. Was tried at York on 2 October and sentenced to death. On the day fixed for his execution he was reprieved. *SHS.2.136.*

CROSBY, WILLIAM, Manchester Regiment. Aged 7, from Whitehaven. Imprisoned Carlisle, Chester Castle. "Was with Townley's Regiment." Nothing more is known of him. He was son of the previous William Crosby. *SHS.2.138.*

CROSBY, WILLIAM, weaver from Whitchurch. Manchester Regiment. Taken and transported 1747. *MR196.*

CULLEN, STEPHEN, Captain, Berwick's French Service. Taken at sea *Louis XV* 28 November 1745, Edinburgh Castle 26 December 1745, Berwick February 1746, Hull. Pardoned on condition of perpetual banishment 3 July 1747. *SHS.2.138.*

CULLINAN, AUGUSTUS, Manchester Regiment. From Dublin. Imprisoned 30 December 1745 Carlisle. Taken at capture of Carlisle. There is no further reference to him. *SHS.2.138, MR196.*

CUNNINGHAM, JOHN, a horse hirer from Dunfermline, imprisoned "treasonable practice" 18 July 1746, Dunfermline, released under General Pardon, 1747. *SHS.2.140.*

CUPID, JOHN, French Service. Gentleman from Lyme, Cheshire. Imprisoned Chester Castle. "Apprehended as a rebel." Nothing more is known about him. *SHS.2.140.*

CURRY, HUGH, French Service. Taken at sea Berwick, Marshalsea. Discharged. *SHS.2.140.*

CUSACK, FRANCIS, Captain, Dillon's French Service. Imprisoned Culloden, Inverness. Pardoned on condition of perpetual banishment 3 July 1747. *SHS.2.140, MR135.*

CUTHBERT, LAUNCELOT, Major, French Royal Scots Cavalry, brother to Castlehill. Taken at Culloden, imprisoned Inverness, Southwark. Discharged and banished. Brother of the Laird of Castlehill, Inverness, who was Sheriff Depute, Inverness, and not a Jacobite. Captain in Lord John Drummond's French Regiment of Royal Scots. He took a prominent part in the operations about Inverury in December 1745. He was captured after Culloden and treated with great severity in Southwark, but subsequently he was recognised as a prisoner of war. He

ultimately becaome Lieut. Col. In his own regiment.
MR.61, SHS.2.142.

DADERICK, PETER, French Service. Imprisoned Marshalsea. Discharged. *SHS.2.142.*

D'AIGULLES or DE GUILLES or DU BOYER, ……, Marquis, Captain, Marine Regiment, French Ambassador to the Prince. Imprisoned Culloden, Inverness. Sent back to France. Joined the Prince in October 1745. Was taken after Culloden and was "prisoner at large." *SHS.2.142.*

D'ANDRION, ……….., Artillery, Irish Piquets. Taken at Culloden. Discharged. *MR135.*

D'ARCY, ……, Captain, Conde's Horse, French Service. Imprisoned 21 February 1746 *Bourbon*. Discharged. Aide-de-camp to Count Fitzjames. Captured off Ostend, 21 February 1746. *SHS.2.142.*

DAILY, THOMAS, Clare's French Service. Imprisoned at sea 28 November 1745, Berwick February 1746, Hull. Discharged. *SHS.2.142.*

DALMAHOY, ALEXANDER, son to Sir Alexander Dalmahoy, Thirleston, Linlithgow. Carried arms in the rebel Life Guards, assisted in carrying off two Dragoon horses from the Parks of Kinneil, and in levying the Excise and malt duty for the rebels. Whereabouts not known. *SHS.8.264.*

DALTON, ………., Artillery, Irish Piquets. Killed at siege of Carlisle. *MR135.*

DAMARY, ……., Lieutenant, Lord John Drummond's Regiment, French Royal Scots Cavalry. Taken at Culloden, imprisoned 17 April 1746 Inverness, Penrith. Discharged. *MR.61, SHS.2.142.*

D'ANDRION, ……., Officer, French Artillery, from France. Imprisoned 17 April 1746 Inverness, Penrith. Discharged. *SHS.2.142*.

DARIEN, JASPER, Bulkeley's French Service. From France. Imprisoned at sea 28 November 1745. Hull. Discharged. *SHS.2.144*.

DAVERT, DAVID, gardener to Kilmarnock, Callender House, Linlithgow. Carried arms in the rebel service, said to be killed. *SHS.8.264*.

DAVIDSON, ALEXANDER, shoemaker in the Canongate, Edinburgh, son of Alexander Davidson. Imprisoned Gask, 7 February 1746 Edinburgh (Canongate), Carlisle, transported March 1747. Is styled in the jail report "servant to the Pretender's son." When brought up for trial he pleaded guilty and was sentenced to death, but reprieved. Evidence from John Smith, George Porteous and John Anderson, Excise Officers. *SHS.2.144, SHS.8.338*.

DAVIDSON, ALEXANDER, shoemaker from Cowgate of Edinburgh, Midlothian. Carried arms in the rebel army. Now a prisoner. Was brought to trial at Carlisle, and pleading guilty, was sentenced to death. *SHS.8.246*, SHS.8.379.

DAVIDSON, HENDRY, mason from Tranent. Was with the rebels at Preston battle in Elcho's Regiment, went with them to England and there deserted. In the neighbourhood. *SHS.8.134*.

DAVIDSON, JAMES, servant to Gordon of Carnousie. Aged 14 from Westchester. Imprisoned Inverness June 1746 *Wallsgrave* Tilbury, Tilbury Fort. Released. "A very wicked boy, servant to Gordon of Carnousie. Has been all over Ireland, Scotland and England." The ship return says he was servant to Lord Lewis Gordon. He gave evidence against Adam Hay and others. This may have been the "James Division" who was in the custody of Dick, the messenger in June 1747. *SHS.2.144.*

DAVIDSON, JAMES, soldier, French Royal Scots Cavalry. From Angus (deserter, Scots Fusiliers). Taken. *MR.62.*

DAVIDSON, JAMES, servant from Myreside, Falkland, Fife, imprisoned Falkland, discharged. "Went servant to Lord Kilmarnock when he joined the rebels, but bore no arms." *SHS.2.146, SHS.8.64.*

DAVIDSON, THOMAS, a tinker from Cupar, Fife, imprisoned on suspicion 3 June 1746 Perth, dismissed on bail 26 May 1747. "Witnesses declare he was seen in arms." *SHS.2.146.*

DAVIDSON, THOMAS, resident from Kelso, Teviotdale. Carried arms with the rebels but in what station not known, he is frequently lunatic and has a wife and several children living upon charity. Now at home. *SHS.8.280.*

DAVIS, ROBERT, taken near Carlisle and imprisoned House of Correction, Whitehaven from 15 January 1745. An English deserter who enlisted in the Duke of Perth's regiment. Transported. *CQS.346.*

DAVIS, THOMAS, Clare's French Service. Imprisoned at sea 28 November 1745, Berwick, February 1746 Hull. Discharged. *SHS.2.146*

DAVIES, ROBERT, jail in Whitehaven. *CQS.359.*

DAWSON, JAMES, Captain or Ensign, Manchester Regiment. Student from Lancashire. Imprisoned 30 December 1745 Carlisle, London. Joined the Prince in October 1745. Executed at Kennington Common 30 July 1746. While at St John's College, Cambridge, he ran away and joined the Manchester Regiment. He was taken prisoner at the surrender of Carlisle, sent to London, and executed. *MR.195, SHS.1.148, SHS.2.146.*

DEACON, CHARLES CLEMENT, Ensign, Manchester Regiment. Born 1930, youngest son of Dr Thomas Deacon, non-jurant Bishop in Manchester. Imprisoned 30 December 1745 Carlisle, London (Southwark). Transported July 1748. Joined the Prince at Manchester in November 1745 and was made ensign of the regiment raised there. He was taken prisoner when the garrison of Carlisle surrendered on 30 December 1745. In due course he was sent to London and sentenced to death. He was present at the execution of his brother Thomas, but was himself reprieved on 30 July 1746, probably on account of his youth, being only 17. He appealed for release on 30 April 1748, but was transported. He had been concerned in an attack on the prison warders. *MR.195, SHS.2.148.*

DEACON, ROBERT, Lieutenant, Manchester Regiment. Second son of Dr Thomas Deacon, the non-juring Bishop in Manchester. Imprisoned 30 December 1745 Carlisle, Kendal. Died at Kendal on his way to London, January 1746. With his two brothers he joined the Prince at Manchester, 30 November 1745, and was appointed Lieutenant in the regiment recruited there. Taken prisoner at the surrender of Carlisle on 30 December 1745, he was sent to London but fell ill on the way, and died at Kendal. *MR.195, SHS.2.148.*

DEACON, THOMAS THEODORE, Lieutenant, Manchester Regiment. Son of Dr Thomas Deacon, the non-juring

Bishop in Manchester. Imprisoned 30 December 1745 Carlisle, London. Executed at Kennington Common, 30 July 1746. He was taken prisoner at the surrender of Carlisle and, along with his two brothers, was sent to London; at his trial one Maddox deponed that Deacon "sat at the table at the Bull Head, Manchester, took down the names of such as enlisted in the Pretender's service, and received a shilling for each. When he was writing he employed himself in making blue and white ribbons into favours, which he gave to the men who enlisted." Maddox was an ensign in the regiment who turned King's Evidence. After execution in London his head was sent to Manchester and stuck up on the Exchange there. *SHS.2.150, MR.195, SHS.1.148.*

DE BOYER, JEAN, Marquis d'Eguilles, Ambassador. Taken at Culloden. Discharged. *MR135.*

DE BUTLER, Le Baron, Captain, Fitzjames' Regiment. Imprisoned 21 February 1746 *Charite*, Berwick. Discharged. Taken at sea. *SHS.2.148.*

DE COOKE, Coronet, Fitzjames' Horse, French Service. Taken at sea? *MR38.*

DE FRAINE, CLAUDE, Drummer, Berwick's Regiment. From France. Imprisoned at sea 28 November 1745, Hull. Discharged. *SHS.2.148.*

DE FRAINE, GLAN, French Service. From France. Taken at sea, imprisoned Hull. Discharged. *SHS.2.206.*

DE GORDON, MIRABELLE, Engineer, French Service. From France. Taken at Culloden, imprisoned Inverness, May 1746. Discharged as a prisoner of war. A French Engineer, who came over with Lord John Drummond, he was very unsuccessful in his plan for the sieges of Stirling and of Fort William. Lord Macleod says he was always drunk. He was taken prisoner in May 1746. *SHS.2.240, MR136.*

D'HORTON, ..., Captain, Lord John Drummond's Regiment. From France. Imprisoned 17 April 1746 Culloden, Inverness, Penrith. Discharged. *MR.61, SHS.2.152.*

DE LA HOIDE or DELEHIDE, NICHOLAS, Berwick's French Service. From France. Imprisoned Marshalsea. Discharged. He gave evidence for Nicholas Glascoe. *SHS.2.150.*

DE LA HOYDE, NICHOLAS, Captain, Berwick's Regiment. Imprisoned 17 April 1746 Inverness, Penrith. Discharged. *SHS.2.148, MR135.*

DELLARD, MICHAEL, Manchester Regiment. Imprisoned Carlisle, Lancaster. Woolcomber from Manchester. Taken at the surrender of Carlisle 30 December 1745. He pleased guilty at his trial on 9 September 1746 and was sentenced to death. Executed at Brampton, 21 October 1746. *SHS.1.148, SHS.2.150, MR197.*

DE LONGUEVIL, CHEVALIER, French Service. From France. Discharged. Applied for permission to go home. *SHS.2.148.*

DEMON, ..., soldier, Frenchman, Lord John Drummond's French Royal Scots Cavalry. From France. Imprisoned 18 March 1746, Perth. Discharged. "Taken north by Duke of Cumberland's army." *MR.62, SHS.2.150.*

DEMPSEY, ROBERT, Bulkeley's French Service. Imprisoned 21 February 1746 at sea, Berwick, February 1746 Hull. Discharged. *SHS.2.150.*

DEMPSEY, WILLIAM, Sergeant, Manchester Regiment. Joiner from Inniskillen, Ireland. Imprisoned 30 December 1745 Carlisle, Chester Castle, York Castle. Executed at York, 1 November 1746. Taken at fall of Carlisle. He pleaded guilty at his trial at York on 2 October 1746 and was sentenced to death. *MR.195, SHS.1.148, SHS.2.150.*

DENHAME, JOHN, gardener, Haddington. Carried arms at Preston battle, left the rebels when they went to England. At home. *SHS.8.134.*

DENNEENE or DENSON, JOHN, Lord John Drummond's Regiment. Aged 22. Imprisoned Inverness June 1746 *Liberty & Property* Tilbury. Transported 1747 from Tilbury. *SHS.2.152.*

DENOTHY or DENATIS or DENATER, JOHN, French Service. Aged 35, wigmaker to to Mr Charles Boyd, Callander House, Linlithgow. Carried arms in the rebel service. Now in York Jail. This man was a Frenchman and was probably exchanged as a prisoner of war. On the other hand, in an enquiry dated 17 January 1749, he is referred to as a prisoner under sentence of death, who had been overlooked. *SHS.8.264.*

DE SAUSSAY, ..., French Engineers. From France. Taken at Culloden, imprisoned 17 April 1746 Inverness, Penrith. Discharged. *SHS.2.148, MR135.*

DES VISMES, JOSEPHE DE VENISE, Berwick's French Service. From France. Taken at sea, Berwick on Tweed. Discharged. *SHS.2.152.*

DE TYRCONNEL, ... Brigadier-General, French Service. Imprisoned 21 February 1746 *Bourbon*, Marshalsea.

Discharged. Captured off Ostend, 21 February 1746. *SHS.2.148.*

DEVANT, MARSEIL, Lieutenant, Saintonge's French Service. Captured at sea on *Esperance* 25 November 1745. Discharged. *SHS.2.152.*

DE VIVIER, PHILIPPE, Berwick's French Service. From France. Imprisoned Berwick on Tweed. Discharged. *SHS.2.148.*

DEWAR, JOHN, resident tailor from St Andrews, Fife, imprisoned 25 February 1746 Perth, 9 August 1746 Carlisle, released under General Pardon, 1747. "Carried arms in the rebel service under the Earl of Kelly, from Preston battle." No further reference to him has been traced. *SHS.2.152, SHS.8.64.*

DEWAR, JOHN, resident of St Andrews, Fife. Carried arms in the rebel service from Preston battle under the Earl of Kelly. Killed at Culloden. *SHS.8.64.*

DEY, THOMAS, turner from Edinburgh. Evidence from William Simpson, David Murray and J. Burnlie, all in Hamilton. *SHS.8.342.*

D'HORTORE, DOUGLAS, Captain French Royal Scots Cavalry. Taken Culloden, discharged. *MR.61.*

DIAMOND or DIAMANT, SAMUEL, Rooth's Regiment, French Service. From Collidge, Devonshire. Imprisoned 23 June 1746 Carzie, 23 June 1746 Dumfries. Released under General Pardon, 1747. Deserter. "Confesses that he deserted from General Wolfe's regiment in Flanders, and came over with Ruthe's French regiment." *SHS.2.152, MR137.*

DICK, JOHN, butcher in Prestonpans. Joined the rebels on their march for England. Prisoner at Edinburgh. *SHS.8.134.*

DICKINSON, WILLIAM, Manchester Regiment. Aged 40, weaver from Lancashire. Imprisoned Carlisle, York Castle. Transported from Liverpool to Antigua 8 May 1747. *SHS.2.154, MR.197.*

DICKINSON or DICCONSON, Lieutenant, Lord John Drummond's Regiment, French Royal Scots Cavalry. From France. Taken at Culloden. Imprisoned 17 April 1746 Inverness, Penrith. Discharged. *SHS.2.154, MR.61.*

DICKSON, JOHN, Duke of Perth's Regiment. From Prestonpans. Imprisoned "on suspicion" 3 May 1745 Prestonpans, 4 May 1746 Edinburgh Castle, 6 May 1746 Canongate. Released under General Pardon, 1747. *SHS.2.154.*

DIETZ, JAMES, French Service, Irish Piquets. From France. Imprisoned 16 December 1745 Stirling Castle. Discharged. "Deserted from the rebels." *SHS.2.154, MR137.*

DIKES or DYKES, MARGARET, aged 22 from Linlithgow, West Lothian. Imprisoned Carlisle, Lancaster Castle. "Well looking." Transported from Liverpool to Antigua 8 May 1747 in *Veteran*, arriving Martinique June 1747. *SHS.2.154, PRO.SP36.12).*

DILLON, JOHN, Captain, Dillon's French Service. From Ireland. Taken at Culloden, imprisoned 17 April 1746 Inverness, Berwick. Pardoned on condition of perpetual banishment. *SHS.2.154, MR135.*

DIVEY, EDMUND, Corporal, Bulkeley's French Service. Imprisoned *Louis XV* at sea 28 November 1745, Berwick, Hull. Discharged. *SHS.2.156.*

DIVER or DIVEER, JOHN, Surgeon, Clare's French Service. From France. Taken at sea. Imprisoned *Louis XV* 28 November 1745, Edinburgh Castle 26 December 1745, Berwick, February 1746 Hull. Pardoned on condition of banishment. *SHS.2.156.*

DOBLINSON, ALEXANDER, jail in Whitehaven. *CQS.359.*

DOCHERTY (DUCKERTY), JOHN, from Ireland, Irish Piquets. Taken and discharged. *MR137.*

DODDS, JAMES, aged 29, farmer from Setonhill Mains, Belton, Haddington, East Lothian. Joined the rebels in the Pretender's Son's Life Guards. Clerk of the rebel stores, Balmerino's Life Guards, imprisoned June 1746 Inverness, prison ship *Wallsgrave*, Tilbury Fort, transported 31 March 1747 from London to Jamaica in *St George or Carteret*, arriving Jamaica 1747. The battle of Prestonpans was fought on his farm, and he stated at his trial that his horses were all taken and he was forced out. He called evidence to this effect, and appealed for mercy, on the ground that his family would be beggared if he were transported; however, this was his fate. Transported 31 March 1747 from London to Jamaica, in *St George or Carteret*, arriving Jamaica 1747. *SHS.2.156, BMHS.30.75, PRO.CO137.58, SHS.8.134.*

DONALDSON, JAMES, Ogilvy's Regiment. Aged 50, wright from Edinburgh. Imprisoned 18 May 1746 Dunblane, 24 May 1746 Montrose, Dundee, 13 August 1746 Canongate, Carlisle. Transported from Liverpool to Virginia, in *Gildart*, arriving Port North Potomac, Maryland 5 August 1747. *SHS.2.158, MR.98, PRO.T1.328.*

DONALDSON, JOHN, Roy Stewart's (Edinburgh) Regiment. Gardener, Ballinloan, Angus (Comrie's Company). Taken at Carlisle. Turned King's Evidence and was discharged. *MR206.*

DONALDSON, THOMAS, from Cupar, Fife, Schoolmaster, Haddington, imprisoned on suspicion Haddington 22 July 1746, Perth. "Acted as salt officer and uplifted the Duty for the rebels." Died 9 September 1746. *SHS.2.158, SHS.8.134.*

DONALDSON, WILLIAM, Gardener from Grangepans, Linlithgow, imprisoned in Leith, Canongate, 8 August 1746 Carlisle. "Servant to Alexander Dalmahoy in the rebellion." Nothing further is know about him. *SHS.2.158, SHS.8.264.*

DONDAL, ..., Lieutenant, Fitzjames' Regiment. From France. Taken at sea 21 February 1746 *Bourbon*, Marshalsea. Discharged. This may have been "Peter Dornall" who appealed for mercy on 3 October 1748. *SHS.2.160.*

DONELLY, JAMES, labourer from Brampton, Cumberland. Imprisoned Chester Castle. "Taken near Ashbourne, Derby, said to have served in Hamilton's dragoons." There is no record of his transportation; he may have died in prison. *SHS.2.156.*

DONGET, JAMES, "Bragg's Regiment, Captain Willock's Company." From Surrey. Imprisoned 27 April 1746 Stirling Castle. This entry probably means that he was a deserter from Bragg's Regiment, and in that case he was probably handed over to the military authorities. *SHS.2.158.*

DONNE, JAMES, Lieutenant, Berwick's French Service. Impisoned at sea Berwick, February 1746 Hull, Tower of London. Discharged. *SHS.2.158.*

DOOLING, DAVID, from Lancashire. Imprisoned Stirling. Released under General Pardon, 1747. *SHS.2.158.*

DOUGHERTY, JOHN, French Service. Aged 30, labourer from Ireland. Imprisoned Carlisle. Transported 1747. He asked not to be sent back to France and was transported. *SHS.2.160.*

DOUGLAS, ALEXANDER, soldier, Lord John Drummond's French Royal Scots Cavalry. "Was a deserter from English. "Owned he had deserted from the King's army in Flanders, enlisted with the French, came over with Lord John Drummond, was apprehended robbing a minister's house near Perth in the retreat of the rebel army." His ultimate disposal is not known. Does not appear in the transportation lists. Imprisoned Coupar Angus, 6 February 1746 Perth, 30 March 1746 Edinburgh, 8 August 1746 Carlisle. SHS.2.160, *MR.62.*

DOUGLAS, ARCHIBALD, tailor from Greenock. Imprisoned 20 June 1746 Stirling. "Broke prison and escaped." *SHS.2.160.*

DOUGLAS, CHARLES WILLIAM, Captain, French Service. From Languedoc, France. Taken at Culloden, imprisoned 17 April 1746 Inverness, Penrith. Discharged. *SHS.2.160, MR135.*

DOUGLAS, D'HORTORE, Captain, Lord John Drummond's French Service. Imprisoned 17 Aprill 1746 Inverness, Penrith. Discharged. He was a signatory to the appeal by Lord Louis Drummond on behalf of Captain James Hay of

the French Royal Scots on 22 September 1746.
SHS.2.160.

DOUGLAS, ERSKINE, surgeon, Hillhead, Annandale Stewartry. Brother to Sir John Douglas of Hillhead. Carried arms with the rebels from the time that they left Edinburgh to their repassing the Forth. Now lurking. *SHS.8.142.*

DOUGLAS, FRANCIS, sailor, Hillhead, Annandale Stewartry. Brother to Sir John Douglas of Hillhead. Carried arms with the rebels from the time that they left Edinburgh to their repassing the Forth. Now lurking. *SHS.8.142.*

DOUGLAS, PATRICK, Roy Stewart's (Edinburgh) Regiment. From Banffshire. Taken at Carlisle. Turned King's Evidence and was discharged. *MR206.*

DOUGLAS, ROBERT, gentleman from Cupar, Fife. Collected the Cess for the rebels, was also in the Rebellion in the year 1715. Whereabouts not known. *SHS.8.64.*

DOW, ALLAN, labourer from Glenfinglas, Callender parish, Perthshire. Carried arms with the rebels, was at the battle of Culloden and killed there. *SHS.8.54.*

DOWAR, JOHN, tailor from St Andrews, imprisoned 10 August 1746 Canongate, released under General Pardon, 1747. *SHS.2.162.*

DOWDLE, MATHEW, Clare's French Service. Imprisoned at sea 28 November 1745, Berwick, February 1746 Hull. Discharged. *SHS.2.162.*

DOWLIN, DAVID, from Lancashire. Imprisoned 27 February 1746 Stirling. Released under General Pardon, 1747. Servant to Colonel Baggot. *SHS.2.162.*

DRUM, PETER, French Service. From France. Imprisoned Marshalsea. Discharged. *SHS.2.162.*

DRUMMOND, ……., factor to Drummond of Perth. Was very active in seducing gentlemen from their duty and loyalty to his majesty. At home. *SHS.8.54.*

DRUMMOND, ALEXANDER, Captain, French Service. From France. Imprisoned 24 March 1746 *Prince Charles* (late *Hazard*, HMS *Sheerness* Berwick. Discharged. *SHS.2.162.*

DRUMMOND, JAMES, soldier, French Royal Scots Cavalry. Taken at Culloden. *MR.62.*

DRUMMOND, JOHN, Lieutenant General, Lord, Cavalry, Royal Scots (French). Escaped. *MR.61.*

DRUMMOND, LEWIS, Lord, Lieutenant Colonel, Lord John Drummond's French Royal Scots. From France. Wounded and imprisoned Culloden April 1746, Inverness 29 June 1746 London (Marshalsea). Discharged. Second son of John Drummond the attainted Earl of Melfort, who was Duke of Melfort in the French Peerage, and took part in the Rising of 1715. Lord Lewis lost a leg at Culloden and was kept in Inverness as a prisoner of war. From Mrs Leith's account of him he could bareley speak English. He was sent to London in June 1746 but was treated as a French prisoner of war. He died in Paris in 1792. The regiment of Royal Scots in the French service was raised at the expense of the attainted Drummond family. *SHS.2.162, MR.61.*

DRUMMOND, ROBERT, Messenger at Arms, Edinburgh, Midlothian. Carried arms in the rebel army.

Whereabouts not known. Evidence from George Robertson, Excise Officer. *SHS.8.246, SHS.8.338.*

DRUMMOND, WALTER, porter from Leith, Midlothian. Carried arms as a Sergeant in Drummond of Perth's Regiment. Whereabouts not known. Evidence from Robert Osburn, and James Boyle, Excise Officers. *SHS.8.246, SHS.8.340.*

DRYSDALE, NATHANIEL, Fitzjames' Horse, French Service, aged 14 from Aberdeen, servant to Barnaval. Taken and discharged. *MR38.*

DUBOIS, JOSEPH, Bulkeley's French Service. From France. Imprisoned at sea 28 November 1745, Berwick, February 1746 Hull. Discharged. *SHS.2.166.*

DUBOIS, WILLIAM, Fitzjames' Regiment. From France. Imprisoned Inverness, Perth, Berwick. Discharged. *SHS.2.166, MR38.*

DUCKERTY, JOHN, Dillon's Regiment, French Service. Sailor from Londonderry. Imprisoned Drummond 25 April 1746, Stirling Castle. Discharged. *SHS.2.166.*

DUCKWORTH, JOHN, Lord John Drummond's Regiment. Soldier, French Royal Scots Cavalry. Aged 25 from Lancashire, "was of Bligh's regiment, taken in Germany." Turned King's Evidence against Charles Oliphant. Imprisoned Inverness, June 1746 *Thane of Fife, James & Mary,* Medway. Discharged. *MR.62, SHS.2.166.*

DUFF, ROBERT, aged 25, painter from Glasgow, imprisoned Canongate, 8 August 1746 Carlisle. Evidence from William Tennent and Robert Kerr, painters in Glasgow. Sick with "a bloody flux. Listed with the rebels after Preston battle and continued to the end." Transported 24

April 1747 from Liverpool to Virginia in *Gildart*, arrived Port North Potomac, Maryland 5 August 1747. *SHS.2.168, PRO.T1.328, SHS.8.274, SHS.8.346.*

DUFF, DANIEL, Roy Stewart's (Edinburgh) Regiment. Labourer aged 26, from Perthshire. Taken at Carlisle. Transported 5 May 1747 from Liverpool to Leeward Islands in *Veteran*, arriving Martinique June 1747. *SHS.2.168, MR206, PRO.SP36.102.*

DUFF, JAMES, Roy Stewart's (Edinburgh) Regiment. From Strathbran, Perthshire. Taken at Carlisle. Transported 1747 from Liverpool *SHS.2.168, MR206.*

DUFF, JOHN, Roy Stewart's (Edinburgh) Regiment. Labourer from Kirktoun, Perthshire. Taken at Carlisle. Transported 22 April 1747 from Liverpool to Virginia in *Johnson*, arriving Port Oxford, Maryland 5 August 1747. *SHS.2.168, MR206, PRO.T1.328.*

DUFFEY, JOHN, French Service. From France. Imprisoned *Soleil* Marshalsea. Discharged. Taken at sea in the *Soleil* privateer on the way to Scotland. *SHS.2.168.*

DULLEN, DAVID, from Lancashire. Imprisoned Killin 25 April 1746 Stirling Castle, Edinburgh. Discharged 18 June 1747. "Servant to Colonel Bagot." *SHS.2.168.*

DUMONT, BAPTISTE, French Service. From France. Imprisoned Berwick on Tweed. Discharged. *SHS.2.168.*

DUMONT, RAULEN, French Service. From France. Imprisoned Marshalsea. Discharged. *SHS.2.168.*

DUN or DUNN, EDWARD, Lieutenant, Rooth's Regiment. From France. Imprisoned *Esperance* 25 November 1745,

Deal. Discharged on condition of perpetual banishment. Captured at sea on the way to Montrose. *SHS.2.170.*

DUNCAN, CHARLES, servant to Duchess of Gordon, from Prestonhall. Went north before the battle of Falkirk and joined Lord Lewis Gordon's Core. Whereabouts not known. *SHS.8.134.*

DUNCAN, JAMES, innkeeper at Ferry Porton Craigs, Fife. Drank the Pretender's health and success to his arms, was in Rebellion 1715. *SHS.8.64.*

DUNCAN, JANE, from Leith, Perth's Regiment, taken at capture of Carlisle, imprisoned 30 December 1745 Carlisle, Chester Castle, released. *SHS.2.170.*

DUNCAN, JOHN, soldier, French Royal Scots Cavalry. Aged 21, from Cornie, Banff. Taken at Culloden. Died? *MR.62.*

DUNCAN, PATRICK, from Fife, Ogilvy's Regiment, imprisoned 25 February 1746 Perth, 9 August 1746 Carlisle. There is no further trace of him. He may have died in prison. *SHS.2.172.*

DUNCAN or DONKIN, WILLIAM, Duke of Perth's Regiment. Aged 15, gardener from Edinburgh. Taken at surrender of Carlisle. Imprisoned 30 December 1745 Carlisle, Chester Castle, Whitehaven, Liverpool. Pleaded guilty at his trial and was sentenced to death, 22 August 1745, but reprieved. *SHS.2.172.*

DUNN, NICHOLAS, Sergeant, Berwick's French Service. From France. Imprisoned at sea 28 November 1745, Berwick, February 1746, Hull. Discharged. *SHS.2.172.*

DURIELL or DURIEN, JASPER, French Service. Imprisoned at sea Berwick, February 1746 Hull. Discharged. *SHS.2.174.*

DYCE, JAMES, Aberdeen. Irish Piquets. Taken at Culloden. *MR137.*

DYER, JAMES, soldier, French Royal Scots Cavalry. Aged 56, from Aberdeenshire. Taken at Culloden. Discharged. *MR.62.*

DYER, RICHARD, Berwick's French Service. Imprisoned at sea 28 November 1745, Berwick, February 1746 Hull. Discharged. *SHS.2.174.*

DYERS, JOHN, Bulkeley's Regiment, Surgeon French Service. From France. Imprisoned *Louis XV* at sea, 28 November 1745, February 1746 Hull. Discharged. *SHS.2.174.*

EAGER, JOHN, 2nd Lieutenant, Clare's French Service. Imprisoned *Louis XV* 28 November 1745, Edinburgh Castle 26 December 1745, Berwick, February 1746 Hull. Taken at sea. Pardoned on condition of perpetual banishment. *SHS.2.174.*

EATON, MICHAEL or MOLINEUX, Manchester Reigment. Weaver from Lancashire. Imprisoned 30 December 1745 Carlisle. Executed 15 November 1746. Taken at capture of Carlisle. Tried at Carlisle 19 September 1746 and sentenced to death. *SHS.2.174, MR197.*

EDDRAC or EDCHAC, JAMES, Bulkeley's French Service. From France. Imprisoned at sea 28 November 1745, Berwick, February 1746 Hull. Discharged. *SHS.2.174.*

EDMONSTONE, PETER or PATRICK, of Newton, Doune. Prisoner May 1746 in Stirling Castle, and Edinburgh.

Dischargd 10 July 1747. "Committed by General Edmonstone's order." "Witnesses saw him at Dunblane when the Pretender's son was there. Another saw him riding towards Dunblane, with James Bruce his ground officer walking before him having something in his breast which Bruce told him was colours he was carrying to Dunblane. Further he saw Newton with the Marquis of Perth and some Frenchmen when they were going to Alloa with their cannon, and Newton there had on a white Cockade. George Mackieson says he observed Newton coming from Dunblane and Newton then told him he had been to kiss the Prince's hand, and returning home had on a white cockade." The Prince and his army were at Doune on 12 September 1745. *SRO.CD27/6/31, SHS.2.176.*

ELLIOT, MICHAEL, Clare's French Service. Taken at sea 28 November 1745, imprisoned Berwick, February 1746 Hull. Discharged. *SHS.2.178.*

ELLIS, JOHN, Sergeant, Manchester Regiment. From Northumberland. Taken at Carlisle 30 December 1745. SHS.2.178, *MR.195.*

ELPHINGSTON, ARTHUR, Lord Balmerino. He was involved in the rebellion of 1715, and thereafter spent many years in France. His father having obtained for him a pardon from the Crown, he returned to Scotland, after an absence of about twenty years. On the outbreak of the new rebellion in 1745, Elphinston was one of the first to join the movement, and was appointed Colonel of the second troop of Life Guards to the Chevalier. He was in all the important conflicts of the campaign, was taken prisoner at Culloden, and carried to London along with other noble prisoners. When arraigned he pleaded not guilty, but was condemned. When brought to the block he behaved with great firmness. Having succeeded to the title and estates only in January 1746, he never enjoyed the latter. He left no issue. *SHS.8.377.*

ELPHINGSTON, JAMES, Regality Baillie, Dalkeith. In company with Andrew Brown, collected £50 of Excise for the rebels, being compelled, witness John Murray's letter. Now at home. *SHS.8.134.*

ELPHINSTONE, JOHN. *RH2/8/104.*

EMLY, ALEXANDER, shoemaker from Edinburgh, Midlothian. Carried arms as a volunteer with the rebels. Now lurking. *SHS.8.248.*

ENDSWORTH, JOHN, Grant's Regiment. From Knottesford. Imprisoned Carlisle, York Castle. Executed York 8 November 1746. Pleaded guilty at his trial on 2 October 1746 and was sentenced to death. *SHS.2.178.*

ERSKINE, ..., gentleman, from Montrose, Forfar. "Enlisted men for the Pretender's service." Whereabouts not known. *SHS.8.248.*

ERSKINE, ALEXANDER, Earl of Kelly, Kelly House, Carnbee, Fife. Was a Colonel in the rebel army from the commencement of the Rebellion, was at the battles of Preston, Falkirk, and Culloden, and in the end of September headed a party who collected the Excise in Fife. Lurking in or about his own house. Of this nobleman the *Caledonian Mercury* of 9 October 1745 reports: "The Right Hon. The Earl of Kellie, who, after his joining the Prince's standard, had gone over to Fife in order to raise men to complete his regiment, is returned to camp, and brought a considerable body of men with him." Having been attainted, he surrendered himself to the Lord Justice-Clerk at Edinburgh, in July 1746. After being detained in prison for three years, he was liberated, and died at Kellie in 1756. *SHS.8.64, SHS.8.373.*

ERSKINE, MARTHA, from Kirkbride, Nithsdale, Grant's Regiment, imprisoned Carlisle, Chester Castle, released. *SHS.2.178.*

ERSKINE, THOMAS, merchant, Kilrenny, Boussie parish, Fife. Has carried arms in the Pretender's son's Life Guards from their first raising. Whereabouts not known. *SHS.8.64.*

ERSKINE, THOMAS, from Nithsdale, Grant's Regiment, taken at capture of Carlisle, imprisoned 30 December 1745 Carlisle, York Castle. No further reference to him. *SHS.2.178.*

ESPLINE, JOHN, merchant, Edinburgh. Evidence from David Morrison, brewer and Jonathan Davidson, wright, both in Abbey. SHS.8.338.

ESPLINE, WILLIAM (JOHN?), from Edinburgh, Baggot's Hussars, imprisoned 18 May 1746 Dunichen, 30 May 1746 Montrose, liberated 3 November 1746. Ground officer to Mr Demster, Dunnottar. "For assisting the rebels." *SHS.2.178, SHS.8.248.*

EVANS, SAMUEL, French Service. From France. Imprisoned 16 December 1745 Stirling Castle, Carlisle, Chester. Released 29 July 1747. Deserted from the rebels. *SHS.2.178.*

FAHY, ..., Lieutenant, Fitzjames' Regiment. From France. Imprisoned *Bourbon* Berwick, Febrruary 1746, Hull. Discharged. Taken at sea 21 February 1746. *SHS.2.178.*

FALCONER, JOHN, shoemaker from Pleasents, St Cuthbert's, Edinburgh, Ogilvy's Regiment, imprisoned 17 March 1746

Edinburgh Castle, 8 August 1746 Carlisle, London, released Oct 1747. He turned Evidence against Major Alexander McLauchlan and Aeneas McDonald. *SHS.2.180, SHS.8.248.*

FALLVRE or FALOZE, HUGH, Lally's Regiment, French Service. From Kerry, Ireland. Imprisoned 1 February 1746 Bridge of Allan, 17 March 1746 Edinburgh Castle. Discharged. "Cadee" (caddie). "Confesses that he is a soldier in Bulkeley's French Regiment and came over with the Picquets to Scotland. *SHS.2.180.*

FARO, ……., Engineer, Spanish Service. Imprisoned 24 March 1746 *Prince Charles* (late *Hazard*) HMS *Sheerness* Berwick. Discharged. *SHS.2.180.*

FARRELL, RORY, Berwick's French Service. Taken at sea 28 November 1745, imprisoned Berwick, February 1746 Hull. Discharged. *SHS.2.186.*

FARRIER, MARK, Manchester Regiment. Englishman. Imprisoned Carlisle, York Castle. "Taken in actual rebellion." There is no further reference to him. *SHS.2.186, MR197.*

FARRIER, WILLIAM, Manchester Regiment. Englishman. Imprisoned Carlisle, York Castle. Escaped. "Taken in actual rebellion." Pleaded guilty and was sentenced to death, but reprieved. He succeeded in escaping before being transported. *SHS.2.186, MR197.*

FERGUSON, DONALD, Piper, Roy Stewart's (Edinburgh) Regiment. *MR205.*

FERGUSON, JOHN, tailor and burgess, Edinburgh, Midlothian. Carried arms in the rebel army. Whereabouts not known.

Evidence from Robert Ramsay, tailor, St Mary's Wynd, Edinburgh. *SHS.8.248, SHS.8.338.*

FERRAL, DON RODRIGO (ROGER O'FARRELL), Captain, Engineers, Spanish Service. From Spain. Taken at sea, imprisoned Berwick on Tweed. Discharged. *SHS.2.190.*

FERVAQUE, CRISPIN, Lance-Corporal, Berwick's French Service. From France. Taken at sea, imprisoned Berwick on Tweed. Discharged. *SHS.2.192.*

FIFE, ALEXANDER, son to Gilbert Fife, tailor, Potterrow, Edinburgh, Midlothian. Employed. Whereabouts not known. Evidence from Robert Ramsay, tailor, St Mary's Wynd, Edinburgh. *SHS.8.248, SHS.8.338.*

FIFE, GILBERT, tailor from Potterow, Edinburgh, Midlothian. Seen under arms and in the livery of the rebel Life Guards. Whereabouts not known. *SHS.8.248.*

FINLAY, GEORGE, heelmaker from Anstruther Easter, Fife. Refused to drink his Majesty's health, casting abusive reflections upon his Sacred Majesty and the Presbyterian Ministers and professing his attachment to the Pretender in the strongest manner. At home. Evidence from John Dawson, servant to James Fleeming, shoemaker in Anstruther Easter, James Fleeming and John Traill and others, shoemakers there. *SHS.8.64, SHS.8.352.*

FINLAYSON, JOHN, aged 24 from Edinburgh, Artillery, imprisoned 16 April 1746 Culloden, Inverness, prison ship *Jane of Alloway* Tilbury, released. In the official list of captures at Culloden he is shown as an "Engineer." He was probably the "Mathematik Instrument Maker" who was "employed about the rebel artillery." He was ultimately released and was at home in August 1747. *SHS.2.192, SHS.8.248.*

FINLAYSON, JOHN, salt watchman from Westpans. Acted as salt watchman for the rebels during their stay in the Lothians. Now at home. *SHS.8.136.*

FINNIE, JAMES, from Glasgow. Evidence from Malcolm Cowbrugh, tennent, and Malcolm Cowbrugh, his son, both in the parish of Campsie, and James Reid, gardner in Herriot's Work, Edinburgh. *SHS.8.346.*

FINNIE, ROBERT, servant to Craigbarneth, Burry, Campsie. Carried arms with the rebels, was at Preston battle and acted as a spy in Campsie. Fled the country. *SHS.8.274.*

FITZGERALD, BRYAN, Corporal, Berwick's French Service. Taken at sea 28 November 1745, imprisoned Hull. Discharged. *SHS.2.192.*

FITZGERALD, CHARLES, *alias* GIBSON, French Service. Imprisoned Holland, London. Released. Wounded at Culloden. Appears to have escaped to Holland where he assumed the *alias* of Gibson. He was arrested there on suspicion, sent to London, and imprisoned until February 1749. Was released. *SHS.2.194.*

FITZGERALD, EDWARD, Clare's French Service. Taken at sea 28 November 1745, imprisoned Berwick, February 1746 Hull. Discharged. *SHS.2.194.*

FITZGERALD, GART or GAREET, Sergeant, Berwick's French Service. Taken at sea 28 November 1745, imprisoned Berwick, February 1746 Hull. Discharged. *SHS.2.194.*

FITZGERALD, PATRICK, Captain, Bulkeley's Regiment. Captured at sea *Esperance* 25 November 1745, Deal,

February 1746 Custom House Smack *Caroline* Greenwich, London, Marshalsea. Died in prison. *SHS.2.194.*

FITZGERALD, STEPHEN, French Service. From Newby, Westmorland. Imprisoned Carlisle, Brampton. "Gentleman." "Pretended to be French." He was tried 9 September 1746 and convicted. Orders issued for his execution on 21 October, but he died in prison before that date. *SHS.2.194.*

FITZGERALD, THOMAS, Lord John Drummond's Regiment. From Kilkenny, Ireland. Imprisoned June 1746 Moidart, 4 February 1747 Glasgow, 4 March 1747 Edinburgh. Discharged but deserted on his way to Berwick 4 March 1747. "Was once in Gardiner's Dragoons, thereafter in the Dutch service, was discharged from both. Thereafter entered the French service and came over to Scotland with Drummond's regiment. Deserted from the rebels before Culloden and surrendered himself. *SHS.2.194.*

FITZGERALD, WILLIAM, 2nd Lieutenant, Bulkeley's French Service. Captured at sea *Esperance* 25 November 1745, imprisoned Deal, February 1746 Customs Smack *Caroline* Greenwich, London, Marshalsea. *SHS.2.196.*

FITZJAMES, ..., Comte de, Major General, French Service. Imprisoned 21 February 1746 *Bourbon* at sea, Tower of London. Discharged upon parole 28 February 1746. From France. Son of the Duke of Fitzjames, who was eldest son of the second son of the Duke of Berwick, natural son of James VII and Arabella Churchill. The latter was created Duke of Berwick in 1687. He became a Marshal of France and was killed in 1734. *SHS.2.196.*

FITZMORRIS, ROBERT, French Service. Imprisoned Marshalsea. Discharged. *SHS.2.196.*

FITZPATRICK, PATRICK, French Service. Imprisoned *Louis XV* at sea, Berwick, Hull. Discharged. *SHS.2.196.*

FITZPATRICK, WILLIAM, Lally's French Service. This man when taken prisoner pleaded that he had been forced to join. His disposal is not known. *SHS.2.196.*

FITZSIMONDS or FITZSYMONDS, JOHN, Corporal, Berwick's French Service. Imprisoned *Louis XV* 28 November 1745 at sea, Berwick on Tweed. From France. Discharged. "He had the liberty of the town, till he drank the Pretender's health, upon which I put him in irons and have him now close." *SHS.2.196.*

FLAMMAND, PAUL, French Service. From France. Imprisoned Marshalsea. Discharged. *SHS.2.196.*

FLANAGAN, PETER, Manchester Regiment. From Arsellaugh, Meath, Ireland. Imprisoned 30 December 1745 Carlisle, Chester Castle. Taken at capture of Carlisle. There is no record of what happened to him. He was not in the transportation lists. *SHS.2.196, MR197.*

FLANDY, MART, Clare's French Service. From France. Imprisoned at sea 28 November 1745, Berwick, February 1746 Hull. Discharged. *SHS.2.196.*

FLASHY, JOHN, Berwick's French Service. From France. Taken at sea 28 November 1745, imprisoned Berwick, February 1746 Hull. Discharged. *SHS.2.196.*

FLEMING, PAUL, French Service. From France. Imprisoned *Soleil* 25 November 1745 at sea, Marshalsea. Discharged. In French Service. Taken at sea in *Soleil* privateer going to Scotland. *SHS.2.198.*

FLETCHER, GEORGE, Captain, Manchester Regiment. Linen-draper from Lancashire, aged 25. Imprisoned 30 December 1745 Carlisle, London (Southwark). Executed at Kennington Common, 30 July 1746. Taken at capture of Carlisle. At his trial it was said he paid 150 guineas for his commission. *MR.195, SHS.1.148, SHS.2.198.*

FLETCHER, JOHN, from Lancashire. Imprisoned Lancaster Castle. "Committed on suspicion." Ultimate disposal unknown. Probably discharged. *SHS.2.198.*

FLINT, AGNES, Glenbucket's Regiment. From Dunbar. Imprisoned 30 December 1745 Carlisle, Chester Castle. Released. With a child of 7. Taken at fall of Carlisle. *SHS.2.198.*

FLINT, JAMES, Irish Piquets, Cadet, from Inverness-shire. Taken at Culloden. Discharged. *MR135.*

FLINT, JOHN, Glenbucket's Regiment. From Berwick. Imprisoned 30 December 1745 Carlisle, York Castle. Pardoned on condition of enlistment 22 July 1746. Taken at capture of Carlisle. Pleaded guilty at his trial on 2 October and was sentenced to death, but reprieved. *SHS.2.198.*

FONDEDRITE, VINESSE, Berwick's Regiment. From France. Imprisoned Inverness, Perth, Berwick. Discharged. *SHS.2.198.*

FORBES, ..., gentleman. Attended the Pretender's son under arms. Whreabouts not known. *SHS.8.248.*

FORBES, ALEXANDER, aged 20 from Wemyss, Fife, "Servant to the Pretender." Duke of Perth's Regiment, imprisoned Larbert, 25 April 1746 Stirling Castle, prison ship *James & Mary,* Medway. Transported 31 March

1747 from London to Jamaica in *St George or Carteret*, arriving Jamaica 1747. *SHS.2.200, MR71, PRO.CO137.58, BMHS.76.*

FORBES, DUNCAN, resident of Kirkcaldy. "Concealed two rebells in his house for which was apprehended but liberate." No other reference to him appears in the Records. Discharged. Now at home. *SHS.2.200, SHS.8.260.*

FORBES, FRANCIS, French Service. From Ireland. Captured at sea *Louis XV* 28 November 1745, imprisoned Edinburgh Castle. Executed 24 January 1746 in Edinburgh. Was found to be a deserter from the Royal Regiment, and was hanged. *SHS.2.200.*

FORBES, JAMES, Roy Stewart's (Edinburgh) Regiment. Printer from Caithness. Taken, pardoned on enlistment. *MR206.*

FORBES, JOHN, wright from Edinburgh. Carried arms as a volunteer in the rebel army. Whereabouts not known. *SHS.8.248.*

FORBES, JOSEPH, journeyman wright from Haddington. Joined the rebels about the time of Preston battle and continued with them till dispersed. Said to be influenced by his uncle, Joseph Robertson, non jurant Minister at Haddington. *SHS.8.136.*

FORBES, ROBERT, Rev, from Leith. Imprisoned 7 July 1745 St Ninians, 7 July 1745 Stirling Castle, 4 February 1746 Edinburgh Castle. Released 29 May 1746. Son of Charles Forbes, schoolmaster of Rayne, Aberdeenshire, the Rev Robert Forbes was an Episcopal clergyman in Leith. When he heard of the Prince's landing, he set off with six friends to join him, but was captured at St Ninians and imprisoned first in Stirling, then in Edinburgh Castle, where he was kept until 29 May 1746. In 1762 he became Bishop of Ross. He died on 18 November 1775. To him we owe the *Lyon in Mourning*, which is one of the most important contemporary chronicles of the 1745. *SHS.2.202.*

FORREST, JAMES, Wright from Falkirk, imprisoned 24 January 1746 Coltness; 26 January 1746 Edinburgh Jail Canongate, 8 August 1746 Carlisle. "For treasonable practises"; was in hospital with "scurvey in his legs." "Says that he was a volunteer for his late Majesty in 1715 and had no concern in the late rebellion, but was taken up on his way to Edinburgh to deliver a Dragoon horse that the rebels had left after the battle of Falkirk." There is no record of him after he got to Carlisle. He may have died. *SHS.2.204.*

FORRESTER, WILLIAM, from Edinburgh, Duke of Perth's Regiment, imprisoned Drummond of Linnoch; 4 May 1746 Stirling Castle. "Soldier in Lord Sempill's Regiment." Deserter. Was probably handed over to the military authorities. *SHS.2.204.*

FOSTE, FRANCIS, French Service. From France. Imprisoned Inverness, Perth, Edinburgh, Berwick. Discharged. "A French soldier." "Mariner." *SHS.2.204.*

FOSTER, THOMAS, Berwick's French Service. Imprisoned at sea 28 November 1745, Berwick, February 1746 Hull. Discharged. *SHS.2.204.*

FOURE, LOUIS, French Artillery, Irish Piquets. From France. Imprisoned York. Acquitted and discharged. Was indicted on a charge of plundering Lord Lonsdale's house of Lowther Hall, in conjunction with one James Jellens and Edmond Clavering. At his trial at York on 2 October 1746 he was acquitted. *SHS.2.20, MR137.*

FOX, GABRIEL or CARBERY, Lieutenant, Dillon's French Service. Taken at Culloden, imprisoned 17 April 1746 Inverness, Penrith, Southwark. Pardoned on condition of perpetual banishment. *SHS.2.206, MR135.*

FOX, THOMAS, from Leicester. Imprisoned Gartmore, 2 May 1746 Perth, 12 May 1746 Stirling Castle, 9 August 1746 Carlisle. "In Guise's Regiment." And therefore a deserter. Was probably handed over to the military authorities. *SHS.2.206.*

FRANCOIS, PHILIP, French Service. From Hanau. Imprisoned June 1746 *Wallsgrave* Tilbury. Discharged. *SHS.2.206.*

FRANCOIS, PHILLIPE, Servant to Captain Burke, Irish Piquets. Taken and acquitted. *MR137.*

FRANDSHAM, ROBERT, Bulkeley's French Service. From France. Imprisoned at sea 28 November 1745, Hull. Discharged. *SHS.2.206.*

FRAPONT, GREGORY, French Service. From France. Taken at sea, imprisoned Hull. Discharged. *SHS.2.206.*

FRASER, HUGH, soldier, French Royal Scots Cavalry. Aged 27, husbandman from from Auchindiach, Inverness. Taken at Culloden. Transported 31 March 1747 from London to Jamaica in St George or Carteret, arriving Jamaica 1747. *SHS.2.212, MR.62, PRO.CO137.58.*

FRASER, HUGH, French Service. From France. Taken at sea in *Soleil* 24 November 1745 on the way to Scotland, imprisoned Marshalsea. Discharged. *SHS.2.212.*

FRASER or FRAZER, WILLIAM (of Dalernig?) from Kiltarlity, Captain, William Frazer's Company, imprisoned February 1746 Clifton; 4 February 1747 Glasgow, discharged 15 July 1747. *SHS.2.218.*

FREGER, ALEXANDER, Clare's French Service. Taken at sea 28 November 1745, imprisoned Berwick, February 1746 Hull. Discharged. *SHS.2.218.*

FRIEJOHN, ANTHONY, Berwick's French Service. From France. Taken at sea 28 November 1745, imprisoned Berwick, February 1746 Hull. Discharged. *SHS.2.218.*

FULTHORP, ROGER, Manchester Regiment. Imprisoned Carlisle. Pardoned on condition of enlistment 22 July 1746. Barber from Warrington. He pleaded guilty when arrained, 16 August 1746. Sentenced to death. "Appeared to be very young." *SHS.2.220, MR197.*

FURNIVALL, THOMAS, Lieutenant, Manchester Regiment. A Manchester warehouseman from Cheshire. Imprisoned 30 December 1745 Carlisle, London. Banished. Taken at capture of Carlisle. Was tried, pleaded guilty and sentenced to death, but was reprieved and banished on condition of never returning. He was concerned in an assault on the warders of the prison. *SHS.2.220, MR.195.*

FYRE, JOHN, carter, Leith. Evidence from Mr Balfour. *SHS.8.342.*

GALL, ALEXANDER, late salt officer from Kirkcaldy, Fife. Joined the rebels after Preston battle and with a strong party and great rigour collected the excise for them to a considerable extent and granted his receipts therefor. Whereabouts not known. Evidence from his receipts to brewers in Fife for Excise. *SHS.8.260, SHS.8.344.*

GALLET, JEAN, Berwick's French Service. From France. Imprisoned Berwick. Discharged. *SHS.2.220.*

GAM, PETER, jail in Whitehaven. *CQS.359.*

GARCY, LAWRENCE, Berwick's French Service. Taken at sea 24 November 1745 *Soleil*, imprisoned Marshalsea. Discharged. *SHS.2.220.*

GARDEE, JEAN, French Service. Taken at sea 24 November 1745 *Soleil*, imprisoned Marshalsea. Discharged. In French service. Taken in *Soleil* privater at sea going to Scotland. *SHS.2.220.*

GARDNER, ALEXANDER, from Linlithgow, Duke of Perth's Regiment, imprisoned 30 December 1745 Carlisle; Lincoln Castle. Taken at capture of Carlisle. Sentenced to be transported, but died in prison before April 1747. *SHS.2.220.*

GARDNER, JAMES, from Airth, Stirlingshire, servant to James Graham, younger of Airth. Imprisoned in Edinburgh. Killed one of His Majesty's dragoons at Stirling. Prisoner at Edinburgh." Released under General Pardon, 1747. Evidence from James Raith, barber in Airth and Alexander Archibald, shoemaker there. *SHS.2.222, SHS.8.56, SHS.8.316.*

GARDNER or GARDINER, NICHOLAS, aged 27, from Lancashire. Imprisoned 29 February 1746 Perth, 10 August 1746 Canongate, August 1746 Carlisle, August 1747 Liverpool. Transported 1747. "In rebel service." "Servant to Clichton." *SHS.2.222.*

GARRETY, CORNELIUS, French Service. Taken at sea, imprisoned Berwick. Discharged. From France. *SHS.2.222.*

GARVEY, LAWRENCE, French Service. Taken at sea, imprisoned Berwick, February 1746 Hull, Marshalsea, London. Discharged. *SHS.2.222.*

GAY, JOSEPH, Lord John Drummond's Regiment. From France. Imprisoned 1745, 6 February 1746 Perth, 10 May 1746 Inverness. Discharged. *SHS.2.222.*

GEDD or GADD, JAMES, printer from Edinburgh, Captain, Perth's Regiment, imprisoned in Carlisle; London. "Acted as printer for the rebels." He was son of William Gedd, goldsmith, Edinburgh, who in 1725 invented the art of stereotyping. After an unsuccessful venture in partnership with some London tradesmen, the Gedds in 1738 resumed business in Edinburgh, and in the following year isued an edition of *Sallust* printed by the new process. Their labours were interrupted by the Jacobite rising of 1745, in which James Gedd took part. James Gedd was made prisoner at Carlisle, sent to London and condemned to death, after pleading gulty; but no sentence was recorded against him, and, through the influence of friends, including the Master of Trinity College, Oxford, and in recognition of his father's invention, he was reprieved and pardoned, and he emigrated to Jamaica. *SHS.2.222, SHS.8.248, SHS.8.379.*

GEOGHEGAN, ALEXANDER, Captain, Lally's French Service. From France. Imprisoned 17 April 1746 Inverness, Penrith. Pardoned on condition of permanent banishment. *SHS.2.224.*

GEOGHEGAN, or GOROGAN, Sir FRANCIS, Captain, Lally's French Service. From Ireland. Imprisoned 30 December

1745 Carlisle Castle, Penrith. Discharged. The Prince gave Sir Francis a commission to raise an English regiment when they reached Preston. The Prince's officers pointed out that, being a Catholic, it was inexpedient to appoint him to command Englishmen; and his commission was consequently withdrawn. He was one of the French officers taken prisoner at Carlisle at its surrender. He styled himself "Commander of the French Artillery" and of the French garrison at Carlisle and subscribed his name "De Geoghegan" in a letter which was captured before the fall of that town. This was "Le Chevalier Georghegan" who was signatory to the protest against the treatment of James Hay. *SHS.2.226.*

GEORGE, JOHN, Lord John Drummond's Regiment. From France. Imprisoned 25 June 1746 from Royal Infirmary, 15 July 1746 Canongate Jail, Edinburgh Tolbooth. Discharged. "Servant to Captain Douglas." *SHS.2.226.*

GERITY, CORNELIUS, Sergeant, Berwick's French Service. From France. Imprisoned Berwick. Discharged. *SHS.2.226.*

GIB or GIBB, JAMES, from Edinburgh, Master of the Household of the Prince, imprisoned 16 May 1746 Leven; 16 May 1746 Kirkcaldy, 19 May 1746 Leith, 14 August 1746 Canongate, discharged on bail 8 May 1747. Excise Officer, Leven. "Clerk to the Pretender's son's kitchen." This man's household accounts are contained in *LYON, ii. 115-132*, and from the narrative of his wanderings it appears that it was entirely an accident that he escaped being sent to Carlisle with other prisoners. *SHS.2.226.*

GIBSON, ROGER, shoemaker from Edinburgh, imprisoned in Holland and London. Was arrested in Holland on suspicion and sent to London, and was in prison for 16 months before his release. *SHS.2.228.*

GILES, RICHARD, resident of Canongate, Edinburgh, Midlothian. Carried arms in the rebel army. Whereabouts not known. Evidence from John Wood, vintner, and Alexander Spark, ale seller, Cannongate. *SHS.8.248, SHS.8.338.*

GILLESPIE, THOMAS, aged 13, from servant from Linlithgowshire, Duke of Perth's Regiment, imprisoned Culloden, Inverness; June 1746 prison ship *Jane of Alloway* Tilbury. The Culloden list. *SHS.2.228.*

GLASCOE or GLASGOW, NICHOLAS, Major, Dillon's Regiment. Irish Piquets. From France. Imprisoned Culloden Inverness, June 1746 *Dolphin* Tilbury, London (Southwark). Acquitted as a rebel but detained as a prisoner of war 10 November 1746 and subsequently discharged to France. Lieutenant in Dillon's Irish-French Regiment, he acted as major and military instructor to the 2nd Battalion Lord Ogilvy's Regiment. He was in charge of the batteries in Montrose harbour when the English sloop *Hazard* was captured on 24 November 1745. He is also said to have acted as military instructor to Lord Ogilvy's 2nd Battalion. He carried out a brilliant little night action at Keith on 20 March 1746 against a body of Campbells, killing 9 and taking 80 prisoners and 30 horses, losing only one man himself. He was taken prisoner after Culloden and sent to London, where he was brought to trial. He pleaded that he was born in France and held a French commission, and was consequently released from the status of rebel, his irons were removed, and he was treated as a prisoner of war. *SHS.2.228, MR135.*

GLASSFOORD, THOMAS, son to Duncan Glasfoord, shipmaster, Borowstounness, Linlithgow. Carried arms in the Pretender's son's Life Guards. Now lurking. *SHS.8.264.*

GLOUDE, DE FRAINE, drummer, French Service. From France. Taken at sea, imprisoned Berwick, February 1746 Hull. Discharged. *SHS.2.230.*

GOFF, JOHN, Dillon's Regiment, Irish Piquets. From France. Imprisoned Culloden, *Pamela* Tilbury, in hospital ship *Mermaid*. Transported 1747. "Apprentice to a clothier in Dublin, lived 14 years there, left that country 8 years after; has the brogue very strong, yet, this is one of Mons. Carpentier's Frenchmen who can't speak English. However he signed a petition with John Lowden. *SHS.2.230, MR137.*

GOLD, JOHN, French Service. From France. Pardoned on condition of permanent banishment 2 July 1747. *SHS.2.230.*

GOLD, THOMAS, French Service. From France. Pardoned on condition of permanent banishment 2 July 1747. *SHS.2.230.*

GOODING or GOODEN, JOHN, from Ireland. Imprisoned Stirling. Discharged. "On suspicion." Declares that he was not concerned in the rebellion. *SHS.2.232.*

GOODWILLIE, JOHN, writer from Edinburgh, Midlothian. Wore tartans with a white cockade and assisted in levying the revenues, etc. Whereabouts not known. Evidence from James Thomson and George Robertson, Excise Officers. *SHS.8.248, SHS.8.338.*

GORDON, GEORGE, innkeeper, West Port, Edinburgh, St Cuthberts parish. Entered a volunteer in the rebel army. Whereabouts not known. *SHS.8.248.*

GORDON, JOHN, weaver from Edinburgh, Midlothian. Carried arms in the rebel army. Whereabouts not known. Evidence from John Sloss, Excise Officer and Deacon Lawson, weaver, Edinburgh. *SHS.8.248, SHS.8.342.*

GORDON, JOHN?, Major French Royal Scots Cavalry. Taken, discharged? *MR.61.*

GORDON, JOHN, from France. Imprisoned 26 July 1746 Tranent, 26 July 1746 Haddington. Discharged. "Aiding and assisting the rebels." He was probably in French Service. *SHS.2.238.*

GORDON, PETER, Rev Father, from London. Imprisoned November 1645 Newgate Messenger's House. Released. Arrested for "treasonable practices." There is some doubt about his identity. In his petition he asked to be allowed to go to any Catholic country, and was sent to Holland on 28 February 1746; there he was described as a "Romish priest." He appealed from Newgate for release in February 1746. *SHS.2.240.*

GORDON, ROBERT, from Canongate, Edinburgh, Glenbucket's Regiment, imprisoned Carlisle, acquitted Oct 1746. Alehouse keeper. Tried at Carlisle 19-26 September 1746 and acquitted in consideration of his having surrendered in time. Evidence from John Izat, chandler and Colin Mitchel, goldsmith, Cannongate. *SHS.2.240, SHS.8.248, SHS.8.338.*

GORDON, ROBERT, of Becomie, Midlothian. Carried arms in the rebel army. *SHS.8.248.*

GORDON, WALTER, aged 24, painter from Midlothian, Balmerino's Life Guards, imprisoned 16 April 1746 Culloden; 17 April 1746 Inverness, June 1746 prison ship

Wallsgrave Tilbury. As there is no further reference to him he probably died. *SHS.2.242, SHS.8.248.*

GORE, JAMES, from London. Imprisoned Huntingtower 30 February 1746, Perth, 12 May 1746 Stirling Castle. "Deserter in rebel service." "Colonel Lee's regiment, Sir P. Halkett's Co." His disposal is unknown. He was probably handed over to the military authorities. *SHS.2.242.*

GORNALL, THOMAS, Manchester Regiment. Imprisoned Lancaster. Discharged February 1747. *SHS.2.242, MR197.*

GOW, THOMAS, shoemaker from Potterow, Edinburgh, Midlothian. Carried arms as a rebel Hussar. Whereabouts not known. *SHS.8.248.*

GOULD, JOHN (Don Juan), Captain, Spanish Service. From Spain. Imprisoned 24 March 1746 *Prince Charles* (late *Hazard*), HMS *Sheerness*, Berwick. Pardoned on condition of perpetual banishment 2 July 1747. The Jail return of 16 July 1746 speaks of him as "a man of good fortune." *SHS.2.244.*

GOULD or GOOLD, THOMAS, Lieutenant, Berwick's Regiment. From France. Imprisoned 17 April 1746 Inverness, Penrith. Discharged. *SHS.2.244.*

GOWDER, JOHN, wright from Hamilton, imprisoned Cardross; 4 May 1746 Stirling Castle, released under General Pardon, 1747. "Baggage man, Sullivan's Regiment." *SHS.2.244.*

GRACE, ROBERT, Captain, Lally's French Service. From France. Taken on *Esperance* 25 November 1745, imprisoned Deal, Tower of London. Pardoned on condition of perpetual exile 2 July 1747. Captured at sea. *SHS.2.244.*

GRAHAM, AL, chapman in Glasgow. Evidence from James Graham, tailor, Al Dick, maltman, and Robert McNair, merchant, all in Glasgow. *SHS.8.346.*

GRAHAM, JAMES, younger of Airth, Stirlingshire. Joined the rebels when they first passed the Forth and carried arms with them. Lurking. Evidence from inhabitants of Airth. *SHS.8.56, SHS.8.316.*

GRAHAM, JOHN, of Kilmordinny, Clobar, with the Laird of Mains. Was Aid de Camp to Lord Strathallan and Lieutenant in his Regiment, he was some years ago an Ensign in the Holland Service in a Scots Regiment. Whereabouts not know. Evidence from Alexander Forrester, vintner, James Forrester, maltman, both in Kilsyth, William Adam, farmer in Craigston in Kilsyth, Alexander Dick, maltman and John Rob, Town Officer, both in Glasgow. *SHS.8.274, SHS.8.346.*

GRAHAM, JOHN, painter from Glasgow, Lanark. Enlisted with the rebels on their retreat from England and left them on their flight to Inverness. Now at home. Evidence from William Tennent, Robert Kerr and Jonathan Borland, painters in Glasgow. *SHS.8.274, SHS.8.346.*

GRAHAM, JOHN, barber from Edinburgh, Midlothian. Carried arms in the rebel army as a volunteer. Whereabouts not known. *SHS.8.248.*

GRAHAM, MUNGO, Writer in Edinburgh, "Commissary Officer" imprisoned 22 January 1746/7 on a ship in Leith Road (Mr Mackenzie Master); 24 January 1746/7 Edinburgh Castle, released June 1747. "On suspicion of treason." *SHS.2.248.*

GRAHAM, WALTER, son to the late Walter Graham, surgeon, Falkirk. Acted as surgeon in the rebel army. Whereabouts not known. *SHS.8.264.*

GRANT, ALLAN, Roy Stewart's (Edinburgh) Regiment. Aged 60, labourer from Strathspey. Deserted. Taken and transported 5 May 1747 from Liverpool in *Johnson*, arriving Port Oxford, Maryland 5 August 1747. *SHS.2.250, MR206, PRO.T1.328.*

GRANT, ANGUS, jail in Whitehaven. *CQS.359.*

GRANT, CHARLES, Roy Stewart's (Edinburgh) Regiment. Aged 19, miller from Abernethy, Inverness-shire. Taken at Carlisle. Transported 5 May 1747 from Liverpool to Leeward Islands in *Veteran*, arriving Martinique June 1747. *SHS.2.252, MR206, PRO.SP36.102.*

GRANT, COLQUHOUN, Lieutenant, Roy Stewart's (Edinburgh) Regiment. Writer from Edinburgh. Pardoned. *MR205.*

GRANT, GRIGOR, glassgrinder from Glasgow, Lanarkshire. Joined the rebels at Glasgow and went off with them. Whereabouts not known. Evidence from Jonathan Jamison, wright and James Alison, maltman, both in Glasgow. *SHS.8.272, SHS.8.346.*

GRANT, JAMES, aged 60, a printer and news writer from Edinburgh, Captain (or Lieutenant), Ogilvy's Regiment. Imprisoned January 1748 Harwich, London, discharged 16 February 1748. Admitted he had been out in the '15. Was on the staff of the *Caledonian Mercury*. Murray of Broughton employed him as printer to the Force. He went to Holland after finding no work to do, and was sent home on suspicion. *SHS.2.256, SHS.8.248, SHS.2.256.*

GRANT, JAQUES, Lieutenant, Lally's French Service. From France. Imprisoned 17 April 1746 Inverness, Penrith. Discharged. *SHS.2.258.*

GRANT, JOHN, barber from Edinburgh. Carried arms as a volunteer. Whereabouts not known. *SHS.8.248.*

GRANT, JOHN, Roy Stewart's (Edinburgh) Regiment. Weaver, aged 34, from Banff. Taken at Carlisle. Transported 5 May 1747 from Liverpool to Virginia in *Johnson*, arriving Port Oxford, Maryland 5 August 1747. *SHS.2.262, MR206, PRO.T1.328.*

GRANT, WALTER, aged 40, barber in Edinburgh, from Teviotdale, Strathallan's Regiment. Imprisoned Inverness; June 1746 prison ship *Jane of Leith* Tilbury, Tilbury Fort. Transported 20 March 1747 from London to Jamaica in *St George or Carteret*, arriving Jamaica 1747. *SHS.2.264, PRO.CO137.58, BMHS.78, SHS.8.248.*

GRANT, WILLIAM, Roy Stewart's (Edinburgh) Regiment. Aged 45, from Inverness. Taken and transported 1747. *MR206, SHS.2.264.*

GRAVENOUR, ROBERT, Sergeant, French Royal Scots Cavalry. From Lancashire (Hay's Company). Taken and transported. *MR.62.*

GRAY, WILLIAM, weaver from Gorbals of Glasgow, Meikle Govan, Lanarkshire. Pedee to one Smith in the rebel Life Guards who enticed him. He is only 15 years of age and engaged when the main body lay at Glasgow. Whereabouts not known. Evidence from James Aird, weaver and James Picken, innkeeper, both in Gorbals at Glasgow. *SHS.8.274, SHS.8.346.*

GRENIER, JEAN, Corporal, Berwick's French Service. From France. Imprisoned Berwick. Discharged. *SHS.2.268.*

GRENSHIRE, JAMES, Manchester Regiment. From Lancashire. Imprisoned 30 December 1745 Carlisle. Taken at capture of Carlisle. Does not appear to have been transported. *SHS.2.268, MR197.*

GROSVENOR, ROBERT, "French Soldier", aged 22 from France. Imprisoned Carlisle. Transported 1747. His name is shown in the transportation list of 26 October 1746, although belonging to the French Service. *SHS.2.270.*

GRUMMELL, MICHAEL, Berwick's French Service. From France. Taken at sea 28 November 1745, imprisoned Berwick, February 1746 Hull. Discharged. *SHS.2.270.*

GRUNDALL, JOHN, conveyed from Penrith to Brough, Westmoreland in the company of 19 other Jacobites. *CQS.354.*

GRUNDALL, ROBERT, conveyed from Penrith to Brough, Westmoreland in the company of 19 other Jacobites. *CQS.354.*

GUDDEN, JOHN, Irishman. Imprisoned 8 April 1746 Stirling, Edinburgh. Discharged 18 June 1747. "On suspicion of being in the rebellion." *SHS.2.270.*

GUIDE, JOSEPH, French Service. From France. Imprisoned Marshalsea. Discharged. *SHS.2.270.*

GUIGNARD, GUILLAUME, Berwick's French Service. Imprisoned Berwick. Discharged. *SHS.2.270.*

GUILLAUME, ENEAS, French Service. Taken at sea on the *Soleil* privateer on the way to Scotland 25 November 1745. Imprisoned Marshalsea. Discharged. *SHS.2.270.*

GYERY, JOHN, Berwick's French Service. Taken at sea 28 November 1745, Imprisoned Hull. Discharged. *SHS.2.272.*

HACKET, CHARLES, barber in Edinburgh, Midlothian. Was a volunteer in the rebel army. Whereabouts not known. *SHS.8.250.*

HACKETT, JOHN, Bulkeley's French Service. Taken at sea *Louis XV* 28 November 1745, Imprisoned Berwick February 1746, Hull. Discharged. *SHS.2.272.*

HADDIN, ALEXANDER, son of John Haddin of Lendrick, Kilmadock parish, Perthshire. Had a commission in the rebel army and went along with them. Whereabouts not known. *SHS.8.56.*

HADDIN, JOHN, of Lendrick, Kilmadock parish, Perthshire. Carried arms in the Pretender's Son's Life Guards. Whereabouts not known. *SHS.8.56.*

HALDANE, ALEXANDER, Lord John Drummond's, French Royal Scots Cavalry. Imprisoned 16 March 1746 Glamis, 7 July 1746 Aberdeen. Discharged. Deserter from Semple's Regiment. "Late of the Welsh Fusiliers. Says he was dismissed from them as being lame and wrong in his judgment, and appears to have been an idiot." *MR.62, SHS.2.272.*

HALE, M, Major French Royal Scots Cavalry, ADC to Lord John, drowned at sea. *MR.61.*

HALLIBURTON, THOMAS, carpenter from Dundee. Carried arms in the rebel army and was active in pressing horses. Whereabouts not known. Evidence from William Begg and Jonathan Chapman, Excise Officers. *SHS.8.250, SHS.8.342.*

HALDEN, ALEXANDER, see *John Halden. SHS.8.373.*

HALDEN, JOHN of Lanrick, Stirling district, and his son, Alexander, are mentioned in precognition taken by the sheriff at the town of Lanark on 21 September 1748, when Christopher Bannatyne, merchant and bailie there, deponed that, upon Christmas Day 1745, a party of rebels came to Lanark, amongst whom were the said John and Alexander Halden, and that the latter came into a room where the declarant and Bailie Wild were sitting, with a party of the rebels with drawn swords, in order to force them to come out to the cross to witness a proclamation of the Pretender, which they were forced to do. The Haldens escaped to the Continent, and the father died in Paris in 1765. *SHS.8.373.*

HAMILTON, ELIZABETH, see CLAVERING.

HAMILTON, GEORGE, of Redhouse, Edinburgh, Captain, Baggot's Hussars. Imprisoned Clifton; York Castle. Tried at York, found guilty, and executed there on 1 November 1746. Was captured at Clifton, and was tried at York, found guilty and executed. It was stated at his trial that he went to the Canongate Church, where several English soldiers were confined after Prestonpans, and threatened them with death if they refused to enlist in the Prince's army. Evidence was produced that actually he had tended the English wounded, but this was rebutted. Evidence from Ninian Trotter, George Robertson and Francis Pringle, Excise Officers. *SHS.2.274, SHS.8.250, SHS.8.338, SHS.8.379.*

HAMILTON, JAMES, "A common fidlar" from Kirkintilloch. Imprisoned 13 January 1746 Linlithgow, 20 January 1746 Leith. Liberated 7 February 1746. *SHS.2.274.*

HAMILTON, JOHN, from Linlithgow, Duke of Perth's Regiment. Imprisoned 30 December 1745 Carlisle; York Castle. Taken at capture of Carlisle. As his name does not appear again he probably died. *SHS.2.274.*

HAMILTON, JOHN, Roy Stewart's (Edinburgh) Regiment. Taken and discharged. *MR206.*

HAMILTON, ROBERT, younger of Kilbrachmant, Fife. Joined the rebels and was at Preston battle. Returned home soon after where he has ever since continued. NB he is disordered in his judgement. Now at home. Evidence from Alexander Gourly, smith in Colinsburgh, Thomas Henderson, servant in Bowes in Ely parish. *SHS.8.260, SHS.8.344.*

HAMILTON, ROBERT, sailor, Woodside, near Glasgow, Lanark. Joined in the very beginning of the rebellion and was in the Life Guards. Was in the party that disarmed the well affected in Baldernock. There was a warrant against him prior to the rebellion for carrying over to the French service men raised in the highlands. Fled south. Evidence from David Findlay of Bogside, Robert Miller, portioner and Robert Finnie, wright, all in Balmor and Baldernock parish, Alexander Dick, maltman in Glasgow, and James Buchanan, stabler there. *SHS.8.274, SHS.8.346.*

HAMPTON, FRANCIS, French Service. From France. Taken at sea, imprisoned Berwick. Discharged. *SHS.2.274.*

HARDBUCKLE, WILLIAM, Manchester Regiment.
Imprisoned Carlisle, York Castle 17 March 1746
Edinburgh Castle, 8 August 1746 Carlisle. "Taken in
actual rebellion." No further reference to him.
SHS.2.276, MR197.

HARGREAVES or HARGRAVE, WILLIAM, Manchester
Regiment. From Lancashire. Imprisoned 30 December
1745 Carlisle, Lancaster Castle. Pardoned on condition of
enlistment 22 July 1748. Taken at capture of Carlisle.
"Of a distempered brain." Tried at Carlisle 18 September
1746 and sentenced to death, but reprieved. *SHS.2.276,
MR197.*

HARPER, WILLIAM, Mr, Episcopal Minister from Bothkiner,
Bothkiner parish, Stirlingshire. Was very active in aiding
and assisting the rebels and waited of the Pretender's Son
at Falkirk. At home. Evidence from James McNear,
sclater in Falkirk and Robert and James McNear, his sons.
SHS.8.56, SHS.8.316.

HARTLEY, GEORGE, Corporal, Manchester Regiment. Aged
18 from Manchester, born at Brinndle, near Preston.
Taken near Warwick Bridge, and imprisoned 30 December
1745 Carlisle, Lancaster Castle, also in House of
Correction, Whitehaven from 15 January 1745. Pardoned
on condition of enlistment 22 July 1848. Was tried at
Carlisle September 1746 and sentenced to death, but
reprieved. *SHS.2.276, MR197, CQS.359.*

HARTLEY, JOHN, Manchester Regiment. Carpenter from
Lancashire. Imprisoned 30 December 1745 Carlisle,
Lancaster Castle. Pardoned on condition of enlistment.
Taken at capture of Carlisle. Was tried at Carlisle 19-26
September 1746 and sentenced to death, but reprieved.
SHS.2.276, MR197.

HARVEY or HARVIE, JAMES, Innkeeper at Linlithgow Bridge, Quartermaster, Kilmarnock's Troops. Carried arms as a quartermaster in Kilmarnock's Troop. Imprisoned Canongate; 8 August 1746 Carlisle, Penrith, executed at Penrith 28 October 1746. He pleaded guilty at his arraignment at Carlisle and was sentenced to death, 22 September 1746. *SHS.2.276, SHS.8.266.*

HARVEY or HARVIE or HERVEY, THOMAS, weaver from Carlisle. Imprisoned Coventry, Lancaster Castle, Carlisle. Pardoned on condition of enlistment 23 July 1748. "Soldier in Colonel Lascelles Regiment" and therefore a deserter. Taken on suspicion. Was tried at Carlisle 19 September 1746 and sentenced to death, with a recommendation to mercy by the jury. He was not executed. *SHS.2.276.*

HATCH or HACK, THOMAS, butcher from Preston, born near Preston, Lancashire. Imprisoned Carlisle and House of Correction, Whitehaven for high treason from 15 January 1745. Stated to have been a butcher of Preston, but referred to by Robert Lea of Whitehaven, as a grocer. Lea says, he remembered "Hatch who was formerly a grocer at Preston when taken was armed with a broad sword, brace of pistols and wore a white cockade." This man appears to have been a lunatic. He was tried 19 September 1746 at Carlisle and acquitted. *SHS.2.278, CQS.346, CQS.359.*

HAXTON, HELENEAS, gentleman from Rathehills, Kilminny, Fife. Carried arms in the rebel army during the whole Rebellion. Lurking in the country. Of the well-known family of Hackston (or Halkerston) of Rathillet. The predecessor of this gentleman fought against the Jacobites in 1715. Heleneas evidently got the benefit of the indemnity, as he lived for many years after the rebellion, and sold his estate in 1772. *SHS.8.64, SHS.8.373.*

HAXTON, ROBERT, surgeon from St Andrews, Fife. Carried arms in the rebel army during the whole Rebellion. Whereabouts not known. Evidence from Robert Bell, merchant in Cupar and .... Daw, widow of William Coupar, late baillie there and David Nicoll Stabler there. *SHS.8.64, SHS.8.352.*

HAY, ANDREW, surgeon from Cupar, Fife. Carried arms in the rebel army during the whole Rebellion. Lurking in Fife. *SHS.8.64.*

HAY, GEORGE, Lieutenant, French Royal Scots Cavalry. Shipmaster, Portsoy. Taken and escaped. *MR.61.*

HAY, JAMES, resident of Haddington. Joined the rebel army at Edinburgh and continued with them till after the battle of Falkirk. *SHS.8.136.*

HAY, JAMES, Captain, Lord John Drummond's French Service. 29 April 1746 surrendered Edinburgh, imprisoned 29 April 1746 Edinburgh Castle, 8 August 1746 Carlisle. Pardoned on condition of permanent banishment 2 July 1747. Brother of Hay of Hopes. He surrendered and was placed in Edinburgh Castle. Here he gave a good deal of information about the battle of Culloden. In due course he was sent to Carlisle, where he was convicted and sentenced to death; an appeal against this, on the ground that he was a French subject, was submitted by Lewis Drummond in September 1746. He was reprieved, but included among those who were sent to London as fit for service in the Regular Army abroad. On the march, however, he was recalled and was eventually sent back to France with the other French troops in October 1747. *SHS.2.278, MR61.*

HAY, PATRICK, workman in Edinburgh. Was a volunteer in the rebel army. Whereaobuts not known. *SHS.8.250.*

HAY, PATRICK, Captain, Clare's French Service. Taken at sea 28 November 1745, imprisoned Hull, February 1746 Berwick. Discharged and banished. Brother of Mr Hay of Duns. *SHS.2.280.*

HAY, WILLIAM, of Edington, Berwickshire, Captain, Spanish Irish Grenadiers. Imprisoned 24 March 1746 *Prince Charles (*late *Hazard), HMS Sheerness,* Berwick, pardoned on condition of permanent banishment 2 July 1747. Grandson of John, 1st Earl of Tweeddale, was brother of the Alexander Hay of Drumelzier of the time. Before committing himself to the Rising he conveyed his estate to his brother. He must have been exchanged as a prisoner of war, and was in communication indirectly with the Prince and Mr Edgar in 1752 when living on the Continent. He was killed at the battle of Torgan in 1760. He was appointed Groom of the Bedchamber to the Chevalier in Nov 1727. *SHS.2.280.*

HAYES, PATRICK, Sergeant, Clare's French Service. Taken at sea 28 November 1745, imprisoned Berwick, February 1746 Hull. Discharged. *SHS.2.280.*

HAYES, PHILIP, Bulkeley's French Service. Taken at sea 28 November 1745, imprisoned Berwick, February 1746 Hull. Discharged. *SHS.2.280.*

HAYES, THOMAS, Manchester Regiment. Labourer from Lancashire. Imprisoned 30 December 1745 Carlisle, Lancaster Castle. Executed at Carlisle, 15 November 1746. Taken at capture of Carlisle. Tried at Carlisle September 1746 and sentenced to death. *SHS.1.148, SHS.2.282, MR197.*

HAYNES, LAWRENCE, Clare's French Service. Taken at sea 28 November 1745, imprisoned Berwick, February 1746 Hull. Discharged. *SHS.2.282.*

HAYNES, OWEN, Sergeant, Clare's French Service. Taken at sea 28 November 1745, imprisoned Berwick, February 1746 Hull. Discharged. *SHS.2.282.*

HAYWOOD, JOHN, from Gloucestershire. Imprisoned Gartmore, 2 May 1746 Perth, 12 May 1746 Stirling Castle. Soldier of Guise's Regiment. As he was apparently a deserter he was probably handed over to the military authorities. *SHS.2.282.*

HEAGEN, (or HEGGANS) JOHN, officer's servant, French Royal Scots Cavalry. Aged 14, from Glasgow. Imprisoned Inverness; June 1746 *Margaret & Mary*, Tilbury. Servant to officer in French service. As there is no further reference to him he probably died. *SHS.2.282, MR.62.*

HEAVIE, JAMES, Berwick's French Service. Taken at sea 28 November 1745, imprisoned Berwick, February 1746 Hull. Discharged. *SHS.2.282.*

HENDERSON, ALEXANDER, portioner of Tranent. Joined the rebels, conducted them the most advantageous way through Tranent the night before Preston battle, for which he received a guinea from Sullivan, a Chief Commander; he publicly insulted the well affected in Tranent, vaunted of his being a Sergeant of the Rebel Artillary, and continued with them till dispersed. Lurking and said to be got to England. *SHS.8.136.*

HENDERSON, DAVID, brewer and glazier from Clackmannan, Clackmannanshire. Drank the Pretender's Son's health as Prince of Wales, and beat the Excise Officer for reproving him. Served the rebels as a spy and message bearer. Furnished their army withnecessaries and spoke very treasonable language, he received from them as a reward, brandy etc, out of the Customhouse of Alloa and had a hand in imprisoning the Excise Officer. Now at home. Evidence from John Donaldson, Robert Henderson, Betty Nasmith, Andrew Tasy, residents in Clackmannan, and Margaret Paterson, resident in Kinnet. *SHS.8.56, SHS.8.148, SHS.8.348.*

HENDERSON, FRANCIS, conveyed from Penrith to Brough, Westmoreland in the company of 19 other Jacobites. *CQS.354.*

HENDERSON, JOHN, of Castlemains, Annandale Stewartry. By profession a writer in Lochmaben. Was committed at Carlisle for drinking treasonable healths; set at liberty and made jailkeeper by the rebels on their getting possession of that place; made his escape when his Royal Highness the Duke re-took that city, and now since the battle of Culloden has been apprehended and is a prisoner in Carlisle. Found guilty, sentenced to death, and executed at Carlisle. *SHS.8.142, SHS.8.378.*

HENDERSON, JOHN, merchant and brewer from Clackmannan, Clackmannanshire. Aided and assisted the rebels as a guide and wore a white cockade. Combined with the rebels, got from them out of the warehouse at Leith, goods which had been seized by the King's officers, showed himself very zealous for the Pretender's interest, had a hand in imprisoning the Excise Officer as above mentioned and often beat, oppressed and insulted the well affected. Now at home. Evidence from John Clark, merchant in Airth, Henry Corbet, Excise Officer there. Evidence also from James Dempster, Johnathon Donaldson, David McViccar, William McViccar, David McLaren, Betty Nasmith, William Steen, and Robert

Wilson, resident sin Clackmannan. *SHS.8.56, SHS.8.148, SHS.8.316, SHS.8.348.*

HENDERSON, THOMAS, from Musselburgh, soldier, French Royal Scots Cavalry, Lord John Drummond's Regiment. Imprisoned 25 April 1746 Canongate, 8 August 1746 Carlisle, London, released. Deserter from service of the Dutch States-General. Again deserted from Lord John Drummond's regiment at Stirling, but was arrested by Marines. He was sent as a witness to London, where he was in the custody of Carrington, the messenger, in June 1747. *SHS.2.284, MR.63.*

HENDRIE or HENRY or HUNDRIE, CHARLES, from Dunbar, Ogilvy's Regiment. Imprisoned 30 December 1745 Carlisle; York Castle, London, released. Taken at capture of Carlisle. Turned King's Evidence. His name is shown in the custody of Carrington, the messenger, June 1747. *SHS.2.284.*

HENRY, JAMES, soldier, from Ireland. Imprisoned Gartmore, 13 May 1746 Stirling Castle. "In General Guise's Regiment." Presumably a deserter. He was probably handed over to the military authorities. *SHS.2.284.*

HENRYSON, JOHN, pupil for the Excise, Edinburgh, Midlothian. Carried arms in the rebel army and was active in pressing horses. Now lurking about Edinburgh. *SHS.8.250.*

HENSON, THOMAS, Manchester Regiment. From Nottingham. Imprisoned 30 December 1745 Carlisle. Taken at capture of Carlisle. There is no further reference to him. *SHS.2.286, MR197.*

HEPBURN RICCART, JAMES, of Keith, living in Canongate, Edinburgh, Midlothian. Carried arms in the rebel Life

Guards, said to be Captain. Whereabouts not known. Evidence from Robert Brown, George Robertson and George Porteous, Excise Officers. *SHS.8.250, SHS.8.338.*

HERBERT, JOHN, French Service. Taken at sea, imprisoned Berwick, February 1746 Hull. Discharged. *SHS.2.286.*

HERRING, JANE (or JANET), washerwoman from East Lothian. Imprisoned 30 December 1745 Carlisle; Lancaster Castle, transported 5 May 1747 from Liverpool to Virginia in *Johnson*, arriving Port Oxford, Maryland, 5 Aug 1747. Taken at fall of Carlisle. *SHS.2.286, PRO.T1.328.*

HERVEY, THOMAS, Manchester Regiment. From Wigan. Imprisoned 30 November 1745 Carlisle. Taken at capture of Carlisle. *SHS.2.286, MR197.*

HERVEY, THOMAS, from Braintree, Essex. Imprisoned Coventry. "On suspicion - soldier in Lascelle's regiment." Deserter; was probably handed over to the military authorities. *SHS.2.286.*

HESPELL, JOSEPH, Clare's French Service. Taken at sea 28 November 1745, imprisoned Berwick, February 1746 Hull. Discharged. *SHS.2.286.*

HEWATT, JAMES, soldier, Lord John Drummond's French Royal Scots Cavalry. Aged 24 from Newcastle. Taken prisoner 25 February 1746 Perth, 10 May 1746 Inverness, June 1746 *Dolphin* Tilbury Fort. Transported 20 March 1747. He was transported in spite of claiming to be a French subject. *SHS.2.286, MR.63.*

HEWIT, EDWARD, butcher from Derby. Manchester Regiment. Taken. Died? *MR197.*

HICK, ROBERT, soldier, French Royal Scots Cavalry. Deserter, Scots Fusiliers. Deserted and taken, pardoned. *MR.63.*

HICKEY, LAURENCE, Bulkeley's French Service. Taken at sea 28 November 1745, imprisoned Berwick, February 1746 Hull. Discharged. *SHS.2.286.*

HICKEY, THOMAS, weaver from Dublin. Imprisoned 27 April 1746 Saltcoats, 27 April 1746 Irvine. Escaped 19 July 1746. *SHS.2.286.*

HIGHLEY, THOMAS, Manchester Regiment. Imprisoned Carlisle, Lancaster Castle. There is no further reference to him. *SHS.2.288, MR197.*

HINCHCLIFFE or HINCHLEY, JOSEPH, tallow-chandler, aged 31 from York. Imprisoned 30 December 1745 Carlisle, York Castle. Transported 8 May 1747 from Liverpool to Antigua. Taken at capture of Carlisle. *SHS.2.288.*

HISLEY, JACQUES, French Service. From France. Imprisoned Marshalsea. Discharged. *SHS.2.288.*

HISTILL, PIERRE, French Service. From France. Imprisoned Marshalsea. Discharged. *SHS.2.288.*

HODGE, DAVID, porter from Leith, Midlothian. Employed as John Aikman in this list, assisted in riffling the Old Stage Coach Lofts of their horses provisions and carried them to the rebels whom he likeways assisted in driving their waggons, etc. Now at home. Evidence from Robert Osburn and James Boyle, Excise Officers, and John Balfour. *SHS.8.250, SHS.8.340.*

HODGSON, EDWARD, aged 21, Englishman. Imprisoned Inverness, June 1746 *Liberty & Property* Tilbury. Transported 31 March 1747. "Follower of rebels from Preston." *SHS.2.288.*

HODGSON, JOHN, Manchester Regiment. Imprisoned Lancaster Castle. "Taken in actual rebellion." There is no further reference to him. *SHS.2.288, MR197.*

HOGAN, THOMAS, Surgeon, Clare's French Service. Taken at sea *Louis XV* 28 November 1745, imprisoned Edinburgh Castle, 26 December 1745 Berwick, February 1746 Hull. Pardoned on condition of permanent banishment 2 July 1747. *SHS.2.288.*

HOLKER, JOHN, Lieutenant, Manchester Regiment. From Lancashire. Imprisoned 30 December 1745 Carlisle, London (Newgate Prison). Escaped June 1746. Taken at capture of Carlisle. He appears to have got away before or during his trial. *SHS.2.288, MR195.*

HOLT, VALENTINE, Sergeant, Manchester Regiment. Aged 20, clothmaker from Lancashire. Imprisoned 30 December 1745 Carlisle, Lancaster Castle, Carlisle. Executed 28 October 1746 at Penrith. Taken at capture of Carlisle. Was tried at Carlisle on 9 September 1746 and pleaded guilty. Was sentenced to death. *MR.195, SHS.2.288, SHS.1.149.*

HOME, DAVID, from Duns, Berwickshire, Captain, Balmerino's Life Guards. Imprisoned Carlisle, executed at Penrith 28 October 1746. Son of the late Laird of Whitefield, Duns, brother of Alexander Home of Manderston. He pleaded guilty at the trial at Carlisle, 9 September 1746, and was sentenced to death. Evidence against him from two of Hamilton's Dragoons.

SHS.2.288, SHS.8.292, SHS.8.326, NAS.GD1/384/32, SHS.8.294.

HOME, GEORGE, aged 30, from Duns, Berwickshire. Writer in Edinburgh, son of George Home of Whitefield. Imprisoned Carlisle; Lancaster Castle, transported 8 May 1747 from Liverpool to Leeward Islands, in *Veteran*, arriving Martinique June 1747. Evidence from George Robertson, Excise Officer. *SHS.2.290, PRO.SP36.102, SHS.8.338.*

HOME, NORWALD, brother to Boghall. Went to Glasgow and received the money with the rebels which they extorted from that city. Now lurking. *SHS.8.266.*

HOME, WILLIAM, aged 14, from Duns, Berwickshire, Cornet, Balmerino's Life Guards. Imprisoned Carlisle, pardoned and went to France, October 1747. Son of Patrick Home, maltster. "Indweller in Duns." He was cousin of Captain David Home who was executed. The Earl of Home petitioned on his behalf. His health broke down in Carlisle Castle. He was offered a pardon if he agreed to serve in the East India Company's service, but refused on account of his health. In the end he got a free pardon. The evidence at his trial showed that "he bore the Pretender's Standard at Falkirk." Evidence against him from two of Hamilton's Dragoons. *SHS.2.290, SHS.8.292, SHS.8.326, NAS.GD1/384/31, SHS.8.294, SRO.CD1/384/3.*

HOME, WILLIAM, Manchester Regiment, from Lancashire. Imprisoned 30 December 1745 Carlisle, Lancaster Castle, Carlisle. Taken at capture of Carlisle. Tried at Carlisle and sentenced to death. As he was not transported he probably died. *SHS.2.290, MR197.*

HOUSTON, DAVID, smith from Wester Wemyss, Fife. Suspected of treasonable practices, was apprehended but admitted to bail. Now at home. *SHS.8.260.*

HOWARD, PATRICK, Corporal, French Service. Imprisoned Carlisle. Transported. In spite of his French service, he appears to have been transported. *SHS.2.290.*

HOWARD, WILLIAM, soldier, Lord John Drummond's French Royal Scots Cavalry. Wounded Falkirk. Imprisoned Stirling Castle. Discharged. Shot through shoulder 3 February 1746. Surgeon's fee 6s.8d. *SHS.2.292, MR.63.*

HUBERT, JOHN, Berwick's French Service. From France. Taken at sea 28 November 1745, imprisoned Berwick. Discharged. *SHS.2.292.*

HUDSON, JOHN, Manchester Regiment, from Lancashire. Imprisoned 30 December 1745 Carlisle. Taken at capture of Carlisle. There is no further reference to him. *SHS.2.292, MR197.*

HULL, JAMES, napkin merchant from Lancashire. Imprisoned 24 April 1746 Dunfermline. Escaped 27 December 1746. *SHS.2.292.*

HUME, GEORGE, son to Alexander Hume, writer, deceased, Edinburgh, Midlothian. Carried arms with the rebels, said to be a prisoner in England. *SHS.8.250.*

HUNT, PHILIP, Sergeant, Manchester Regiment. Barber from Wigan. Imprisoned 30 December 1745 Carlisle, Lancaster Castle. Executed at Penrith, 28 October 1746. Taken at capture of Carlisle. When tried he said he had been forced to enlist by Lord George Murray "as the rebels passed by," and was seized by the Highlanders, but at the same time pleaded guilty and was sentenced to death. *MR.195, SHS.1.149, SHS.2.292.*

HUNTER, JOHN, Ensign, Manchester Regiment. From Northumberland. Taken at capture of Carlisle 30 December 1745, imprisoned London. Acquitted and discharged 17 July 1746. Tried on 17 July 1746. Evidence was brought that he had run away eleven miles but was made to return on pain of death, and that he was tied to a horse to prevent his escaping. *MR.195, SHS.2.294.*

HUNTER, WILLIAM, Sergeant, Manchester Regiment. From Newcastle. Taken at capture of Carlisle 30 December 1745, imprisoned York Castle. Executed at York, 8 November 1746. He pleaded guilty at his trial on 2 October and was sentenced to death. *SHS.1.149, SHS.2.294, MR197.*

HURST, JAMES, soldier, Lord John Drummond's French Royal Scots Cavalry. Aged 24, from Newcastle, "Popish schoolmaster in Lancashire." Imprisoned Inverness, Tilbury Fort. No further reference to him, he probably died. *MR.63, SHS.2.294.*

HUSSEY, JACQUES, French Service, French. Taken at sea in the *Soleil* privateer going to Scotland 24 November 1745, imprisoned Marshalsea. Discharged. *SHS.2.294.*

HYNES or HYND, BENEDICT ANTHONY, Lieutenant, Spanish Service. Imprisoned 24 March 1746 *Prince Charles* (late *Hazard*) HMS *Sheerness* Berwick, London. Pardoned on condition of permanent banishment 2 July 1747. *SHS.2.294.*

ILLAH, WILLIAM, Roy Stewart's (Edinburgh) Regiment. Taken at Carlisle. Died? *MR206.*

INE, DENIS, French Service, from France. Taken at sea, imprisoned Hull. Discharged. *SHS.2.296.*

IRVINE, CHARLES, resident in Prestonpans. Acted as salt officer and uplifted duty for the rebels during their stay in Edinburgh. Now at home. *SHS.8.136.*

IRVINE, EDWARD, of Sysbie, Stewartry of Annandale. Guided the rebels and their baggage from Ecclefechan to Graitney on their way to Carlisle. Whereabouts not known. *SHS.8.142.*

IRVINE, JAMES, aged 34, shoemaker from Gribton, Nithsdale, Dumfries-shire. Imprisoned Aberdeen; Canongate, 8 August 1746 Carlisle. Transported 22 April 1747 from Liverpool to Virginia in *Johnson*, arriving Port Oxford, Maryland 5 August 1747. "Carried arms in rebel service." Was concerned in bringing in arms from the Spanish ship at Peterhead to Aberdeen. *SHS.2.298, PRO.T1.328.*

IRVINE, JAMES, jnr, of Gribton, Nithsdale. Carried arms in the rebel service. Whereabouts not known. *SHS.8.142.*

IRVINE, JOHN, of Whitehill, Stewartry of Annandale. Was active in pressing horses for the service of the rebels on their march from Moffat to Carlisle, and threatened the constables that would not give their assistance. Now at home. *SHS.8.144.*

IRVINE, JOHN, French Service, from Ireland. Captured at sea on the way to Montrose in *Louis XV* 28 November 1745, imprisoned Edinburgh Castle. Hanged Edinburgh 24 January 1746. Was found to be a deserter from Ligonier's Foot. *SHS.2.298.*

IRVINE, WILLIAM, from Gribton, Kirkcudbright. Imprisoned 17 December 1745 Edinburgh "on suspicion." Liberated 26 December 1745. "Refused to drink His Majesty's health; went a considerable way to wait on the Pretender's son, and it's general opinion that he forced his son into the Rebellion." *SHS.2.298.*

IRVINE, WILLIAM, of Gribton, Kirkcudbright Stewartry. Refused in a public company to drink his Majesty's health; went a considerable way to wait on the Pretender's son but missed him and it's the general opinion of the country that he forced out his son into the rebellion. Now at home. *SHS.8.144.*

JACKSON, JAMES, Fitzjames' Regiment, from Ireland. Imprisoned 29 June 1746 Glenbucket Aberdeen, 2 August 1746 Canongate. Discharged 17 February 1747. "Confesses he is an Irishman and came from France to Scotland as a soldier in said regiment and was at the battle of Culloden." *SHS.2.300, MR38.*

JACKSON, RICHARD, Manchester Regiment, from Lancashire. Taken at capture of Carlisle 30 December 1745, imprisoned Lancaster Castle. His disposal is unknown. *SHS.2.300, MR197.*

JAMES, JOSEPH, conveyed from Penrith to Brough, Westmoreland in the company of 19 other Jacobites. *CQS.354.*

JAMES, JOSEPH, conveyed from Penrith to Brough, Westmoreland in the company of 19 other Jacobites. *CQS.354.*

JAMIESON, JOHN, gentleman from Clackmannan. On suspicion of treason. Imprisoned 22 January 1746/47 on board a ship in Leith Road (Robertson, Master); 24 January 1746/7 Edinburgh Castle, discharged. *SHS.2.302.*

JARDIN, GUILLAUME, Berwick's French Service, from France. Imprisoned Berwick. *SHS.2.302.*

JAY, THOMAS, Manchester Regiment. Imprisoned Carlisle, London. Released. Turned King's Evidence against many of the Carlisle prisoners. *SHS.2.302, MR197.*

JEFFRAYS (alias HULBART), DANIEL, writer from London (Westminster). Imprisoned May 1746 Annan, 16 July 1746 Edinburgh Tolbooth. Discharged. "On suspicion of treason." "Carrying arms." "Did see him marching with the rebels." *SHS.2.302.*

JEHANNOT, ... Treasurer, French Picquets. Taken at sea *Bourbon*, imprisoned Hull, Marshalsea. Discharged. *SHS.2.302.*

JELENS, JOHN JAMES, French Service. From France. Imprisoned York Castle. Pardoned on condition of enlistment 22 July 1748. "Taken in actual rebellion." At his trial at York on 2 October 1746 he was charged with being concerned in plundering Lord Lonsdale's house of Lowther Hall. He pleaded he was a servant of a Dutch officer, but it was ruled that he had acquired a local allegiance to the Crown. Consequently he was sentenced to death. On the day fixed for the execution he was reprieved. *SHS.2.304.*

JOHNSTON, ANDREW, aged 18, from Canongate, Edinburgh, Kilmarnock's Regiment. Imprisoned 9 May 1746 Musselburgh, 16 July 1746 Canongate, Carlisle, London, pardoned on condition of enlistment 22 July 1748. Son of Johnston of Knockhill. He was styled "Kilmarnock's servant." In the list of prisoners sent to Carlisle on 8

August 1746 the words "to be well used" are written against his name. At his trial at Carlisle on 19 September 1746 he pleaded guilty and was sentenced to death, but was reprieved. He gave evidence against several prisoners in London. *SHS.2.304.*

JOHNSTON, ANDREW, late servant to the Duke of Hamilton. From Abbay, Canongate, Midlothian. Carried arms in the rebel army. Now prisoner in Carlisle. Evidence from David Morrison, brewer and Jonothan Davidson, wright in the Abbey. *SHS.8.250, SHS.8.338.*

JOHNSTON, ANDREW, eldest son of James Lesslie Johnston of Knockhill, Annandale Stewartry. Carried arms with the rebels from the time they left Edinburgh till dispersed. Now lurking. One of this name, styled "son of Knockhill," was brought to trial at York, and, pleading guilty, was sentenced to death. *SHS.8.142, SHS.8.380.*

JOHNSTON, or JOHNSON, HUGH, Manchester Regiment. Aged 27, weaver from Walton, Lancashire. Imprisoned 30 December 1745 Carlisle, Lancaster Castle. "Blind of an eye." Taken at capture of Carlisle. Transported to Antigua 8 May 1747. *SHS.2.304, MR197.*

JOHNSTON, JAMES, from Edinburgh, Midlothian, late a cadet in Lee's Regimen. Was a Captain of volunteers in the rebel service. Whereabouts not known. *SHS.8.250.*

JOHNSTON, JAMES, son of James Johnston, Merchant, from Edinburgh, Midlothian. Was a Captain in the Duke of Perth's Regiment. Whereabouts not known. Evidence from Alexander Strang, George Robertson and Francis Pringle, Excise Officers. *SHS.8.250, SHS.8.338.*

JOHNSTON, JAMES LESSLIE, of Knockhill, Annandale Stewartry. Carried arms with the rebels from the time they left Edinburgh till dispersed. Now lurking. *SHS.8.142.*

JOHNSTON, JOHN, Manchester Regiment. Aged 30, husbandman from Lancashire. Imprisoned Carlisle, York Castle. Transported to Antigua 8 May 1747. *SHS.2.306, MR197.*

JOHNSTON, JOHN, weaver from Edinburgh. Imprisoned 20 May 1746 Dundee, discharged 12 August 1746. Taken on suspicion of treason. *SHS.2.306.*

JOHNSTON, JOHN, aged 13, from Argyle, Officer's Servant, Irish Piquets. Taken, died? *MR137.*

JOHNSTON, RICHARD, Manchester Regiment. Comb maker from Lancaster, also Kilmarnocks. Imprisoned 3 May 1746 Stirling Castle, Carlisle. Transported 24 February 1747 from Liverpool to Virginia in *Gildart,* arriving Port North Potomac, Maryland 5 August 1747. *SHS.2.306, MR197, PRO.T1.328.*

JOHNSTON, WILLIAM, of Lockarby, Whitewinehaws, Stewartry of Annandale. Was very assisting to the rebels in their march through Annandale to England and when some of their baggage they left at Blackfoord was carried off by the country people, caused intimation to be made at several Church Doors that if they did not return it they should suffer military execution. Now at home. *SHS.8.144.*

JONES, CHARLES, Berwick's French Service. From France. Imprisoned Berwick. Discharged. This man appears to have belonged to Berwick's regiment in the French service. He was taken prisoner and pleaded that he had been forced. *SHS.2.306.*

JONES, MICHAEL, Bulkeley's French Service. From France. Taken at sea *Louis XV* 28 November 1745, imprisoned Berwick, February 1746 Hull. Discharged. *SHS.2.306.*

JOY, THOMAS, Manchester Regiment. Weaver from St Michael's, Dublin. Imprisoned 30 December 1745 Carlisle, Chester Castle. Discharged. Taken at capture of Carlisle. *SHS.2.306, MR197.*

JUE, DENIS, Berwick's French Service. From France. Taken at sea 28 November 1745, imprisoned Hull. *SHS.2.306.*

KAVANAGH, DANIEL, Berwick's French Service. From France. Taken at sea 28 November 1745, imprisoned Berwick, February 1746 Hull. Discharged. *SHS.2.308.*

KAVANAGH, EDMUND, Berwick's French Service. From France. Taken at sea 28 November 1745, imprisoned Berwick, February 1746 Hull. *SHS.2.308.*

KEIGHLEY or KEIGHTLY, THOMAS, Manchester Regiment. Englishman. Imprisoned Carlisle. Pardoned on condition of enlistment 22 July 1748. Pleaded guilty at his trial on 19 September 1746 and was sentenced to death, but reprieved. *SHS.2.308, MR197.*

KEIGHRY, MICHAEL, Clare's French Service. From France. Taken at sea 28 November 1745, imprisoned Berwick, February 1746 Hull. Discharged. *SHS.2.308.*

KEIR or KER, PATRICK, Wright from Moultrie Hill, St Cuthbert's, Midlothian, "carried arms." Imprisoned 18 July 1746 Morpeth; Carlisle, executed Carlisle 15 November 1746. Was offered his life to give evidence against Sir Archibald Primrose but refused it. He himself pleaded guilty, and was sentenced to death. Evidence from Robert Harvie and James Jack, brewers in Ediburgh. *SHS.2.308, SHS.8.250, SHS.8.338, SHS.8.380.*

KEITH, JAMES, aged 20, servant from Glenbervie, Fife. Imprisoned at Lord Strathallan's house; 4 May 1746 Stirling Castle, Carlisle, transported 24 February 1747 from Liverpool to Virginia in *Gildart*, arriving Port North Potomac, Maryland 5 August 1747. "Carried arms, mounted Guards and acted as ground officer on the Estate of Marischal for the Rebels." *SHS.2.310, PRO.T1.328.*

KELL, ..., Lord John Drummond's Regiment. From France. Imprisoned Perth 18 February 1746. Discharged. *SHS.2.310.*

KELLIE, Earl of ALEXANDER ERSKINE, of Kellie House, Carnbee, Fife, Colonel. Imprisoned 11 July 1746 surrendered at Kinghorn; 11 July 1746 Edinburgh Castle, liberated 11 October 1749. "Subsisted himself in prison." Alexander Erskine, 5th Earl of Kellie, joined the Prince in Oct 1745. He was at the battles of Preston, Falkirk and Culloden, and, in September 1745 headed a party which collected the Excise in Fife. The Lord Justice Clerk wrote of him as a person "of understanding of an inferior size, not many removes from the very lowest." He surrendered the day before the final date on which surrenders were accepted. He remained for three years in Edinburgh Castle, and was never brought to trial, though he was excepted from the Act of Pardon of June 1747. The original report on him, dated 22 November 1746 says he "was seen in Highland dress and in arms with the rebels and was reputed a Colonel." *SHS.2.310.*

KELLIE, JOHN, joiner from Edinburgh. Imprisoned on suspicion 13 January 1746 Edinburgh, 20 January 1746 Leith. Discharged on bail 7 February 1746. *SHS.2.310.*

KELLIE, JOHN, French Service. Pardoned on condition of enlistment in Brig. Gen. Fowkes' regiment at Gibraltar 24 September 1746. There is no explanation of this pardon. No other man was sent to Gibraltar.* *SHS.2.310.*
* see Charles Young

KELLY, THOMAS, Bulkeley's French Service. From France. Taken at sea 28 November 1745, imprisoned Berwick, February 1746 Hull. Discharged. *SHS.2.310.*

KENDELA or KENDAL, ULTANO, Colonel, Spanish Service. From Spain. Imprisoned 15 April 1746 near Dunrobin, Inverness, London. Pardoned on condition of leaving the country and not returning 21 July 1747. Captured with the Earl of Cromarty near Dunrobin, 15 April 1746. Mrs Leith, describing the condition of the prisoners in Inverness after Culloden, says there was "Colonel Kendela, a gentleman in the Spanish Service. It was he that came to the Island of Barra and landed the arms that were found there." She says also that he was "one of the most religious men I ever was acquainted with and Englishman born." *SHS.2.312.*

KENDRIE, JAMES, soldier, Lord John Drummond's Regiment, French Royal Scots Cavalry. From Derry, Ireland. Taken 25 February 1726 Perth, imprisoned 12 May 1746 Inverness, Berwick. Discharged. *MR.63, SHS.2.312.*

KENNEDY, ..., Major, Irish Brigades French Service. (Uncle to Lochiel). Imprisoned Inverness, 22 September 1746 Edinburgh Castle. Discharged February 1747. *SHS.2.312, MR136.*

KENNEDY, ARCHIBALD, aged 18, jeweller's/goldsmith's apprentice from Edinburgh. Carried arms in the rebel army. Artillery. Imprisoned Carlisle; York Castle, executed York 8 November 1746. "Servant to Col

Grant." "Taken in actual rebellion." A statement was put in by Alexander Shaw, "Attorney at Law" in Edinburgh, in his favour, saying that when he joined the Prince's Army the shops were all shut and the youths, being idle, mixed with the rebels. Kennedy pleased guilty at his trial and was sentenced to death. It was also stated that at the siege of Carlisle he was "an active gunner but very young." Evidence from James Ker, goldsmith and Robert Brown, Excise Officer both in Edinburgh. *SHS.2.314, SHS.8.250, SHS.8.338.*

KENNEDY, BARNARD, Clare's French Service. From France. Taken at sea, imprisoned Berwick, February 1746 Hull. Discharged. *SHS.2.314.*

KENNEDY, MARTIN, French Service. From France. Taken at sea, imprisoned Hull. Discharged. *SHS.2.316.*

KENNEDY, MAURICE, Clare's French Service. Taken at sea 28 November 1745, imprisoned Berwick, February 1746 Hull. Discharged. *SHS.2.316.*

KENNEDY, PHILIP, French Service. From France. Taken at sea imprisoned Marshalsea. Discharged. *SHS.2.316.*

KENNEDY, THOMAS, Major, Bulkeley's French Service. From France. Taken at sea 28 November 1745, imprisoned Berwick, February 1746 Hull. Pardoned conditionally on leaving the country 22 October 1748. He stated he had been naturalised in 1733 and had entered the French army as a boy in 1729. *SHS.2.316.*

KENNY, JOHN, French Service. From France. Taken at sea 28 November 1745, imprisoned Berwick. Discharged. *SHS.2.316.*

KER or KERR, HENRY, of Graden, aged 43, Graden, Teviotdale, Colonel, ADC to Lord George Murray, Spanish Service. Imprisoned May 1746 Braes of Angus; London, House of Mr Ward, messenger. Tried at St Margaret's, Westminster, and found guilty. His counsel alleged "that he was an officer in the Spanish service; but soon gave up that point." The evidence showed that he was very active in the Rebellion; took and harshly treated Captain Vere on 2 December 1745 within three miles of the royal army, then at Newcastle - the said Captain Vere being called "principal spy" of the Duke's army "by the rebel journal published at Glasgow." Kerr was also alleged to have "endeavoured to rally the rebels at Culloden after they were broke." Released on condition of never returning 1748. Born in 1702, he served in the Spanish army 1722-1728, and then returned to Scotland. Throughout the campaign he was ADC to Lord George Murray. It was he who captured the English spy, Weir. When captured he was tried for his life and claimed to be a Spanish officer, but was sentenced to death on 15 Nov 1746. He was however reprieved through the good offices of the Prussian ambassador and placed in the house of a messenger. In 1748 he was released and went abroad. He died, as a Lieutenant Colonel in the Spanish army in 1751. *SHS.2.318, SHS.8.280, SHS.8.381.*

KER or KERR, JAMES, merchant from Traquair, Peebles-shire. Imprisoned Edinburgh Castle; 15 February 1746 Edinburgh Jail, liberated 5 May 1746. "Taken on suspicion of corresponding with the rebels." *SHS.2.318, SHS.8.84.*

KER, ROBERT, Lieutenant, Lord John Drummond's French Service. Aged 18, from France. Imprisoned Inverness, June 1746 *Jane of Leith* Tilbury. Died in prison 1746. *SHS.2.318.*

KERR, EUGENE, French Service. From France. Taken at sea, imprisoned Marshalsea. Discharged. *SHS.2.318.*

KERR, JAMES, of Crommack, Ayrshire. Imprisoned 24 December 1745 Dumbarton, died 5 June 1747. *SHS.2.318.*

KERR, JOHN, French Picquet. Imprisoned 16 December 1746 Stirling Castle. Discharged. "Deserted from the rebel service." *SHS.2.318, MR137.*

KERR, MARK, pupil for the Excise, from Edinburgh, Midlothian. Commanded as Lieutenant in the rebel army. Whereabouts not known. Evidence from Jonathan Chapman, Excise Officer and Robert Kerr, porter in the Excise Office. *SHS.8.250, SHS.8.342.*

KERR, ROBERT, Lieutenant, French Royal Scots Cavalry. Taken, died in prison 1746. *MR.61.*

KETTLE, JOHN, Berwick's French Service. From France. Taken at sea, imprisoned Marshalsea. Discharged. *SHS.2.320.*

KILLEN, JOHN, Berwick's French Service. From France. Taken at sea, imprisoned Berwick, February 1746 Hull. Discharged. *SHS.2.320.*

KILMARNOCK, WILLIAM BOYD, fourth Earl of, Callender House, Linlithgow. Aged 41. 16 April 1746 surrendered after Culloden, imprisoned Inverness, 28 April 1746 HMS *Exeter*, 20 May 1746 Tower of London. Was Lieutenant in Pitsligo's Horse and uplifted 12 shillings and 6 pence from a distiller as his Excise. When only 10 years old he went with his father to oppose Lord Mar in 1715. Succeeded to the Earldom in 1717. After the battle of Prestonpans he joined the Prince, and was made Colonel.

He was taken prisoner at Culloden, having mistaken a troop of English for his own men. His estates, greatly encumbered when he succeeded, were not relieved by his mode of living, which he himself acknowledged to be "careless and dissolute." The embarrassments under which he lay on these accounts impelled him to risk all in the cause of the Pretender. He was taken at Culloden, and tried at Westminster along with the other rebel lords. He pleaded guilty, was condemned, and beheaded on Tower Hill on 18 August 1746. After being sentenced he appealed for mercy to George II and the Duke of Cumberland. His Lady, Anne Livingstone, daughter of the Earl of Callendar, who was attainted in 1716, seems to have sympathised with the Jacobites, and went north with their army when they left Stirling. The eldest son of Lord Kilmarnock succeeded in 1758 to the Earldom of Errol. *SHS.8.266, SHS.8.381, SHS.2.320.*

KINCAID, JAMES, of Degreen, Falkirk parish, Stirlingshire, yearly rent £25. Was very active in assisting the rebels day and night. Robbed the country of horses, drank the Prentender'sson as Prince of Wales, wishing damnation to his Majesty. At home. Evidence from Robert Mckie, deput Baillie in Airth and his spouse, and Archibald Gilchrist, baker there. *SHS.8.56, SHS.8.316.*

KINCHLEY, JOSEPH, Manchester Regiment. Imprisoned Carlisle. Transported to Antigua 8 May 1747. *SHS.2.320, MR197.*

KING, CHARLES, from Edinburgh, Duke of Perth's Regiment. Imprisoned 19 February 1746 Burnston; 19 February 1746 Musselburgh, escaped 26 July 1746. *SHS.2.320.*

KING, LAUCHLANE, salt watchman from Edmonston pans. Acted as watchman under the rebels during their stay in that part of the country. Now at home. *SHS.8.136.*

KIRKLAND, ROBERT, from Glasgow. Imprisoned Gartmore; 2 May 1746 Perth, 12 May 1746 Stirling Castle. "Rebel service." Soldier in Guise's Regiment and a deserter. He was probably handed over to military authorities. *SHS.2.324.*

KORCAN, PEIRCY or PEIRCEY, Berwick's Regiment, Corporal French Service. From France. Taken at sea 28 November 1745, imprisoned Berwick, February 1746 Hull. Discharged. *SHS.2.326.*

LA BOUCHE, JEAN CLAUD *alias* JOHN GEORGE, French Service. From France. Imprisoned Edinburgh Castle, 11 August 1746 Canongate, Berwick. Discharged. *SHS.2.326.*

LACASE, JOHN, Bulkeley's French Service. From France. Taken at sea 28 November 1745, imprisoned Berwick, February 1746 Hull. Discharged. *SHS.2.326.*

LACKEY or LAKEY, JOHN, Berwick's French Service. From France. Captured at sea. Imprisoned Hull. Discharged. *SHS.2.328.*

LACKEY, JOHN or JAMES, aged 16, weaver from Edinburgh. Imprisoned Carlisle; York Castle. Transported 5 May 1747 from Liverpool to Leeward Islands in *Veteran*, arriving Martinique June 1747. *SHS.2.328, PRO.SP36.102.*

LACKEY or LEAK, WILLIAM, Manchester Regiment. Imprisoned Carlisle. Pardoned on condition of enlistment 22 July 1748. Was tried and sentenced to death in September 1746 with recommendation to mercy. *SHS.2.328, MR197.*

LAFAGUE, HIPPOLOYTE, Lieutenant, French Navy. From France. Imprisoned Perth, Berwick on Tweed. *SHS.2.326.*

LAING, THOMAS, Roy Stewart's (Edinburgh) Regiment. Lead miner from Aberdeenshire. Taken and transported 24 February 1747 from Liverpool to Virginia in *Gildart*, arriving Port North Potomac, Maryland 5 August 1747. *SHS.2.328, MR206, JAB.2.432, PRO.T1.328.*

LALOCHE, PIERRE, Sergeant, Lally's French Service. From Toulouse, France. Taken at capture of Carlisle 30 December 1745, imprisoned Marshalsea. Discharged. *SHS.2.326.*

LAMB, JAMES, aged 25, clockmaker from Edinburgh, Artillery. Taken at the capture of Carlisle. Imprisoned 30 December 1745 Carlisle; York Castle, Lincoln Castle. Transported 8 May 1747 from Liverpool to Leeward islands in *Veteran* arriving Martinique June 1747. *SHS.2.330, PRO.SP36.102.*

LA MOTTE, FRANCIS, Lally's Picquet French Service. From France. Imprisoned 1 February 1746 Stirling, 7 February 1746 Stirling Castle, 13 February 1746 Canongate Jail, 16 July 1746 Royal Infirmary, Edinburgh, 13 December 1746 Carlisle, Berwick. Discharged. *SHS.2.328.*

LANDERS, MICHAEL, French Service. From France. Taken at sea *Louis XV*, imprisoned Berwick, Hull. Discharged. *SHS.2.332.*

LA PAGE, CARLO, Lally's Picquet French Service. From France. 1 February 1746 Ford of Frew, 17 March 1746 Edinburgh Castle, Berwick. Discharged. *SHS.2.328.*

LARGER, ANDREW (ALEXANDER), aged 40, weaver from Dublin. Imprisoned Carlisle, York Castle, Lincoln Castle. Transported 22 April 1747. *SHS.2.330.*

LARRIE or LARY or LERY, CORNELIUS, Lally's Regiment, French Service. Cadie from Kerry, Ireland. Imprisoned 1 February 1746 Ford of Frew, 17 March 1746 Edinburgh Castle. Discharged. "Confesses that he came over with the French Picquets." *SHS.2.330.*

LASHLEY, WILLIAM, Pilot, French Service. From France. Taken at sea *Louis XV*, Berwick. Discharged. *SHS.2.330.*

LAUDEN, JAMES, Fitzjames' Horse French Service. From Hampshire. Taken and transported. *MR38.*

LAUDER, ARCHIBALD, a boy, from Duns, Berwickshire, Ogilvy's Regiment. Imprisoned Carlisle; York, London, released. "Son to Robert Lauder, junior of Bailmouth in Duns." "Joined the rebels and went with them to England." Evidence against him from two of Hamilton's Dragoons. Turned King's Evidence against many of the Carlisle prisoners. *SHS.2.332, SHS.8.326, SHS.8.294.*

LAUDER, CHARLES, procurator from Haddington. Acted as salt officer and collector for the rebels, said to have been with them at Perth before they came to Edinburgh. Now at home. *SHS.8.136.*

LAUDER, GEORGE, surgeon from Edinburgh. Imprisoned 16 April 1746 Culloden, Inverness; 28 May 1746 Edinburgh, London, liberated 7 January 1747. He and John Rattray were confined in Inverness Church with many wounded prisoners, but their instruments were taken away. He was liberated after a few days, at the request of Lord President Forbes. After his release he was again arrested and sent to

London. He was finally released 7 January 1747. *SHS.2.332*.

LAUDER, JAMES, merchant in Potterow, St Cuthberts, Midlothian. Carried arms in the rebel Life Guards. Whereabouts not known. *SHS.8.250*.

LAUDER, JAMES, merchant apprentice, Edinburgh, Midlothian. Carried arms in the rebel Life Guards. Whereabouts not known. Evidence from George Porteous, Excise Officer and Robert Ramsay, tailor, Edinburgh. *SHS.8.250, SHS.8.338*.

LAUDER, ROBERT, junior, of Bailmouth, East Lothian. Joined the rebels and went with them to England. Whereabouts not known. *SHS.8.294*.

LAUNEY, THOMAS, Clare's French Service. From Ireland. Imprisoned Edinburgh Castle, April 1746 Royal Infirmary Edinburgh. Discharged. *SHS.2.332*.

LAWRIE, JOHN, salt watchman from Prestonpans. Continued in the exercise of his office under the rebels. Now at home. *SHS.8.136*.

LAWSENT or LAUSENT, NICOLAS, French Service. Taken at sea, imprisoned Berwick. Discharged. *SHS.2.334*.

LAWSON, ROBERT, Manchester Regiment. Imprisoned 30 December 1745 Carlisle. Taken at capture of Carlisle. There is no further reference to him. *SHS.2.334, MR197*.

LAWSON, THOMAS, born near Cupar, Fife. Arrested for High Treason and held in the House of Correction at Whitehaven since 15 January 1745. Taken at Cockermouth. He was tried, condemned and executed at Carlisle. No. 3342 in S & A of Ogilvy's regiment, a chapman of Alyth, Perthshire. According to his petition, he was forced out, and was "carried along with them to Carlisle." "Did desert from them before they left that place in order to march southwards, and for that reason was imprisoned by them in the Castle of Carlisle, and left there until their return from Derby..... Being then set at liberty by them did again attempt to desert them, but was taken prisoner at the Scots Gate of Carlisle without having any arms upon him the day the rebels retreated from Carlisle, so that was forced to remain in that city until was taken from the rebels." Tried, convicted and sentenced to death at Carlisle, but sentence reduced to transportation. S & A say he attempted to escape, was sent to Liverpool for transportation, but fell ill, and could not be shipped: was reported still suffering from stone in January, 1749, and was pardoned and released in February, 1749. (No. 1533): no mention however of Whitehaven. *CQS.344.*

LAWSON, WILLIAM, soldier from Durham. Imprisoned Clackmannan, 4 May 1746 Stirling Castle, Carlisle. A deserter. Transported 24 February 1747 from Liverpool to Virginia in *Gildart*, arriving Port North Potomac, Maryland 5 August 1747. *SHS.2.334, PRO.T1.328.*

LEA, HUMPHREY, Manchester Regiment. From Lancashire. Taken at capture of Carlisle, 30 December 1745. No further reference to him. *SHS.2.336, MR197.*

LEARY, DANIEL, French Service. From France. Imprisoned Carlisle, Berwick. Pardoned on condition of permanent banishment, 2 July 1747. *SHS.2.336.*

LEATHERBARROW, RICHARD, Manchester Regiment. Aged 32, weaver from Winwick, Lancashire. Imprisoned Carlisle, Lancaster Castle. Transported 1747. *SHS.2.336, MR197.*

LE BLANE, ..., Commissary of Artillery, French Service. From France. Taken at sea 21 February 1746 *Bourbon*, imprisoned Marshalsea, London. Discharged. *SHS.2.336.*

LE DUC, THOMAS, Berwick's French Service. From France. Taken at sea, imprisoned HMS *Sheerness*, Berwick. Discharged. *SHS.2.336.*

LEE, SAMUEL, Manchester Regiment. Tailor from Lancashire. Taken at capture of Carlisle 30 December 1745, imprisoned Lancaster Castle, Carlisle. Pardoned on condition of enlistment 22 July 1748. Pleaded guilty at his trial on 19 September and was sentenced to death, but reprieved. *SHS.2.338, MR197.*

LEITH, ROBERT, baillie from Pittenweem, Fife, Stonywood's Regiment. Imprisoned London, released February 1748. This was probably the Bailie who went in person to the brewers and forbid them to pay their excise duty to the Revenue, but to the rebels, and told them he would protect them for so doing and he himself attended the rebels at their collecting the Revenue. At home. Evidence from Janet Todie, victualer in Pittenweem and Janet Mason, wife of William Thomson, brewer there. *SHS.2.340, SHS.8.66, SHS.8.352.*

LENNIE, THOMAS, Corporal, Clare's French Service. From Ireland. Imprisoned Canongate, 15 July 1746 Edinburgh Tolbooth. Discharged. *SHS.2.340.*

LE PAGE, CARLO, Clare's French Service. From France. Imprisoned Edinburgh Castle, Berwick. Discharged. "He is a soldier in Clare's Regiment, and came over with them." *SHS.2.336.*

LESLIE, ALEXANDER, in jail in Whitehaven. *CQS.359.*

LESSLIE, JAMES, gentleman to the Duchess of Gordon, from Prestonhall. Went north before the battle of Falkirk and joined the rebels under Lord Lewis Gordon. Now lurking in Edinburgh. *SHS.8.136.*

LESSLIE, WILLIAM, Mariner from Montrose, Captain *Prince Charles*, Irish Piquets. Taken and discharged. *MR136.*

LIGHTFOOT, JOHN, soldier, French Royal Scots Cavalry. From Greenock, Lord John Drummond's French Service. Imprisoned 27 April 1746 Dunsmiln; 27 April 1746 Montrose, 13 May 1746 Inverness. Discharged. *SHS.2.340, MR.63.*

LILLE, ALEXANDER, yr, journeyman wright from Haddington. Imprisoned 15 January 1746 Haddington, 7 August 1746 Canongate. Discharged. Carried arms with the rebels and came to Haddington well mounted, supposed to be a spy. Now in prison. *SHS.2.342, SHS.8.136.*

LINCH or LYNCH, DAVID, Berwick's French Service. From France. Taken at sea, imprisoned Berwick, February 1746 Hull. Discharged. *SHS.2.342.*

LINCH, HUMPHREY, Drummer, French Service. From France. Taken at sea *Louis XV*, imprisoned Berwick, Hull. Discharged. *SHS.2.342.*

LINDSAY, ALEXANDER, shoemaker from Canongate-head, Edinburgh. Imprisoned 5 February 1746 Edinburgh, discharged 21 February 1746. "On suspicion." *SHS.2.342, SHS.8.250.*

LINDSAY, MARTIN, tried as a Jacobite 1746. *SRO.CD.254/708.*

LINDSAY, PETER, aged 46, gentleman from Wormistone, Crail, Fife, Kilmarnock's Regiment. Imprisoned 30 June 1746 Dundee, 8 August 1746 Carlisle. Executed at Brampton 21 October 1746. Son of John Lindsay of Wormistone, commissary clerk, St Andrews. Tenant to Rt Hon Lord Justice Clerk. Was "wardrobe keeper Holyrood." "Carried arms and assisted in levying the Cess and Excise." He was tried at Carlisle and sentenced to death, but does not appear to have been executed, and his ultimate disposal is unknown. At his trial the Crown Solicitor said he had been "wardrobe keeper" at Holyrood House. This is probably the Captain Patrick Lindsay, who was taken prisoner in Angus in July 1746, and carried to Dundee. There was a Patrick Lindsay executed at Brampton, but he is described as a farmer at Wester Deans, Tweeddale. *SHS.2.344, SHS.8.66, SHS.8.374.*

LINDSAY, ROBERT, weaver from Haddington. Was a volunteer with the rebels at Preston battle, deserted when they went to England. Now at home. *SHS.8.136.*

LINGLEY, JAMES, French Service. From France. Taken at sea *Louis XV*, imprisoned Berwick, February 1746 Hull. Discharged. *SHS.2.344.*

LITHGOW, GEORGE, from Bothwell. Imprisoned 3 February 1746 Kinross; 4 February 1746 Edinburgh. "Late of Barrel's Regiment, " and therefore presumably a deserter. Disposal is unknown; he was probably handed over to the military authorities. *SHS.2.344.*

LIVER, JAMES, "sailor" from Lancashire. Imprisoned 3 May 1746 Stirling Castle. Discharged. *SHS.2.346.*

LIVESAY or LIVESLEY, JOHN, Manchester Regiment. Aged 17, cordwainer from Lancashire. Imprisoned Carlisle, Lincoln Castle. Transported 1747. *SHS.2.346, MR197.*

LIVINGSTON, JAMES, late postmaster, Falkirk. Carried arms in the rebel Life Guards. Now lurking. *SHS.8.266.*

LOCKHART, PETER, smith from Bannockburn, St Ninians parish, Stirlingshire. Drank the Pretender's son as Prince of Wales, speaking most indecently and maliciously of his Majesty. At home. Evidence from Margaret Logan, spouse to John Logan, brewer in Bannockburn, Robert Davidson, weaver in Glasgow and Henry Corbet, Officer of Excise in Airth. *SHS.8.56, SHS.8.316.*

LOCHEAD, JOHN, merchant from Alloa, Clackmannanshire. Purchased from the rebels a very considerable quantity of goods that had been seized for his Majesty's behoof and got them at under value. At home. Evidence from Robert Adam and John Dick, shipmasters in Airth. *SHS.8.56, SHS.8.316.*

LONGING, ANDREW, Manchester Regiment. From Ireland. Taken at capture of Carlisle 30 December 1745. No evidence of transportation. *SHS.2.348, MR197.*

LORIMER, JAMES, Musician from Edinburgh. Imprisoned "on suspicion" Carlisle, discharged. *SHS.2.348.*

LORRY, JACQUES, French Service. Stocking weaver from Hampshire. Taken at sea, imprisoned Berwick. Discharged. "Went 5 years agone to France. This is one of Mon. Carpentier's Frenchmen, yet he has signed a petition to His Majesty acknowledging his guilt and begging for transportation. *SHS.2.348.*

LOTHIAN, ANDREW, brewer and precentor to the Unqualified Meetinghouse, Cellardyke, parish of Kilrenny, Fife. Paid the whole of his own duty and demanded and received the Revenue from other liable therein, which he also paid to the rebels whom he caused use severities on the people, he prayed for the prosperity of the rebels and shows himself upon all occasions to be disaffected. At home. Evidence from James Simpson, town treasurer of Cellardyke, Marjory Alison his wife, Marjory Alison their servant and Thomas Anderson brewer there. *SHS.8.66, SHS.8.352.*

LOUDON, JOHN, soldier, French Royal Scots Cavalry. Weaver from Lanark, Lord John Drummond's Regiment. Imprisoned 3 May 1746 Dumbarton, discharged 29 January 1747. *SHS.2.348, MR.63.*

LOW, ALEXANDER, aged 37, Whitesmith from Lancashire. Imprisoned Carlisle, Lincoln Castle, 24 July 1746 Chester Castle. Transported to Antigua 8 May 1747. *SHS.2.350.*

LOWMAN, WILLIAM, Manchester Regiment. Imprisoned 30 December 1745 Carlisle. Taken at capture of Carlisle. Nothing more is known about him. *SHS.2.352, MR198.*

LOWRANCE, ISAAC, conveyed from Penrith to Brough, Westmoreland in the company of 19 other Jacobites. *CQS.354.*

LOWTHER, ARCHIBALD, from Dunbar, Artillery. Imprisoned 30 December 1745 Carlisle. Taken at capture of Carlisle. No further reference to him. *SHS.2.352.*

LUCAS, JEREMIAH, French Service. Taken at sea, imprisoned Marshalsea. Discharged. *SHS.2.352.*

LUGTON, SIMON, tailor from Edinburgh. Imprisoned 2 January 1746 Edinburgh; 8 August 1746 Carlisle,

Liverpool, transported November 1748. Carried arms as a volunteer. "Almost an idiot." He was tried at Carlisle on 19 September 1746 and sentenced to death. He was not, however, executed, as his name appears in a list of 13 prisoners at Carlisle who were pardoned and sent to Liverpool for transportation. *SHS.2.354, SHS.8.250, SHS.8.380.*

LUMSDAILE, ANDREW, writer from Edinburgh, Midlothian. Carried arms in the rebel army as a volunteer. Whereabouts not known. *SHS.8.250.*

LYON, MICHAEL, Colonel Rooth's French Picquet. Tailor from Dublin. Imprisoned Drummond of Linnoch, 4 May 1746 Stirling Castle, Carlisle. Transported 1747. *SHS.2.354, MR137.*

McARTHUR, JOHN, Roy Stewart's (Edinburgh) Regiment. Brewer from Inverness. Taken at Carlisle. Died? *MR206.*

McARTHUR, JOHN, Officer, Duke of Perth' Regiment, from Callendar. Imprisoned Callendar, 4 May 1746 Stirling Castle. Discharged 29 April 1746. *SHS.3.18.*

McAULAY, JAMES, Roy Stewart's (Edinburgh) Regiment. Taken at Carlisle. Transported 1747. *MR206, SHS.3.18.*

McBEATH, MARMDUKE, powder flask maker, Canongate, Midlothian. Was one of the Hussars and very active in levying money for the rebels, with them at all the battles and to the end. Now lurking about Edinburgh. Evidence from Ninian Trotter, George Robertson and James Easson, Excise Officers. *SHS.8.252, SHS.8.340.*

McCARTNEY, AGNES, aged 18, from Belfast. Taken at capture of Carlisle. Imprisoned 31 December 1745

Carlisle, Chester Castle, York Castle. Tranported 1747. *SHS.3.22.*

McCARTY, CURN (or CHARLES), Ensign, Bulkeley's French Service, from France. Captured at sea *Esperance*, imprisoned 25 November 1745 Deal, February 1746 Custom House smack *Caroline* Greenwich, Marshalsea. Discharged. *SHS.3.22.*

McCARTY, TIMOTHY, Fitzjames' Horse, from France. Imprisoned at sea February 1746 Berwick, Canterbury. Discharged. This man reported an attempt to get him and others to escape and rejoin the Prince in France, 17 June 1747. *SHS.3.24.*

McCARTY, WILLIAM, French Service, from France. Imprisoned at sea Berwick, February 1746 Hull. Discharged. *SHS.3.24.*

McCONNIE, ROBERT, brewer from Drumachie, Fife. Was engaged in the rebellion, active in robbing the country of horses, etc. Hanged by the rebels. *SHS.8.260.*

McCORMACK, ORMESBY, Manchester Regiment, from Antrim, Ireland. Taken at capture of Carlisle. Imprisoned 30 December 1745 Carlisle, London. Turned King's Evidence against Townley and others and was discharged. *MR198, SHS.3.28.*

McCORMACK, NICHOLAS, French Service. Taken at sea, imprisoned Berwick, February 1746 Hull. Discharged. *SHS.3.28.*

McCRECY, JAMES, labourer from Milton, Roy Stewart's (Edinburgh) Regiment. Taken. *MR207.*

McCULLEN, JAMES, from Grantley. Roy Stewart's (Edinburgh) Regiment. Taken at Carlisle. Died? *MR207.*

McCULLOCH (McCALAGH), JAMES, from Perth. Roy Stewart's (Edinburgh) Regiment. Taken at Carlisle. Died? *MR207.*

McCULLOCH, WILLIAM, servant to Kilmarnock, Callender House, Linlithgow. Carried arms in the rebellion. Prisoner. *SHS.8.266.*

McDERMID, ARCHIBALD, Mason. Imprisoned 10 March 1746 Stirling, discharged 14 July 1746. "In the rebellion." *SHS.3.32.*

McDERMOT, DUDLEY, Lieutenant, Rooth's Regiment, Irish Piquets, French Service, from France. Taken at Culloden 17 April 1746, imprisoned Inverness, Marshalsea. Pardoned on condition of permanent banishment 2 July 1747. *MR136, SHS.3.32.*

McDERMOT, THOMAS, Captain, Rooth's Regiment, French Service, Irish Piquets, from France. Taken at Culloden 17 April 1746, imprisoned Inverness, Marshalsea. Pardoned on condition of permanent banishment 2 July 1747. *MR136, SHS.3.34.*

McDONAGH, JEAN, Lieutenant, Dillon's Regiment, French Service, Irish Piquets. From France. Taken at Culloden 17 April 1746, imprisoned Inverness, Marshalsea. Pardoned on condition of permanent banishment 2 July 1747. *MR136, SHS.3.34.*

McDONALD, AENEAS, Banker in Paris. 13 May 1746 surrendered to General Campbell, imprisoned 14 June 1746 Dumbarton Castle, 30 August 1746 Edinburgh

Castle. Pardoned conditionally on banishment 7 July 1748. He was one of the small party who accompanied the Prince to Scotland. His brother was Donald McDonald of Kinlochmoidart. He was committed to Newgate 27 May 1747, and was excepted from the "Act of Grace." On 2 July he escaped from Newgate by throwing snuff in the turnkey's eyes; but, being shod with loose slippers, he was recaptured while running down Warwick Lane. At his trial, 10 December 1747, he said he was French and was educated there; but it was proved that he was born in Scotland, and kept St Andrew's Day. He was recommended to mercy when sentenced to death, and was placed in the charge of a messenger. On 28 May 1748 he was committed to Newgate. He received a conditional pardon involving perpetual banishment, dated 7 July 1748, but was not released until 11 December 1749, a creditor having secured hi further detention for debt. He returned to France, where he was killed during the Revolution. *SHS.3.34.*

McDONALD, ALEXANDER, soldier, French Royal Scots Cavalry. Deserter. Transported 7 February 1746. *MR.63.*

McDONALD, ALEXANDER, French Service, from France. Captured at sea in the *Soliel* privateer while going to Scotland. Imprisoned at Marshalsea. Discharged. *SHS.3.42.*

McDONALD, ANGUS, French Service. From France. Captured at sea in the *Soleil* privateer while going to Scotland. Imprisoned Marshalsea. *SHS.3.46.*

McDONALD, CLEMENTINA, aged 16, from Edinburgh. Clanranald's Regiment. Imprisoned Carlisle and Chester Castle. Taken at fall of Carlisle. Released *SHS.1.216, SHS.3.50, SHS.3.50.*

McDONALD, DONALD, from Edinburgh, Riding Master to Kilmarnock's Horse. Imprisoned 1 February 1746 St Ninians; Edinburgh Castle, 13 December 1746 Edinburgh Jail. Released under General Pardon, 1747. "Confesses that he served Lord Kilmarnock as a riding master during the rebellion." *SHS.3.56.*

McDONALD, DONALD, of Benbecula (Clan Ranald's), Paymaster, French Royal Scots Cavalry. Taken, pardoned. *MR.61.*

McDONALD, DONALD, Cadet, Rooth's French Royal Scots Cavalry. Captain, Lord John Drummond's Regiment. Imprisoned at Inverness and Edinburgh Castle. Had been in French Army since 1742. Wounded at Stirling, taken at Culloden. Discharged. *MR.61, SHS.3.54.*

McDONALD, FRANCIS, of Ballycastle, Ireland. Imprisoned HMS *Furnace* Tilbury. Discharged April 1747 "there being no evidence against him." Was charged with raising men in Ireland for the Prince. *SHS.3.60.*

McDONALD, HUGH, servant to Clanranald, from Ballycastle, Ireland. Imprisoned HMS *Furnace* October 1746 Tilbury, House of Dick, mesenger. Released 10 June 1747. Turned King's Evidence agaisnt Francis McDonald, and was in 1747 in the custody of Dick the messenger; was released on 10 June 1747. *SHS.3.62.*

McDONALD, Sir JOHN, Colonel, Fitzjames' Horse, Inspector of Cavalry, French Service. Taken at Culloden 16 April 1746, imprisoned Inverness, Penrith. Pardoned on condition of permanent banishment 2 July 1747. An officer in the French army, from France, who came over with the Prince from France. He surrendered on Culloden day and was "suffered to go out upon his parole amongst other French prisoners at Penrith. *MR38, SHS.3.64.*

McDONALD, JOHN, servant to Captain, Chalmers of Gadyart, Ayrshire. Joined the rebel army when first at Perth. Whereabouts not known. *SHS.8.292.*

McDONALD, JOHN of Crowlin, Captain, Irish Brigade, French ervice. Imprisoned Fort William April 1746. Released January 1747. From France. Second son of Angus McDonald of Scotus, and officer in the Irish Brigade of the French Army. He arrived in Lochbroom after Culloden, bringing with him letters for the Prince and £3000. He was captured by Captain Ferguson, who mistook him for Barisdale. Was detained at Fort William for nine months and then released for want of evidence. *SHS.3.66, MR136.*

McDONALD, JOHN, Lieutenant, French Royal Scots Cavalry. Brother to Glenaladale. *MR.62.*

McDONALD, JOHN, aged 14 from Argyle, Officer's Servant, Irish Piquets. Taken and transported. *MR137.*

McDONALD, RANALD, Edinburgh. Imprisoned Edinburgh, 8 August 1746 Carlisle. Transported 24 February 1747 from Liverpool to Virginia in *Gildart*, arriving Port North Potomac, Maryland 5 August 1747. A member of the City Guard who joined the Prince. When brought up for trial he pleaded guilty and was sentenced to death, but reprieved. *SHS.3.76, PRO.T1.328.*

McDONOUGH, JOHN, French service. Captured at sea, imprisoned Marshalsea. Discharged. *SHS.3.80.*

McDOUGAL, JOHN, Piper's Servant, French Royal Scots Cavalry. From Inverness-shire. Taken at Culloden. *MR.62.*

McDOUGAL, KATHERINE from Edinburgh. Imprisoned December 1746 Edinburgh Castle, London, in Dick the messenger's house. Discharged. On suspicion. Sister of John Murray of Broughton. She was the wife of an Edinburgh wine merchant, and was concerned in the disposal of a part of the Prince's treasure, and was committed to the Castle by the Lord Justice Clerk. The only later reference to her is that she was in the custody of Dick the messenger in June 1747. *SHS.3.84.*

McDUER, PETER, sailor from Dogheda, Ireland. Imprisoned Crieff 25 April 1746, Stirling Castle. Released under General Pardon, 1747. *SHS.3.84.*

McDUFF, JAMES, Roy Stewart's (Edinburgh) Regiment. Labourer from Ballincreughen, Perthshire. Taken at Carlisle. Transported 22 April 1747, from Liverpool to Virginia in *Johnson*, arriving Port Oxford, Maryland 5 August 1747. *MR207, SHS.3.84, PRO.T1.328.*

McEWAN, JAMES, son to John McEwen, shoemaker, Stirling. Accepted of a commission in the rebel army. Whereabouts not known. *SHS.8.56.*

McEWAN, JOHN, yr of Muchlie, Captain, Roy Stewart's (Edinburgh) Regiment. Killed at Culloden. *MR205.*

McEWAR or MacKEWAR, PATRICK, Englishman. Imprisoned Carlisle. Was probably captured at surrender of Carlisle. Was tried 19-26 September 1746 at Carlisle and acquitted. *SHS.3.86.*

McFARLANE, ALEXANDER, "School doctor" from Kinghorn, Fife. Imprisoned 14 May 1746 Kinghorn. Discharged. Treasonable practices. "Suspected of assisting in the escape of two rebels found in Duncan Forbes' house." *SHS.3.88, SHS.8.260.*

McFARLANE, JAMES, soldier, French Royal Scots Cavalry. From Perthshire. Taken and discharged. *MR.63.*

McFARLANE, JAMES, Roy Stewart's (Edinburgh) Regiment. From Perth. Taken at Carlisle. Died? *MR207.*

McFARLANE, JOHN, servant from Glenfinglas, Callander, Perthshire. Carried arms with the rebels in England, and was at battle of Culloden. Lurking. *SHS.8.56.*

McFARLANE, JOHN, Roy Stewart's (Edinburgh) Regiment. Labourer from Denmore, Perthshire. Taken at Carlisle. Drowned. *MR207.*

McFARLANE, JOHN, Roy Stewart's (Edinburgh) Regiment. From Perthshire. Taken at Carlisle. Died? *MR207.*

McFARLANE, MALCOLM, from Linlithgow, Clanranald's Regiment. Imprisoned 12 January 1746 Linlithgow, 20 January 1746 Leith, 7 February 1746 Edinburgh. Discharged. *SHS.3.88.*

McFARLANE, THOMAS, smith in Doune, Stirlingshire. Evidence from William McLellan, purse master in Doune and his spouse, William Christy, baker there, Duncan McNicol, brewer there, and his spouse, and Allan Stewart, vintner there. *SHS.8.318.*

McGHIE, WILLIAM, glazier from Dumfries, Nithsdale. Imprisoned 30 April 1746 Dumfries, London, house of Mr Carrington, messenger. Liberated 2 April 1747.

"Common man." "Suspected of aiding ye rebels." "Was employed to go from Dumfries to Carlisle to reconnoitre the King's army and bring forward rebel stragglers, which he did." He subsequently became King's Evidence against Aeneas Macdonald, Lord Balmerino, and others. He was kept in a messenger's house until after 10 June 1748, and was then released. *SHS.3.90, SHS.8.144.*

McGILL, GEORGE, surgeon from Kimbock, Fife. Carried arms in the rebel service from after the battle of Preston till Culloden. Whereabouts not known. Evidence from David Paterson in Dairsie and Thomas Shepherd in Cambuck Miln. *SHS.8.66, SHS.8.352.*

McGRIGOR, ALEXANDER, tradesman from Miltoun, Callander parish, Perthshire. Carried arms into England with the rebels. Said to be forced. Returned home. *SHS.8.58.*

McGRIGOR, ALEXANDER ROY, labouring man, from Callander, Perthshire. Carried arms in the rebel service and was at battle of Culloden. Said to be forced. At home. *SHS.8.58.*

McGRIGOR, DOUGAL, tradesman from Miltoun, Callander parish, Perthshire , Callander parish, Perthshire. Carried arms into England with the rebels. Said to be forced. Returned home. *SHS.8.58.*

McGRIGOR, JOHN, gardener from Back of Canongate, South Leith, Midlothian. Carried arms and was at the battle of Preston. Whereabouts not known. Evidence from James and William Fleemings etc, brewers in Caldton. *SHS.8.252, SHS.8.340.*

McGRIGOR, PATRICK, tradesman from Miltoun, Callander parish, Perthshire. Carried arms into England with the rebels. Said to be forced. Returned home. *SHS.8.58.*

McHUMISH, JOHN, pedler from Bridge of Turk, Callander parish, Perthshire. Carried arms in the rebel service and was at Falkirk and Culloden battles. Lurking. *SHS.8.58.*

McINHONNEL, JOHN, brewer from Bridge of Kelty, Callander parish, Perthshire. Acted as a Sergeant in the rebel army. Returned home. *SHS.8.58.*

McINNES, ..., Lieutenant, French Service. Imprisoned January 1747 Tower of London. Discharged. There is nothing to identify this officer. *SHS.3.98.*

McINNES, ARCHIBALD, servant from Stirlingshire, Stewart of Ardshiel's Regiment. Imprisoned Dunblane, 27 April 1746 Stirling Castle. Released under General Pardon, 1747. *SHS.3.100.*

McINTOSH, JOHN, in jail in Whitehaven. *CQS.359.*

McIVER, WILLIAM, factor to the Earl of Traquair, Tweeddale. Imprisoned 15 February 1746 Edinburgh Jail. Released 11 May 1746. "Suspected of aiding the rebels." *SHS.3.106, SHS.8.84.*

McKENNY, KENNETH, journeyman goldsmith, Edinburgh. Evidence from Dougal Ged and Edward Lothian, goldsmiths in Edinburgh. *SHS.8.338.*

McKENZIE, ALEXANDER, shoemaker and shopkeeper, Canongate, Edinburgh, Midlothian. Carried arms in the rebel army. Whereabouts not known. Evidence from John and William Parks, journey shoemakers, Edinburgh. *SHS.8.252, SHS.8.340.*

McKENZIE, KENNETH, journeyman goldsmith, Edinburgh, Midlothian. Carried arms in the rebel army. Whereabouts not known. *SHS.8.252.*

McKENZIE, RODERICK, timber merchant from Fisheraw. Joined the rebel army at Edinburgh, supposed to have continued with them till dispersed. Whereabouts not known. *SHS.8.138.*

McKENZIE, SIMON, Roy Stewart's (Edinburgh) Regiment. Aged 26 from Inverness-shire. Taken at Carlisle. Executed 8 November 1746. *MR207.*

McKENZIE, WILLIAM, saltman from Cockenzie. Continued in the exercise of his office for the rebels. Now at home. *SHS.8.138.*

McKILLOP, JOHN, maltster from Stirling. Imprisoned 13 January 1746 Linlithgow, 20 January 1746 Leith. Liberated 7 February 1746. *SHS.3.136.*

McKNOBY, ARCHIBALD, servant from Damhead of Aberdour, Fife. Joined the rebels. Whereabouts not known. *SHS.8.260.*

McLACHLAN, DONALD, tenant, Lochiel's Regiment. Imprisoned 1 February 1746 Stirling, 7 February 1746 Stirling Castle, Edinburgh. Discharged 18 June 1747. In hospital with fracture of leg. Surgeon's fee, 6s.8d. *SHS.3.140.*

McLACHLAN, DUNCAN, farmer, from Dumbarton, Glengyle's Regiment. Imprisoned 9 March 1746 Dumbarton. Escaped 2 February 1746. *SHS.3.140.*

McLAREN, ARCHIBALD, farmer in Curnoch, Callander parish, Perthshire. Assisted the rebels with money being forced thereto or to send a man. At home. *SHS.8.58.*

McLAREN, DONALD, Captain, Appin Stewart's Regiment. Drover from Western Invernentie, Balquhidder. Imprisoned 19 July 1746 Braes of Leny, Stirling, Edinburgh, Canongate. Escaped August 1746. He was captured, with some others, while living in a hut in the Braes of Leny. Defending himself he was wounded in the thigh. "When on his way to Carlisle strapped to a dragoon, he cut the strap, threw himself over the cliff and escaped. This incident occurred on Erickstane Brae at the hollow formerly called Annandale's Beefstand but now McLaren's Leap. After his escape he went back to his own country and remained in disguise until the Act of Indemnity. *SHS.3.142.*

McLAUCHLAN, JOHN, wright from Doune, Stirlingshire. Evidence from John Christy, multerer in Doune Miln, John Mitchel, merchant there, Alexander Campbell, gunsmith there, James Kemp, innkeeper there and James and William Taylors both innkeepers there. *SHS.8.318.*

McLAUCHLAN, JOHN ROY, brewer in Callander, Perthshire. Went to Edinburgh in rebel service, took the benefit of the Indemnity in November 1746. At home. *SHS.8.58.*

McLEAN, DONALD, Surgeon. Irish Piquets, French Service. Taken at Culloden and imprisoned in Inverness. Discharged. *MR136, SHS.3.146.*

McLEAN, HECTOR, porter, servant to James Reid, Leith, Midlothian. Was forced out into the rebellion by his said master. Now at home. Evidence from the neighbourhood. *SHS.8.252, SHS.8.340.*

McLEAN, JAMES, aged 19, nailmaker from Stirling, Duke of
Perth's Regiment. Imprisoned 30 December 1745
Carlisle, York Castle, Lincoln Castle. Taken at capture of
Carlisle. Transported Antigua 8 May 1747 from
Liverpool to Leeward Islands in *Veteran*, arriving
Martinique June 1747. *SHS.3.148, MR74,
PRO.SP36.102.*

McLEAN, LACHLAN, Roy Stewart's (Edinburgh) Regiment.
From Argyllshire. Taken at Culloden. *MR207.*

McLEAN, PATRICK, sailor from Ireland. Lord John
Drummond's French Royal Scots Cavalry. Imprisoned
Drummond of Lunnoch, 4 May 1746 Stirling Castle.
Released under General Pardon, 1747. *MR.63,
SHS.3.152.*

McLEAN, PETER, Corporal, French Royal Scots Cavalry.
Aged 28. Taken at Carlisle, transported 1747.
SHS.3.152, MR.62.

McLEISH, WILLIAM, servant to Roy Stewart, Edinburgh.
Evidence from James Easson, Excise Officer. *SHS.8.340,
MR205.*

McLEOD, ALEXANDER, aged 50, from Nithsdale. Carrier.
Imprisoned 24 February 1746 Perth, 4 May 1746 Stirling
Castle, Carlisle, York Castle, Lancaster Castle.
"Belonged to Guise's Regiment and was therefore a
deserter." Transported 1747. *SHS.3.156.*

McLEOD, ALEXANDER, son to Mr John McLeod, Advocate,
Muiravenside. Was engaged in the rebellion.
Whereabouts not known. *SHS.8.266.*

McLEOD, JOHN, imprisoned 13 August 1745 Edinburgh
Tolbooth. Released. The *Scots Magazine* reported that,

shortly after the Prince's landing, John McLeod, who had recently come over from Holland, was imprisoned on 13 August 1745 on suspicion. Ultimately released. This may have been John McLeod of Muiravonside, Stirling, Advocate, grandson of Sir Normal McLeod of Bernera. *SHS.3.162.*

McMAHON, ANDREW, Captain, Hainault's French Service. Taken 24 March 1746 *Prince Charles* (late *Hazard*); Sheerness, Berwick. Aged 24 from France. Pardoned on condition of permanent banishment 2 July 1747. *SHS.3.166.*

McMAHON, CLAUD, Captain, Berwick's French Service. From France. Taken 24 March 1746 *Prince Charles* (late *Hazard*); Sheerness, Berwick. Pardoned on condition of permanent banishment 3 July 1747. *SHS.3.166.*

McMAHON, MORGAN, Lieutenant, Ultonia's Regiment, Spanish Service. From France. Imprisoned Fort William, Fort Augustus, 11 August 1746 Inverness, Perth, Canongate, Berwick. Pardoned on condition of banishment 20 October 1748. *SHS.3.166.*

McMANUS, HENRY, French Service, from Ireland. Taken *Louis XV* 28 November 1745, imprisoned Edinburgh Castle. Hanged Edinburgh 24 January 1746. Captured at sea. Found to be a deserter from Hamilton's Dragoons. *SHS.3.166.*

McNAB, DONALD, farmer from Brae Leing, Callander parish, Perthshire. Carried arms and first went south and thereafter north with the rebels. Whereabouts not known. *SHS.8.58.*

McNAB, FINLAY, labourer from Stirling. Imprisoned on suspicion 2 February 1746 Cambus Wallace, 7 February

1746 Stirling Castle, 13 February 1746 Leith. Discharged. *SHS.3.170*.

McNAUGHTON, COLIN, from Jamaica. Imprisoned Edinburgh Castle, 15 January 1746 Edinburgh Jail "on suspicion". Discharged. *SHS.3.170*.

McNAUGHTON, JOHN, journeyman watchmaker, Canongatehead, Edinburgh, Midlothian. Was at Preston battle and boasted that he killed Colonel Gardner there. Now a prisoner in Carlisle. This was the "stalwart Highlander" who killed the famous Colonel Gardner at the battle of Prestonpans. He is described as an Edinburgh workman. Tried at Carlisle, he was found guilty, and executed there on 18 October 1746. *SHS.8.252, SHS.8.380*.

McNEAL, JOHN, Manchester Regiment, from Lancashire. Tried and pardoned on enlistment. *MR198*.

McNEAL, RICHARD, Manchester Regiment, from Lancashire. Tried and transported 1747. *MR198*.

McNEILL, PATRICK, Roy Stewart's (Edinburgh) Regiment. From Perthshire. Taken at Carlisle. Died? *MR207*.

McPHERSON, JAMES, Captain, Spanish-Irish Grenadiers. Imprisoned 24 March 1746 *Prince Charles* (late *Hazard*), Sheerness, Berwick. Pardoned on condition of permanent banishment. Shown in the lists as "Don Diego McPherson." *SHS.3.176*.

McRAE JAMES, Lieutenant, Spanish Service, Irish Piquets. Taken at Dunrobin. Discharged. *MR136*.

MACAY, JAMES, Clare's French Service. Captured at sea 28 November 1745, imprisoned Berwick, February 1746 Hull. Discharged. *SHS.3.108*.

MACKENSEN, JOHN, Manchester Regiment. From Lancashire. Taken. Turned King's Evidence. Discharged. *MR198, SHS.3.2.*

MACKMAN, NICHOLAS, Corporal, Berwick's French Service. From France. Taken at sea 28 November 1745, imprisoned Berwick, February 1746 Hull. Discharged. *SHS.3.2.*

MACKRALL, JOHN, Clare's French Service. From France. Taken at sea 28 November 1745, imprisoned Berwick, February 1746 Hull. Discharged. *SHS.3.2.*

MACKSUNN (McSWEEN?), ARCHIBALD, Innkeeper from Linlithgow. Imprisoned 13 January 1746 Linlithgow, 20 January 1746 Leith. Discharged on bail 7 February 1746. *SHS.3.184.*

MACRAE, JAMES, Lieutenant, Spanish Service. Imprisoned 15 April 1746 Sutherland, HMS *Hawk*, London. Discharged. Taken along with the Earl of Cromarty, several officers, and 150 men. *SHS.3.182.*

MACRAITH or MACROTH, JAMES or JOHN, Captain, Berwick's French Service. Taken on *Louis XV*, imprisoned 28 November 1745 Edinburgh Castle, 26 December 1745 Berwick, February 1746 Hull. Pardoned on condition of permanent banishment 2 July 1747. From France. This man was one of the Kintail Macraes. *SHS.3.182.*

MADAY, JAMES, Clare's French Service. From France. Taken at sea 28 November 1745, imprisoned Berwick, February 1746 Hull. Discharged. *SHS.3.2.*

MADDEN, MARK, Fitzjames' Horse. Imprisoned 10 February 1746 Kippen, 25 February 1746 Stirling. From Galway, Ireland. In hospital with fever. Surgeon's fee 4s. "Discharged from Fitzjames' Horse and taken at Kippen by Countrymen." Discharged. *SHS.3.2.*

MADDOCK or MADDOX, SAMUEL, Ensign, Manchester Regiment. Apothecary's apprentice in Manchester. From Cheshire. Taken at capture of Carlisle, 30 December 1745. Imprisoned London (Southwark). He turned King's Evidence against Francis Townley and the other officers of his regiment. Transported 1747. *MR.195, SHS.3.2.*

MAGNALD, JOHN, Manchester Regiment. Taken. Died? *MR198.*

MAGGENIS or GENNIS, MURTOUGH (MURDOCH), Captain, Dillon's French Service. From France. Taken on *Esperance* (late *Soleil*), 25 November 1745 Deal. Pardoned on condition of permanent banishment 2 July 1747. Captured at sea on the way to Montrose. A petition was sent in by him on 4 June 1747 for permission to return to France. *SHS.3.2.*

MAGINNIES, JAMES, Berwick's French Service. From France. Taken at sea 28 November 1745 imprisoned Berwick, February 1746 Hull. Discharged. *SHS.3.2.*

MAGNALL or MACKNELL, JOHN, Manchester Regiment. Taken at Carlisle, imprisoned Lancaster Castle, Carlisle. "Taken in actual rebellion." Nothing more is known about him. He was not transported, and may have died. *SHS.3.4.*

MAGRATH, NICHOLAS, French Service. Imprisoned Carlisle, Berwick. Pardoned on condition of permanent banishment 2 July 1747. *SHS.3.4.*

MAHONY, DENNIS, Lieutenant, Bulkeley's Regiment. Taken *Louis XV* 28 November 1745, imprisoned Edinburgh Castle, 26 December 1745 Berwick, February 1746 Hull. Pardoned on condition of permanent banishment 2 July 1747. Captured at sea off Montrose. *SHS.3.4.*

MAHONY, DERBY, Lieutenant, Bulkeley's Regiment. Captured at sea off Montrose, *Louis XV*, 28 November 1745. Imprisoned Edinburgh Castle, 26 December 1745 Berwick, February 1746 Hull. Pardoned on condition of permanent banishment, 2 July 1747. *SHS.3.4.*

MAIDEN, ..., surgeon from Crail, Fife. Drank the Pretender's health and his son's, and vaunted that he had got 20 libs of their money. At home. Evidence from Alexander Oliphant, Alexander Mapsie, Andrew Jamieson, all in Crail, and John Ross, excise officer there. *SHS.8.66, SHS.8.352.*

MAIN, or MAYNE, JAMES, from Alloa, Stirlingshire, Sergeant, Grant's Regiment, brewer or tallow chandler. Imprisoned Chester; York Castle, executed York 1 November 1746. "Joined the rebels before Preston battle and went with them to England. London prisoner." He pleaded guilty at his trial on 6 October and was sentenced to death, but does not appear in the list of those executed. Evidence from James Haig, innkeeper in Alloa and William and James Davidson, baillies there. *SHS.3.4, SHS.8.148, SHS.8.348, SHS.8.378.*

MAITLAND, JOHN, Artillery, from Armagh, Ireland. Aged 30, gardener. Imprisoned 30 December 1745 Carlisle, Lincoln Castle. Transported 1747. *SHS.3.6.*

MALCOLM, JAMES, younger of Balbeddie, Fife. Joined the rebels and assisted them in collecting the Excise. Whereabouts not known. Evidence from John McGill, merchant, Kirkcaldy, Messrs Alexander Steedman, late Provost and others in Kirkcaldy. *SHS.8.260, SHS.8.344.*

MALCOLM, JAMES, Officer in Lord George Murray's Regiment. From Tullibardine. Imprisoned 3 February 1746 Dunblane, 7 February 1746 tirling Castle, 13 February 1746 Leith. Discharged. Ground officer to Duke of Perth. *SHS.3.6.*

MALONEY, JOHN, Corporal, Clare's French Service, from France. Imprisoned at sea 28 November 1745 Berwick, February 1746 Hull. Discharged. *SHS.3.6.*

MANN, JAMES, Ensign, Roy Stewart's (Edinburgh) Regiment. Aged 20, baker from Dunkeld. Taken at Carlisle. Transported 5 May 1747 from Liverpool to Leeward Islands in *Veteran*, arriving Martinique June 1747. *SHS.3.6, MR205, PRO.SP36.102.*

MANSFIELD, WILLIAM, from Shropshire. Imprisoned Alloa, 25 April 1746 Stirling Castle. Discharged. "Servant to the Pretender." *SHS.3.6.*

MAR, (MARR), ALEXANDER, Roy Stewart's (Edinburgh) Regiment. Aged 33, butcher. Taken and transported 1747. *MR206.*

MARNERY, JOHN, Manchester Regiment. Taken. Died? *MR198.*

MARNYNE, VALENTYNE, Captain, Clare's French Service, from France. Imprisoned at sea 28 November 1745 Berwick, Hull. Discharged. *SHS.3.8.*

MARRIS, THOMAS, Roy Stewart's (Edinburgh) Regiment. Taken. Died? *MR206.*

MARSHAL, DONALD, Roy Stewart's (Edinburgh) Regiment. From Perthshire. Taken at Carlisle. Died. *MR206.*

MARSHALL, JAMES, from Dundee, Officer's Servant, Irish Piquets. Taken and discharged. *MR137.*

MARSHALL, JOHN, labouring man from Alloa. Joined the rebels after Preston battle and continued with them. Whereabouts not known. Evidence from Robert Thomson, Charles White and James Paton, all brewers in Alloa. *SHS.8.148, SHS.8.348.*

MARSHALL, JOHN, writer from Kinross. Gave the rebels intelligence of arms, hid in the country, etc. Now at home. Evidence from James Stuart, Sheriff Depute in Kinross, William Lendrum, excise officer in Kirkintilloch and James Dunbar, servitor to Sir John Bruce Hope of Kinross. *SHS.8.148, SHS.8.348.*

MARTIN, DENNIS, Clare's French Regiment, from France. Imprisoned at sea 28 November 1745 Berwick, February 1746 Hull. Discharged. *SHS.3.8.*

MARTIN, JOHN, soldier, French Royal Scots Cavalry. Aged 42, stocking weaver from Stonehaven, Kincardineshire. Taken and transported 31 March 1747 from London to Jamaica in *St George or Carteret*, arriving Jamaica 1747. *SHS.3.8, MR.63, PRO.CO137.58*

MASH, JAMES, Manchester Regiment. From Lancashire. Imprisoned 30 December 1745 Carlisle, Lancaster Castle. Taken at capture of Carlisle. No further reference to him. *MR198, SHS.3.6.*

MASON, BENJAMIN, Sergeant, Glenbucket's Regiment. Weaver from Abbey Lease, Queen's County, Ireland. Imprisoned 31 December 1745 Carlisle, Chester Castle, York Castle. Pleaded guilty at his trial on 2 October and was sentenced to death. *SHS.3.10.*

MASTERTON, FRANCIS, of Parkhill, Alloa. Joined the rebels on their coming to Edinburgh and got a Commission in their Army. Whereabouts not known. Three persons evidences against the Laird of Clackmannan. Condition of Mansion House - habitable. Rental £250. *SHS.8.148, SHS.8.348*

MATTHEWS, ANNE, Manchester Regiment. From Newton, Kildare, Ireland. Imprisoned Carlisle, Chester. Discharged. *SHS.3.12.*

MATTHEWS, BARNABAS, Manchester Regiment. Aged 24 from Lancashire. Imprisoned 30 December 1745 Carlisle. Pleaded guilty and was sentenced to death, August 1746. Executed at Carlisle, 15 November 1746. *SHS.1.150, MR198, SHS.3.12.*

MATTHEWS, FRANCIS, Cadet, Bulkeley's French Service, from France. Imprisoned *Louis XV* 28 November 1745, Edinburgh Castle, 26 December 1745 Berwick, February 1746 Hull. Captured at sea off Montrose. *SHS.3.14.*

MATTHEWS, GEORGE, Cadet, Bulkeley's French Service, from France. Captured at sea *Louis XV* 28 November 1745 Edinburgh Castle, 26 December 1745 Berwick, February 1746 Hull. Discharged. *SHS.3.6.14.*

MATTHEWS, MATTHEW, Manchester Regiment. Weaver from Naas, Co. Kildare, Ireland. Imprisoned 30 December 1745 Carlisle, Chester Castle, York Castle.

Taken at capture of Carlisle. "A poor deaf man." He pleaded guilty at his trial on 2 October 1746, was sentenced to death, but was reprieved. Transported 21 July 1748. *SHS.3.14, MR198, SHS.3.14.*

MATTISON, THOMAS, conveyed from Penrith to Brough, Westmoreland in the company of 19 other Jacobites. *CQS.354.*

MAUL, HENRY, a clerk in the Stamp Office, Edinburgh, Midlothian. Carried arms with the rebels and was most active in seizing horses for their use. Whereabouts not known. *SHS.8.266, SHS.8.252.*

MAURICE, ..., Lieutenant, Berwick's Regiment, from France. Imprisoned 24 March 1746 *Prince Charles* (late *Hazard*); HMS *Sheerness* Berwick. Discharged. *SHS.3.14.*

MAXWELL, ADAM, Roy Stewart's (Edinburgh) Regiment. Aged 17, labourer. Taken at Carlisle. Transported 22 April 1747. *Mr206, SHS.3.14.*

MAXWELL, JAMES, of Kirkconnal, Kirkcudbright Stewartry. Served in the Pretender's son's Life Guards till the defeat at Culloden. Whereabouts not known. *SHS.8.144.*

MAXWELL, KATHARINE, Lady, spouse to the Earl of Nithsdale, William Maxwell, Terragles, Nithsdale. Attended the Young Pretender most of the time he was in Edinburgh and Dumfries, was most active in promoting his interest and had the principal hand in engaging William Maxwell of Carruchan to join the rebels. She likewise made a present of a horse and chaise to the person commonly called Duke of Perth. Now at home. *SHS.8.144.*

MAXWELL, ROBERT, aged 50 from Edinburgh, imprisoned Edinburgh; Carlisle, pardoned on condition of enlistment 22 July 1747. "Said to be a natural brother of Sir William Maxwell of Monreith." Writer. "Carried arms." At his trial he pleaded guilty, and he petitioned for mercy because he had surrendered in Edinburgh. He said he was only a clerk, unpaid, and that he merely noted down and gave receipts for corn and straw brought in for the army. He was condemned, but was reprieved on 10 November 1746. On 13 October 1747 he appealed against the commutation of his sentence to enlistment, and explained that he had been forced. There is nothing to show what was the result of his appeal. Evidence from George Robertson and Francis Pringle, Excise Officers. *SHS.3.16, SHS.8.340, SHS.3.16.*

MAXWELL, ROBERT, from Stewartry of Kirkcudbright, Lieutenant, Lord John Drummond's Regiment, French Royal Scots Cavalry. Imprisoned 23 June 1746 Longwood; 23 June 1746 Dumfries, London. Pardoned on condition of permanent banishment 3 July 1747. The Dumfries Jail return shows that on 1 March 1747 he was handed over to a military escort as a deserter from Price's Regiment. *SHS.3.16, MR.62, SHS.3.16.*

MAXWELL, WILLIAM, Captain, of Carruchan, Kirkcudbrightshire, Chief Engineer, imprisoned 30 December 1745 Carlisle. Escaped 30 December 1747. Acted as Chief Engineer in the defence of Carlisle against Cumberland. When the town surrendered on 30 December 1745 and during the process of capitualtion he escaped over the city wall and got clear away. *SHS.3.16, SHS.8.144, SHS.3.16.*

MAXWELL, WILLIAM, from Dumfries, Lord John Drummond's Regiment, French Royal Scots Cavalry. Imprisoned 25 April 1746 Quarrelwood; 25 April 1745

Dumfries, discharged 2 February 1747. "Gentleman."
"Son to James Maxwell of Barricleugh." *SHS.3.16, MR.62, SHS.3.16.*

MAXWELL, WILLIAM, son to James Maxwell of Barncleugh, Dumfries, Nithsdale. Carried arms with the rebels. Now a prisoner. *SHS.8.144.*

MAXWELL, WILLIAM, Sir, of Sprinkell, Annandale Stewartry. Entertained one called Major Brown and William Maxwell of Carruchan, two rebels, after they had made their escape over the walls of Carlisle and provided them in horses to carry them to the rebel army at Glasgow. Now at home. *SHS.8.144.*

MAXWELL, WILLIAM, Esq, called Earl of Nithsdale, Terragles, Nithsdale. Went to Edinburgh and waited some time upon the Pretender's son. Now at home. *SHS.8.144.*

MEAGHER, PATRICK, Lieutenant, Bulkeley's Regiment, from France. Captured at sea *Louis XV* off Montrose, 28 November 1745 Edinburgh Castle, 26 December 1745 Berwick, February 1746 Hull. Pardoned on condition of permanent banishment 3 July 1747. *SHS.3.16.*

MEALY, LAWRENCE, mariner on the *Hawk* sloop of war. Imprisoned on suspicion of having deserted, having no pass on 14 May 1746 in Montrose. *SHS.3.186.*

MEAN, JOHN, Manchester Regiment, from Lancashire. Tried and transported 31 March 1747. *SHS.3.186, MR198.*

MEIKLEJOHN or MEIKLE, JOHN, soldier aged 31, from Stirling. Deserter from Royal Scots. "Stack's Company." Imprisoned Inverness June 1746, *Alexander and James,*

Liberty, Medway. Transported 31 March 1747 from London to Barbados in *Frere*. *BMHS.83, SHS.3.186*.

MEIN or MEAN, ISABEL, from Alloa, Grant's Regiment. Imprisoned Carlisle, Chester Castle. Released. *SHS.3.186*.

MELLIN, JAMES, Manchester Regiment. Weaver aged 23 from Preston, Lancashire. Taken at capture of Carlisle. He was sentenced to death, but his disposal is unknow. May have died. Does not appear in transportation lists. *MR198, SHS.3.186*.

MELVIL, ROBERT, aged 30, carrier, from Edinburgh. Imprisoned on suspicion 28 January 1746 Edinburgh Jail. Discharged 8 February 1746. *SHS.3.188*.

MENEY, JOSEPH, Berwick's French Service. From France. Taken at sea 28 November 1745, imprisoned Berwick. Discharged. *SHS.3.188*.

MENZIES, JAMES, Lieutenant, Roy Stewart's (Edinburgh) Regiment. From St Germaine, France. Taken at Carlisle, imprisoned 31 December 1745 in Carlisle, and Marshalsea. He appears to have shown that he was a French subject. Discharged. *MR205, SHS.3.188*.

MENZIES, JOHN, Mr, gentleman from Edinburgh, Midlothian. Captain of volunteers in the rebel army. Whereabouts not known. *SHS.8.252*.

MENZIES, JOHN, son to Robert Menzies, late Innkeeper, St Ninians, Stirling. Was paymaster in Menzies of Schian's Regiment. Whereabouts not known. *SHS.8.266*.

MENZIES, JOHN, paymaster, Menzies of Schien's Regiment. From St Ninians. Imprisoned Canongate. Discharged.

Son of Rob Menzies, innkeeper; portioner of St Ninians. "Witnesses state that he was in arms with the rebels and acted as Quartermaster." It was possibly this man who was subsequently arrested in Holland on suspicion and sent ot London and confined in Carrington's House. *SHS.3.188.*

MENZIES, JOHN, from Edinburgh. Writer in Edinburgh. Imprisoned "on suspicion" July 1746 Aberdeen, 2 August 1746 Canongate. Discharged. *SHS.3.188.*

MENZIES, ROBERT, farmer from Callander. Imprisoned "on suspicion" 31 March 1746 Stirling. Discharged 29 April 1746. *SHS.3.188.*

MERCER, ROBERT, of Aldie, brother to Lord Nairn. Joined early in the rebellion, was active in forcing out others and was made a Colonel. Whereabouts not known. Evidence from John Kelly of Newbigging, Adam Colvill, tacksman of Aldie Parks and William Colvill, brewere in Crook of Devon. Condition of Mansion House - habitable. Rental £400. *SHS.8.148, SHS.8.348.*

MERCER, SIMON, Clare's French Service. Taken at sea 28 November 1745, imprisoned Berwick, February 1746 Hull. Discharged. From France. *SHS.3.190.*

MERVYN, VALENTINE, Clare's French Service. Taken at sea in *Louis XV*, imprisoned 6 December 1745 Edinburgh Castle, 26 December 1745 Berwick, Hull. Pardoned on condition of permanent banishment. *SHS.3.190.*

MIDDLETON, ALEXANDER, wright from Leuchars, Fife. Carried arms in the rebel service from after the battle of Preston till Culloden. Whereabouts not known. *SHS.8.66.*

MIDDLETON, PATRICK, surgeon from Edinburgh, Midlothian. Carried arms in the rebel Life Guards. Whereabouts not known. *SHS.8.252.*

MILL, ALEXANDER, of Newmilln, Callander parish, Stirlingshire. Seized boats for the rebels passage. Transported their arms with horses and abused his Majesty's soldiers when prisoners. At home. *SHS.8.58.*

MILL, DAVID, son of Alexander Mill of Newmilln, Callander parish, Stirlingshire. Very active in aiding and assisting the rebels and transporting their arms. At home. *SHS.8.58.*

MILL, THOMAS, son of Alexander Mill of Newmilln, Callander parish, Stirlingshire. Very active in aiding and assisting the rebels and transporting their arms. At home. *SHS.8.58.*

MILLER, ALEXANDER, servant to Lord George Murray, from Benvie. Served his master in the rebellion. Whereabouts not known. *SHS.8.252.*

MILLER, CHARLES, servant from Hawick. Imprisoned 27 April 1746 Leslie, Leith, Canongate 25 June 1746. Released 20 March 1747. Servant to Mr Scott of Atherstonshiells. "In arms at Leslie." This was probably the man who was ill in prison in December 1746. "He declares that he served his master, a rebel officer, during the rebellion but never carried arms." *SHS.3.192.*

MILLER, FARQUHAR (FARCHER), Duke of Perth's Regiment. Aged 50, gardener from Edinburgh. Imprisoned Kippen, 1 May 1746 Stirling Castle, Carlisle. Transported 24 February 1747 from Liverpool to Virginia in *Gildart*, arriving Port North Potomac, Maryland 5 August 1747. *SHS.3.194, MR74, PRO.T1.328.*

MILLER, JAMES, Manchester Regiment. Tried and pardoned on enlistment. *MR198.*

MILLER, JOHN (JEAN), Berwick's French Service. Taken at sea, imprisoned Berwick. Discharged. From France. *SHS.3.194.*

MILLER, WALTER, hostler from Linlithgow. Imprisoned 13 January 1746 Linlithgow, 20 January 1746 Leith. Liberated 2 July 1746. *SHS.3.196.*

MILLS, GEORGE, from Penrith. Imprisoned Carlisle, York. Escaped 10 August 1747. He was tried at York on 6 October 1746 and pleaded guitly. No other trace of this man's history has been found until 17 January 1749, when Lord Stanhope asked the Sheriff of Yorkshire how he had escaped. *SHS.3.196.*

MILLS, WILLIAM, Manchester Regiment. Aged 23, from Lancashire. Imprisoned York Castle, Lincoln. Tried and transported to Antigua 8 May 1747. "Taken in actual rebellion." Pleaded guilty at his trial 2 October 1746, was sentenced to death, but was reprieved. *MR198, SHS.3.196.*

MILN, ALEXANDER, of Newmiln, Airth, Stirlingshire. Yearly rent £40. Evidence from John Dick, shipmaster in Airth and Alexander Hodge, brewer there. *SHS.8.316.*

MILN, DAVID, son of Alexander Miln, of Newmiln, Airth, Stirlingshire. Yearly rent £40. Evidence from John Dick, shipmaster in Airth and Alexander Hodge, brewer there. *SHS.8.316.*

MILN, DAVID, from Linlithgow. Probably a deserter from Navy. Imprisoned 1 February 1746, 13 February 1746

Leith. Sent to a King's ship, Leith Roads, as innocent. *SHS.3.196.*

MILN, THOMAS, son of Alexander Miln, of Newmiln, Airth, Stirlingshire. Yearly rent £40. Evidence from John Dick, shipmaster in Airth and Alexander Hodge, brewer there. *SHS.8.316.*

MILN, THOMAS, from Linlithgow. Probably a deserter from the Navy (see also David Miln). Imprisoned 1 February 1746, 13 February 1746 Leith. Sent to a King's ship, Leith Roads, as innocent. *SHS.3.198.*

MISSIN, TADDY, from France, French Service. Taken at sea, imprisoned Marshalsea. Discharged. Servant to Colonel Nugent. *SHS.3.198.*

MITCHELL, DONALD, slater from Doune, Stirlingshire. Evidence from John Christy, multerer in Doune Miln, John Mitchel, merchant there, Alexander Campbell, gunsmith there, James Kemp, innkeeper there and James and William Taylors both innkeepers there. *SHS.8.318.*

MITCHELL, DUNCAN, carrier from Doune, Stirlingshire. Evidence from Patrick Ferguson, merchant in Doune and James Taylor, merchant there. *SHS.8.318.*

MITCHELL, JOHN, aged 48, alehouse-keeper from Edinburgh, Glengarry's Regiment. Imprisoned Inverness, Tilbury Fort. Transported 20 March 1747. This may have been the John Mitchell, alehouse keeper, and servant to Lord Elcho, who "carried arms, was at Preston battle, carried off a Dragoon horse from thence, and was in the rebellion to the end." Evidence from William Lithgow, maltster, Jonathan Brown and his servant, Calton. *SHS.3.200, MR159, SHS.8.252, SHS.8.340.*

MITCHELL, ROBERT, journeyman goldsmith, Edinburgh, Midlothian. Carried arms in the rebel army. Whereabouts not known. Evidence from Robert Gordon and Robert Low, goldsmiths in Edinburgh. *SHS.8.252, SHS.8.338.*

MITCHELL, THOMAS, goldsmith, Potterow, St Cuthberts, Midlothian. Was in arms as a rebel Hussar. Whereabouts not known. Evidence from Robert Ramsay, tailor, St Mary's Wynd, Edinburgh. *SHS.8.252, SHS.8.340.*

MITCHELL, WILLIAM, saltman from Cockenzie. Continued in the exercise of his office for the rebels. Now at home. *SHS.8.138.*

MOIR, HENRY, surgeon at Kelso, "But had little business and no estate." Roxburghshire, Private, Balmerino's Life Guards. Imprisoned Inverness, London (Southwark). Brother of Robert Moir. He was tried 22 January 1747 and sentenced to death, but reprieved 12 February 1747. The Duke of Queensberry, on 12 February 1747, wrote to Newcastle recommending him for pardon. Transported September 1748. *SHS.3.202, MR48.*

MOIR, ROBERT, from Kelso, Private, (an idle young fellow). Joined the rebel army at Edinburgh. Balmerino's Life Guards. Imprisoned Inverness, London (Southward). Transported to America, September 1748. Brother of Henry Moir and farmer near Kelso. Tried 22 January 1747 and sentenced to death but was reprieved 12 February 1747. The Duke of Queensberry wrote on 12 February 1747 to Newcastle recommending that he be pardoned. *SHS.3.204, MR49, SHS.8.280.*

MOIR, or MORE, of Leckie, WILLIAM MONTGOMERY, Stirlingshire. Imprisoned on suspicion 13 September

1745 House of Leckie; 6 February 1746 Edinburgh Castle. "Subsists himself." By his declaration before Sheriff Napier he denies to have had correspondence with the person called the Duke of Perth. Yet there is a letter in Mr Solicitor Home's custody wrote and signed by Leckie directed to the Duke wherein he acknowledges to have received a letter from him." According to *Lyon in Mourning*, Leckie's name was George. Dr Blaikie says that Leckie, in September 1745, belong to George Moir. *SHS.3.204*.

MOITOU, LOUIS, French Service, from France. Taken at sea *Soleil*, privateer going to Scotland, imprisoned Marshalsea. Discharged. *SHS.3.204*.

MOLLEN, JAMES, Englishman, Manchester Regiment. Imprisoned Carlisle. Tried at Carlisle September 1746 and sentenced to death. No further reference to him; as he was not transported he probably died. *SHS.3.204, MR198*.

MOLLOY, PHILLIPE, Quartermaster, Fitzjames' Horse, French Service. Taken at Culloden 17 April 1746, imprisoned Inverness, Penrith. From France. Discharged. *MR38, SHS.3.204*.

MONEY, JAMES, napkin merchant from Yorkshire. Imprisoned 24 April 1746 Dunfermline. Escaped 27 December 1746. *SHS.3.204*.

MONTEITH, ALEXANDER, sorter of Yearn, Kinross. Joined the rebels and continued with them. Whereabouts not known. Evidence from James Stuart, sheriff depute in Kinross, William Lendrum, excise officer in Kirkintilloch and James Dunbar, servitor to Sir John Bruce Hope of Kinross. *SHS.8.148, SHS.8.348*.

MONTIGNY, CHARLES, Berwick's French Service. Aged 24, from France. Taken on *Prince Charles* at sea, imprisoned Berwick. Discharged. *SHS.3.206.*

MOORE, WILLIAM, Coronet, Fitzjames' Horse, French Service. Aged 26 from Ireland. No commision. Taken at Culloden, imprisoned Inverness June 1746, *Jane of Alloway* Tilbury, Marshalsea. Pardoned on condition of permanent banishment 2 July 1747. *MR38, SHS.3.206.*

MOORE, WILLIAM, French Service, from France. Imprisoned Marshalsea. Pardoned on condition of permanent banishment 2 July 1747. *SHS.3.206.*

MORGAN, DAVID, Captain, Manchester Regiment. Barrister from Monmouthshire. Imprisoned London. Executed at Kennington Common, 30 July 1746. He joined the Prince's army at Preston on 27 November 1745 and accompanied him to Derby, but refused to return to Scotland with him. The Prince consulted him a good deal, and he was called "the Pretender's Counsellor." He left the army at Ashbourne on 6 December to go to London to procure intelligence for the Prince. He was tried 18 July 1746 and sentenced to death, and was executed at Kennington along with Townley and several other English officers. *MR.195, SHS.1.150, SHS.3.208.*

MORGAN, DAVID MORRIS, French Service, from France. Pardoned on condition of permanent banishment 2 July 1747. *SHS.3.208.*

MORGAN, JOHN, Corporal, French Royal Scots Cavalry (Lord John Drummon's). Aged 20, sailor from Longford, Ireland, "deserted from General Phillip's." Transported 31 March 1747. *MR.62, SHS.3.210.*

MORGAN, PETER (or PATRICK), Roy Stewart's (Edinburgh) Regiment. From Fodderletterm, Banff. Taken and transported 22 April 1747 from Liverpool to Virginia in *Johnson*, arriving Port Oxford, Maryland 5 August 1747. *SHS.3.210, JAB.2.438, MR207, PRO.T1.328,*

MORISON, DAVID, aged 15, servant from Dunfermline; a youth. Imprisoned on suspicion 26 February 1746 Perth. Discharged on baill 17 June 1747. "Confesses that he served a reel officer." *SHS.3.212.*

MORISON, RICHARD, barber "wig maker" from Edinburgh, Valet de Chambre to the Prince. Imprisoned 15 May 1746 Leven; 16 May 1746 Kirkcaldy; 19 May 1746 Leith; 7 August 1746 Canongate; 8 August 1746 Carlisle; November 1746 London, in house of Dick the messenger. Released after 8 July 1748. "Attended the Young Pretender." "Went along with him as his barber." He and Mr Gib escaped after Culloden to Leven, Fife, where they were caught on 15 May. He was sent to Carlisle, tried and condemned. On 12 November 1746 he was reprieved and sent to London to give evidence regarding the Prince. Like others who were employed as witnesses he was ultimately released after 8 July 1748. *SHS.3.212, SHS.8.252, SHS.8.380.*

MORRIS, DAVID, Lieutenant, Berwick's French Service. From France. Taken at sea, imprisoned HMS *Sheerness*, Berwick. Discharged. *SHS.3.210.*

MORRIS, EDWARD, aged 22, servant from London. Irish Piquets, French Service. Imprisoned Loch Tay, 1 May 1746 Perth, 12 May 1746 Stirling Castle, Carlisle. He asked to be sent back to France, but was transported 1747. *MR137, SHS.3.210.*

MORRIS, NICHOLAS, Sergeant, Bulkeley's French Service. From France. Taken at sea *Louis XV*, imprisoned 28 November 1745 Berwick, Hull. Pardoned on condition of permanent banishment 2 July 1747. *SHS.3.210.*

MORRIS, NICHOLAS, Captain, Bulkeley's French Service. From France. Captured at sea *Louis XV*, off Montrose, imprisoned 28 November 1745 Edinburgh Castle, 26 December 1745 Berwick, Hull. Pardoned on condition of permanent banishment. *SHS.3.210.*

MORRIS, WILLIAM, Manchester Regiment. From Derbyshire. Taken at capture of Carlisle and imprisoned there 30 December 1745. No further reference to him. *MR198, SHS.3.210.*

MORSEY, EDMUND, from France, Bulkeley's French Service. Taken at sea, 28 November 1745 Berwick, February 1746 Hull. Discharged. *SHS.3.212.*

MORSH (MARSH?), SAMUEL, mariner from London. Imprisoned 28 May 1746 Fettercairn, 29 May 1746 Montrose. Sent back to the Navy. "The wine help *(sic)* in a man of war; on suspicion of having deserted - no pass." *SHS.3.212.*

MOSS, PETER, Lieutenant, Manchester Regiment. Imprisoned 30 December 1745 Carlisle, London. Turned King's Evidence and was discharged. *MR.195, SHS.3.212.*

MOSS, WILLIAM, Captain, Manchester Regiment. From Lancashire. Taken and imprisoned 30 December 1745 Carlisle, London (Newgate Prison). Excaped July 1746. He appears to have escaped before or during his trial. *MR.195, SHS.3.214.*

MOUSE, JAMES, from London (deserter Colonel Scott's Regiment). Irish Piquets, French Service. Imprisoned 18

May 1746 Linton, Leith, 20 May 1746 Edinburgh Jail. Declares that he deserted in Flanders in order to come home, but, being taken prisoner by the French, he enlisted with them and came over with the French Picquets. Discharged 17 February 1747. *MR137, SHS.3.214.*

MOWLONY, WALTER, hatmaker from Ireland. Imprisoned 27 April 1746 Saltcoats, 27 April 1746 Irvine. Escaped 19 July 1746. *SHS.3.214.*

MUCKARSY, or McKASAW, MAGNUS, carter from Edinburgh. Imprisoned 1 February 1746 Stirling; 13 December 1746 Edinburgh Jail from Canongate. Released under General Pardon, 1747. "Forced to carry baggage." *SHS.3.214.*

MUCKLE, ROBERT, aged 60, labourer from Duns, Berwickshire. Imprisoned Cockermouth, Carlisle, 22 July 1746 Whitehaven. "For high treason in levying war." He was probably trying to desert when he was caught. Transported 1747. *SHS.3.214.*

MUIR, ADOLPHUS, servant to James Reid, Leith, Midlothian. Assisted in pillaging the Old Stage Coach lofts and carrying off provisions for the rebel horses. Now at home. Evidence from John Balfour. *SHS.8.252, SHS.8.340.*

MURDOCH or MURDO, WILLIAM, aged 40, wool merchant from Callander, Perthshire. Acted as an Ensign in the rebel army, was thrice forced out and as often deserted. Transported from Liverpool to Virginia in *Johnson*, arriving Port Oxford, Maryland 5 August 1747. *SHS.8.58, SHS.3.216, PRO.T1.328.*

MURPHY, RICHARD, Captain, Lally's French Service. Imprisoned 17 April 1746 Inverness, Penrith. Pardoned on condition of permanent banishment. From Ireland. *SHS.3.216.*

MURRAY, ANTHONY, of Grante, Culross. Joined the rebel army after Preston battle and continued with them. Whereabouts not known. Evidence from Dougal Ged and Robert Low, goldsmiths in Edinburgh. *SHS.8.148, SHS.8.338.*

MURRAY, ANTHONY, journeyman goldsmith, Edinburgh, Midlothian. Carried arms in the rebel army. Whereabouts not known. *SHS.8.252.*

MURRAY, DAVID, from Leith. Evidence from Fullarton and Cairns, distillers in Leith. *SHS.8.340.*

MURRAY, Sir DAVID of Stanhope (Peebles), Bart. Aged 17, Captain, Baggot's Housars, ADC to the Prince. Imprisoned Whitby, York Castle. Pardoned Sept 1748 on condition of his leaving the country. The 4th baronet, grandson of Sir David, who was father to John Murray of Broughton. He was captured at Whitby trying to escape to Holland in disguise after the battle of Culloden and taken to York, where he was tried and sentenced to death, but conditionally pardoned in September 1748 through the interest of Lord Hopetoun and others. He went abroad and died in exile in 1770. The Ardnamurchan estate, in which lay his famous lead quarry of Strontian, was forfeited and sold for £33,700. In December 1748 he was in the retinue of the Prince in Paris, and was arrested and put in confinement until the whole party left the country. After his death, although forfeited, the title was assumed by his uncle John Murray. *SHS.3.216, SHS.8.252, SHS.8.380.*

MURRAY, JAMES, surgeon from Edinburgh, "in rebel service." Imprisoned 1 February 1746 Stirling, 13

February 1746 Leith, 7 August 1746 Canongate, 8 August 1746 Carlisle. Acquitted and released 26 September 1746. *SHS.3.218, SHS.8.252, SHS.8.380.*

MURRAY, JAMES, merchant in Airth, Stirlingshire. Evidence from John Watson, shipmaster in Airth and John Scott, wright there. *SHS.8.316.*

MURRAY, JOHN, surgeon from Edinburgh, Midlothian. Carried arms as a volunteer in the rebel army. Whereabouts not known. *SHS.8.252.*

MURRAY, JOHN, son of James Murray, merchant from Airth, Stirlingshire. In the rebel service from their first crossing the Forth. Lurking in Dollar parish about Hillfoot. *SHS.8.58.*

MURRAY, JOHN, aged 30, weaver from Annandale, Manchester Regiment. Imprisoned 30 December 1745 Carlisle, York Castle. Taken at capture of Carlisle. Not transported, probably died. *SHS.3.218, MR198.*

MURRAY, JOHN, late Clerk to Collector of the Customs, Alloa. Joined the rebel army at the beginning. Assisted in collecting the Excise at Clackmannan and continued with them. Whereabouts not known. *SHS.8.148.*

MURRAY, JOHN, of Broughton, Tweeddale, aged 30, Secretary to Prince Charles Edward. Imprisoned 29 June 1746 Tweeddale; Edinburgh Castle, 19 July 1746 Tower of London. Released after May 1747 but not pardoned until 7 June 1748. The Prince's Secretary and adviser, Broughton did more than any other man to damage the success of the operations of the 1745, and turned traitor in the end. When his master had escaped after the dispersion of his followers, Murray sought refuge with his relative Mr Hunter of Polmood, but was seized and carried to London.

As soon as he was captured he turned King's Evidence, primarily against Lord Lovat, but also against the leading Jacobites generally. Lord Lovat charged him as being "the most abandoned of mankind." He was never brought to trial but was frequently under examination by the Crown lawyers. In July 1747 he begged to be removed from the Tower and to be sent to a messenger's house. In due course he was pardoned, and it is said, though this is doubtful, that he was given a pension of £200. The letter of pardon bears date 7 June 1748. In 1770 he assumed the baronetcy of his nephew, Sir David Murray. In 1771 he was placed in an asylum, and died in 1777. *SHS.3.218, SHS.8.376, SHS.8.84.*

MURRAY, PATRICK, of Dollair or Doloray (Dullany), Clackmannanshire, younger, Lord George Murray's Regiment. Imprisoned Nov 1745 Airdrie; 7 February 1746 Perth, 1 April 1746 Edinburgh Castle, 8 August 1746 Carlisle. Executed 14 November 1746, buried in St Cuthbert's Churchyard. Goldsmith in Stirling. A volunteer. Commonly called "Cowley Murray." On suspicion of treason. When taken prisoner he declared that he had surrendered under the terms of Wade's proclamation. "Witnesses declare that they had seen him viewing the rebel trenches at Perth with the rebel Governor and that he frequently was in company with the rebel Governors of Perth. Others allege that he attended the non-jurant Episcopal Meeting House." He was tried at Carlisle and sentenced to death. Lord Albemarle reported on 5 February 1747 that Murray was a JP and Sheriff Clerk. *SHS.3.218.*

MURRAY, PATRICK, Bulkeley's French Service. Taken at sea 28 November 1745, imprisoned Berwick, February 1746 Hull. Discharged. From France. *SHS.3.220.*

MURRAY, ROBERT, a writer, Edinburgh, Elcho's Life Guards. Imprisoned 29 April 1746 South Queensferry, 30 April 1746 Edinburgh, 8 August 1746 Carlisle. Pardoned on condition of enlistment 22 July 1748. "Son to Spittlehaugh." "Appears to be very young." Was tried and condemned to death, but reprieved. *SHS.3.220, SHS.8.252, SHS.8.380.*

MUSHET, WILLIAM, wright from Edinburgh, Midlothian. Carried arms in the Pretender's son's Life Guards. Whereabouts not known. Evidence from Robert Ramsay, tailor, St Mary's Wynd, Edinburgh. *SHS.8.252, SHS.8.340.*

NAIRN, ..., Deputy Paymaster, from Edinburgh. Imprisoned 16 April 1746 Culloden, Inverness. There is no further reference to him, and he may have died. *SHS.3.222.*

NAIRN, JOHN, Lieutenant, Lord John Drummond's French Service, Royal Scots Cavalry. (Clan Ranald's). Taken at Culloden 17 April 1746, imprisoned Inverness, Marshalsea. Pardoned and banished. *MR.62, SHS.3.222.*

NAIRN, ROBERT, aged 22, from Stirling, Ogilvy's Regiment. Imprisoned 25 April 1746 Dunsmilne, 26 April 1746 Montrose, 13 May 1746 Inverness, June 1746 prison ship *Jane of Leith*, Tilbury, Southwark. Discharged. This is the individual who turned King's Evidence at Southwark. *SHS.3.222.*

NAIRN, ROBERT, from Edinburgh, Duke of Perth's Regiment. Imprisoned Culloden, Inverness. Escaped ? March 1747. In the official Culloden list he is styled "Deputy Paymaster." He was badly wounded at Culloden, having an arm nearly cut off. He was captured, along with McDonald of Belfinlay, about 18 April 1746, and put in the cellar of a private house. With the assistance of some ladies and one Anna McKay he escaped in March 1747. *SHS.3.222.*

NAIRN, THOMAS, The Hon, Lieutenant, Lord John Drummond's Regiment. Taken at sea *Esperance* 25 November 1745 Deal, February 1746 Customs Smack *Caroline* Greenwich, London, Marshalsea. Pardoned on condition of permanent banishment 2 July 1747. Seventh son of John, 3rd Lord Nairn. He died at Sancerre in France in April 1777. *SHS.3.222.*

NEAVY, DAVID, merchant from Edinburgh, Midlothian. Carried arms as a volunteer in the rebel army. Whereabouts not known. *SHS.8.254.*

NELSON, JAMES, conveyed from Penrith to Brough, Westmoreland in the company of 19 other Jacobites. *CQS.354.*

NESBIT (or NISBIT), JOHN, aged 21, tutor from Falkirk, soldier, French Royal Scots Cavalry, Lord John Drummond's Regiment. Imprisoned Inverness June 1746 prison ships *Alexander & James,* and *Liberty.* Transported from Tilbury 1747. Tutor to Sir Alexander McKenzie's children. *SHS.3.224, MR63.*

NEWTON, JOHN, Manchester Regiment. Aged 16, cotton weaver from Lancashire. Imprisoned 30 December 1745 Carlisle, Lancaster Castle. Taken at capture of Carlise. Transported 22 April 1747 from Liverpool to Virginia in *Johnson,* arriving Port Oxford, Maryland 5 August 1747. *SHS.3.226, MR198, PRO.T1.328.*

NEWTON, WILLIAM, Irish Piquets. Deserted. Taken and discharged. *MR137.*

NEWTON, WILLIAM, "Soldier, French Picquet", imprisoned 16 December 1745 Stirling Castle. Discharged. "Deserted from the rebels." *SHS.3.226.*

NICCOL, ROBERT, mason, Cannongate, Edinburgh. Evidence from James Purdie, skinner and George Robertson, Excise Officer, Edinburgh. *SHS.8.340.*

NICHOLSON, JAMES, Lieutenant, Perth's Regiment. coffeehouse keeper, Leith, Midlothian. "Had a commission in the rebel army and bore arms. Greatly oppressed the country in seizing horses, arms, etc for the rebels' use. Now lurking. Was taken at the surrender of Carlisle. It was reported "he broke the capitulation by endeavouring to make his escape." Tried in London on 31 July, and condemned to death. Executed Kennington Common 2 August 1746. *SHS.3.228, SHS.8.254, SHS.8.380.*

NISBETT, JOHN, Lord John Drummond's French Service. Taken at Culloden, imprisoned Tilbury Fort. Transported? On 20 March 1747 Mons. Carpentier claimed this man as a French subject, but it is not clear whether he got his discharge. His name is in the list of those condemned to transportation, but in the special report on Carpentier's claims, he has "discharged" after his name. *SHS.3.228.*

NIVINS, NINIAN, Rev, Episcopal Minister. *SRO.CH12/12/110.*

NORRIS, NICHOLAS, Captain, Bulkeley's Regiment. Taken at sea *Louis XV* 28 November 1745, February 1746 Hull. Discharged. *SHS.3.338.*

NORRIS, THOMAS, Manchester Regiment. From Lancashire. Taken 30 December 1745 at capture of Carlisle. No further reference to him. Died? *MR198, SHS.3.228.*

NORWALL, ..., of Boghall, from Bathgate, Linlithgow. Imprisoned 29 September 1746 Linlithgow. Released 2 October 1746. He had a brother out with the Prince, and was himself under suspicion. His house was searched on 29 April 1746 to see if he had any Jacobites in hiding. He was taken prisoner and conveyed to Linlithgow, but was released in two or three days, by order of the Lord Justice Clerk. *SHS.3.228.*

NOWLAN, THOMAS, Captain, Baggot's Hussar's. Imprisoned Inverness June 1746, *Jane of Leith*, Tilbury Fort. Aged 30, smith and farmer in France, from Carlow, Ireland. Transported 1747. *SHS.3.230.*

NUGENT, ..., Lieutenant, Bulkeley's Regiment. Imprisoned 24 March 1746 *Prince Charles* (late *Hazard*), HMS *Sheerness*, Berwick. Pardoned on condition of banishment. *SHS.3.230.*

NUGENT, ..., Brigadier General, French Service. Taken at sea on *Bourbon* 21 February 1746, imprisoned Berwick. Pardoned on condition of banishment. *SHS.3.230.*

NUGENT, CHARLES, Cornet, Fitzjames'. Imprisoned Marshalsea, London. Discharged 1747. Taken at sea, from France. *SHS.3.230.*

NUGENT, EDWARD, Captain, Dillon's Regiment. Irish Piquets. Taken at Culloden. Discharged. *MR136.*

NUGENT, FRANCOIS, Quartermaster, Fitzjames' Horse, French Service. Imprisoned at Culloden 17 April 1746, Inverness, London. Pardoned on condition of permanent banishment 2 July 1747. From France. "Appointed to exercise the function of Quartermaster to the French troops in Scotland." Taken at sea. *MR38, SHS.3.230.*

NUGENT, JOHN, Lieutenant, Fitzjames' Horse. 17 April 1746, imprisoned Inverness. Pardoned on condition of permanent banishment 2 July 1747. *SHS.3.230.*

NUGENT, PATRICK, Quartermaster, Fitzjames' Horse, French Service. Taken at Culloden. Pardoned on condition of permanent banishment 2 July 1747. *MR38, SHS.3.230.*

OAT or OAK, HENRY, slater from Doune, Stirlingshire. Imprisoned Leith "on suspicion." Was sick, 18 May – 18 June 1746. Liberated on petition on bail of £50, 3 June 1746. Evidence from John Christy, multerer in Doune Miln, John Mitchel, merchant there, Alexander Campbell, gunsmith there, James Kemp, innkeeper there and James and William Taylors both innkeepers there. *SHS.8.318, SHS.3.236.*

OATT, WILLIAM, from Doune, Stirlingshire. Evidence from Donald Campbell, gunsmith in Stirling and James Taylor, merchant in Doune. *SHS.8.318.*

O'BERNE (O'BRIEN?), FRANCOISE, Lieutenant, Clare's French Service. From France. Taken at sea 28 November 1745 *Louis XV*, imprisoned Edinburgh, Berwick, Hull. Pardoned on condition of permanent banishment 2 July 1747. *SHS.3.230.*

O'BRIEN or O'BRYAN, BARRY, Lieutenant, Berwick's French Service. Taken at sea 28 November 1745, imprisoned Berwick, February 1746 Hull. Discharged. *SHS.2.232.*

O'BRIEN, BERNARD, Lieutenant, Clare's French Service. Captured at sea *Louis XV* 18 November 1745, imprisoned

Edinburgh Castle, 26 December 1745 Berwick, February 1746 Hull. Pardoned on condition of permanent banishment 2 July 1747. *SHS.3.232.*

O'BRIEN, JAMES, Clare's French Service. Taken at sea 28 November 1745, imprisoned Berwick, February 1746 Hull. Discharged. *SHS.3.232.*

O'BRIEN, JOHN, Captain, Paris Militia. Irish Piquets. Taken at Culloden 17 April 1746, imprisoned Inverness, Marshalsea (London). Pardoned on condition of permanent banishment 2 July 1747. From Ireland. *MR136, SHS.3.232.*

O'BRIEN or O'BRAIN, JOHN, aged 23, cook from Cork, Ireland. Imprisoned 1 May 1746 Perth, 10 August 1746 Canongate, Carlisle. Transported 1747. *SHS.3.232.*

O'BRYEN, THEOBALD, Lieutenant, Berwick's French Service. Imprisoned February 1746 Berwick, Hull. Pardoned on condition of permanent banishment 2 July 1747. Taken at sea. *SHS.3.232.*

O'BRYEN, THOMAS, Berwick's French Service. Taken at sea 28 November 1745, imprisoned Berwick, February 1746 Hull. Discharged. *SHS.3.232.*

O'DANIEL, ..., Lieutenant, Bulkeley's Regiment, Irish Piquets. Taken at Culloden 17 April 1746. From France. Pardoned and banished 2 July 1747. *SHS.3.232. MR136.*

O'DONALD, CALEMB, Clare's French Service. Taken at sea 28 November 1745, imprisoned Berwick, February 1746 Hull. Discharged. *SHS.3.232.*

O'DONOGHUE, FRANCIS, Captain, Lord John Drummond's French Royal Scots Cavalry. Taken at Culloden, 17 April

1746, imprisoned Inverness, Hull. Pardoned and banished 2 July 1747. From France *MR.61, SHS.3.234.*

O'DONOHUE, JOSEPH, French Service. Taken at sea, imprisoned Berwick, February 1746 Hull. Pardoned on condition of permanent banishment 2 July 1747. *SHS.3.234.*

O'DONOGHUE or O'DONHUE, TERENCE, Bulkeley's French Service. Taken at sea 28 November 1745, imprisoned Berwick, February 1746 Hull. Discharged. *SHS.3.234.*

O'DONNELL, JOHN, French Service. Imprisoned Marshalsea. Discharged. *SHS.3.234.*

O'FARRELL, RODERICK, Cornet (Captain?) Fitzjames' Spanish Service. Taken at sea *Charite* 21 February 1746, imprisoned Berwick, Hull, London. Pardoned on condition of permanent banishment 2 July 1747. *SHS.3.234.*

OFFARD, CHARLES, "Rebel Service", taken at Culloden 17 April 1746. Hanged 30 April 1746. Deserter from Dejean's Regiment, taken at Culloden. *SHS.3.236.*

OGDEN, THOMAS, Manchester Regiment. Weaver aged 34 from Manchester. Taken at capture of Carlisle 30 December 1745, imprisoned York Castle. Transported to Antigua 8 May 1747. *MR198, SHS3.236.*

OGSTON, JAMES, weaver from Grange Pans, Linlithgow. Carried arms in the rebel Life Guards, assisted in carrying off his Majesty's Dragoon Horses from Kinneil Parks and in levying the Excise for the rebels. Whereabouts not known. *SHS.8.266.*

O'HANLON, JAMES, Rooth's French Service. Captured at sea *Esperance*, 25 November 1745 Deal, *Caroline* Greenwich, Marshalsea. Discharged. *SHS.3.234.*

O'KEIFE, EUGENE, Lieutenant, Berwick's French Regiment. Irish Piquets. From France. Taken at Culloden 17 April 1746, imprisoned Inverness, Berwick, Hull. Pardoned on condition of permanent banishment 2 July 1747. *SHS.3.234, MR136.*

OLDBECK, ANTOINE, Berwick's French Service. Taken at sea and imprisoned in Berwick. Discharged. *SHS.3.242.*

OLDHAM or OLDHORN, WILLIAM, weaver from Lower Darren, Lancashire. Duke of Perth's Regiment. Imprisoned Carlisle and Chester. Drowned at Liverpool when going on board a ship for transportation 5 May 1747. *SHS.3.242.*

OLIPHANT, CHARLES, Lieutenant French Royal Scots Cavalry. Excise Officer, Aberdeen. Taken and transported September 1748. *MR.62, SHS.3.242, JAB.2.374.*

OLIPHANT, THOMAS, wright, late baillie and present elder in the Church, from Anstruther Wester, Fife. Assisted in carrying a barrel of gunpowder to the rebels and drank the Pretender's health. At home. Evidence from Alexander Stephen, porter in Leith, George Robertson and Kathleen Reid, then servants to Mrs Rolland, etc. *SHS.8.66, SHS.8.352.*

OLTON, JOHN, Elcho's Regiment. From Shropshire. Imprisoned 21 February 1746 Perth, 9 August 1746 Carlisle. Northing more is known of him after he got to Carlisle. He probably died. *SHS.3.242.*

O'NEAL, JAMES, Bulkeley's French Service. Taken at sea 28 November 1745, imprisoned Berwick, February 1746 Hull. Discharged. *SHS.3.234.*

O'NEAL, TIMOTHY, Corporal, Bulkeley's French Service. Taken at sea *Louis XV*, imprisoned Berwick, Hull. Discharged. *SHS.3.234.*

O'NEILLE or O'NEIL, FELIX, Captain, Lally's French-Irish Regiment. Imprisoned North Uist or Benbecula, July 1746, 30 September 1746 Inverness, HMS *Triton*, 22 October 1746 Edinburgh Castle. Released on parole February 1747 and exchanged. From France. He was the son of a brigadier in the Spanish army, and himself served in the latter until 1744. He then joined Lally's French-Irish regiment as Captain. He was sent over from France to the Prince in March 1746 by the Duc de Richelieu. After Culloden he accompanied the Prince on his wanderings until 28 June. He then went to North Uist, where he was taken prisoner and sent to Edinburgh Castle. In February 1747 he was released on parole and subsequently exchanged as a French prisoner of war. *SHS.3.236.*

ORAM, ALEXANDER, vintner from Cupar, Fife. Was very active in levying the public money for the rebels and compelling people to pay: distribute money to some sick rebels at Cupar and was always disaffected. At home. Evidence from Mary Dott, spouse to William Melvill, brewer in Cupar. Helen Morris, and Grisell Kilkpatrick, servants to Mr Oram. *SHS.8.66, SHS.8.352.*

O'REILLY, ..., Colonel, French or Spanish Service. Irish Piquets. Killed at Culloden. *MR136.*

O'REILLY, PIERRE, Lieutenant, Berwick's Regiment, Irish Piquets. Taken at Culloden 17 April 1746, imprisoned Inverness. Pardoned and banished. *MR136, SHS.3.236.*

ORROCK, WALTER, shoemaker and council deacon, Edinburgh, Midlothian. The day of Preston battle came riding furiously up the Canongate with a white cockade, crying Victory, Victory, the Prince has won the day, and alighting at the Netherbow Port, shut it against the flying soldiers, by which means several of them fell into the hands of the rebels. Now at Dubbieside near Leven in Fife. Evidence from John and James Aitkin, wrights, Thomas Beatson, baker, and David Beatson, hosier in Cannongate. *SHS.8.254, SHS.8.340.*

OSTLER, JOHN, Duke of Perth's Regiment. "Gentleman .... genteel", from Lincolnshire. Imprisoned Carlisle, Lancaster Castle. Transported to Antigua 8 May 1747. *SHS.3.244.*

OSWALD, JAMES, gardener, Tullibardine, soldier, Lord John Drummond's French Royal Scots Cavalry. Imprisoned Crieff, 2 May 1746 Perth, 12 May 1746 Stirling Castle, Edinburgh. Discharged 17 July 1747. "Witnesses assert that he marched and did duty with the rebel army, wore the White Cockade, and bore arms." *MR.63, SHS.3.244.*

PALSTON, HENRY, "a French prisoner". Imprisoned 20 March 1746/47 Edinburgh Castle. Released under General pardon, 1747. *SHS.3.244.*

PARK (PARKE), THOMAS, Sergeant, Manchester Regiment. Shoemaker from Lancashire. Taken at capture of Carlisle. Imprisoned 30 December 1745 Carlisle, Lancaster Castle. Pleaded guilty at his trial on 19 September 1746 and was sentenced to death. Executed at Brampton 21 October 1746. *MR.195, SHS.3.244, SHS.1.150.*

PARKER, ALEXANDER, Roy Stewart's (Edinburgh) Regiment. Barber from Elgin. Taken at Carlisle. Executed 8 November 1746. *MR207.*

PARKER, JAMES, aged 30, pedlar at Greenock, Renfrewshire, Duke of Perth's Regiment. Imprisoned 25 April 1746 Brechin, 29 April 1746 Montrose, 13 May 1746 Inverness, June 1746 prison ship *Dolphin*, Tilbury Fort. Discharged. Turned King's Evidence against Allan Cameron and others at Southwark trials. *SHS.3.244.*

PARKER, WILLIAM, from Yorkshire. Imprisoned 30 December 1745 Carlisle. Taken at capture of Carlisle. No further trace of him. He probably died. *SHS.3.246.*

PARKINSON, HENRY, Manchester Regiment. From Lancashire. Taken at capture of Carlisle 30 December 1745, imprisoned Lancaster Castle. No further reference to his disposal. *MR198, SHS.3.246.*

PARROT, JOSEPH, from Warwick. Imprisoned for high treason in House of Correction, Whitehaven since 15 January 1745. *CQS.346, CQS.359.*

PATERSON, CHARLES, Carter's servant, from Leith, Midlothian. Assisted in taking and carrying provisions to the rebel horses and driving their waggons, etc. Now about Leith. Evidence from John Balfour. *SHS.8.254, SHS.8.340.*

PATERSON, ROBERT, from Haddington, Artillery. Imprisoned 30 December 1745 Carlisle, Lincoln Castle. Taken at capture of Carlisle. Died in prison 1746. *SHS.3.248.*

PATERSON, ROBERT, Manchester Regiment. From Lancashire. Taken at capture of Carlisle 30 December 1745. Imprisoned Lincoln Castle. Transported to Antigua 8 May 1747. *SHS.3.246, MR198.*

PATON, ARCHIBALD, Manchester Regiment. Joiner. "Taken in actual rebellion." Pleaded guilty when tried 2 October 1746 and was sentenced to death, but reprieved. Transported 21 July 1748. *SHS.3.248, MR198.*

PATON or PATTEN, GEORGE, aged 20, brewer's servant from Dirleton, East Lothian, Duke of Perth's Regiment. Imprisoned Torwood, 1 May 1746 Stirling Castle, Carlisle. Transported 1747. *SHS.3.248.*

PATON or PATTEN, JAMES, shoemaker from Edinburgh. Imprisoned 3 May 1746 Edinburgh Castle, 5 May 1746 Edinburgh Jail. Released under General pardon, 1747. Suspicion of carrying arms. "Says his father forced him to drive the rebel waggons." *SHS.3.248.*

PATON, JOHN, servant to Broughton, Traquhair, Tweedale. Went out in the beginning of the rebellion with his said master. Whereabouts not known. *SHS.8.84.*

PATTEN, CHRISTOPHER, from Yorkshire. Imprisoned 19 April 1746 Inverness. Released under General Pardon, 1747. "For aiding and assisting to the Pretender." *SHS.3.248.*

PATTIE, JAMES, servant from Ballcornie, Carnbee parish, Fife. Went along with the Earl of Kelly at first and carried arms till defeat at Culloden. Now in Balcormie, with his father, Peter Pattie. *SHS.8.68.*

PATTIE, WALTER, from Fife, Ogilvy's Regiment. Imprisoned 29 November 1746 Perth. "Enlisted" 14

August 1747. This probably means that he enlisted in the Army in order to escape transportation, but his name does not appear in the official lists. *SHS.3.248.*

PATTON, ARCHIBALD, from East Lothian, Ogilvy's Regiment. Imprisoned 30 December 1746 Carlisle. Taken at capture of Carlisle. No further reference to him. *SHS.3.248.*

PECASSAN or PECKASE, FRANCIS, soldier, Lord John Drummond's French Royal Scots Cavalry. From France. Taken 1 February 1746 in Ford of Frew, imprisoned 17 March 1746 Edinburgh Castle. Discharged. *MR.63, SHS.3.248.*

PENDLETON, JOHN, Manchester Regiment. Aged 15, weaver, Dutch loom, from Manchester. Taken at capture of Carlisle 30 December 1745, imprisoned Carlisle, Lancaster Castle. Transported 1747. *SHS.3.250, MR198.*

PENSTON, ROBERT, gardner from Tranent. Assisted in conducting the rebels through Tranent the night before Preston battle and gave them intelligence. Now at home. *SHS.8.138.*

PERKINS, JOHN, Officer, French Service, Irish Piquets. Imprisoned Inverness and Marshalsea. Pardoned on condition of permanent banishment 2 July 1747. *MR136, SHS.3.250.*

PETRIE, JOHN, ale-house keeper, Cowgate Edinburgh. Imprisoned Edinburgh Castle, 11 August 1746 Canongate, Carlisle. "Carried off several Dragoon horses from Preston, wearing soldiers' accoutraments besmeared with blood and a white cockade." He was acquitted. Evidence from Robert Beatson, baker, John Smith and Robert

Brown, Excise Officers. *SHS.3.252, SHS.8.254, SHS.8.340, SHS.8.380.*

PETRY, CHARLES, from Stirling, "son to one of the soldiers of the Castle. On suspicion of discovering what was doing in the Castle." Imprisoned 7 February 1746 Stirling Castle. Discharged. *SHS.3.252.*

PETTS, WILLIAM, soldier, Lord John Drummond's French Royal Scots Cavalry. From France. Taken 7 February 1746, imprisoned in Stirling Castle. Discharged. *MR.63, SHS.3.252.*

PHILLIPS, CORNELIUS JOSEPH, Lord John Drummond's Regiment. Taken at sea *Soleil* November 1745, imprisoned Marshalsea. From France. Discharged. *SHS.3.252.*

PHILP, ROBERT, shoemaker from Crail, Fife. Assisted in burning one of his Majesty's boats, was frequently with the rebels, drinking the Pretender's health and his son's under discharges of fire arms and is a known enemy to the present government. At home. Evidence from John Morris and George Anderson, both in Crail. *SHS.8.66, SHS.8.352.*

PICKERING, CHRISTOPHER, Sergeant, Berwick's French Service. Imprisoned HMS *Sheerness*, Berwick. From France. Discharged. *SHS.3.252.*

PIERY, JOHN, servant to Traquair, Tweedale. Joined the rebels when in possession of Edinburgh. Whereabouts not known. *SHS.8.84.*

PILONE, FRANCIS, Bulkeley's French Service. Taken at sea *Louis XV;* 28 November 1745 imprisoned in Berwick,

February 1746 Hull. Discharged. From France. *SHS.3.252.*

PIRSON, JOHN, Bulkeley's French Service. Taken at sea, imprisoned Berwick, February 1746 Hull. Discharged. *SHS.3.254.*

PITH, JAMES, porter from Leith, Midlothian. Was in the rebellion and served as carter to the rebels. Now in Leith. Evidence from his fellow porters. *SHS.8.254, SHS.8.340.*

PLIVISOCH, WALTER, from Edinburgh, Roy Stuart's Regiment. Imprisoned 30 December 1745 Carlisle. Taken at capture of Carlisle. There is no further reference to him. Pobably died. *SHS.3.254, MR207.*

PLUNKETT, CHRISTOPHER, Lieutenant, Berwick's Regiment. Taken at sea *Louis XV* 28 November 1745, imprisoned Edinburgh Castle, 26 December 1745 Berwick, February 1746 Hull. From Ireland. Pardoned on condition of permanent banishment 2 July 1747. *SHS.3.254.*

PLUNKETT, NICHOLAS, Clare's French Service. Taken at sea *Louis XV*, imprisoned Hull. Discharged. *SHS.3.254.*

PLUNKETT, PATRICK, Clare's French Service. Taken at sea *Louis XV*, imprisoned Berwick, February 1746 Hull. Discharged. *SHS.3.254.*

POITEU, PIERRE, French Service. Imprisoned 17 March 1746 Edinburgh Castle. Discharged. *SHS.3.254.*

PONCEAN, JEAN, French Service. "Servant. Imprisoned Marshalsea. Discharged. *SHS.3.254.*

PONNER, JEAN, Berwick's French Service. Taken at sea *Prince Charles*, imprisoned Berwick. Discharged. *SHS.3.254.*

POO, ANTHONY, soldier, Lord John Drummond's French Royal Scots Cavalry. From France. Taken Bucklyvie 25 February 1746, imprisoned Stirling Castle. Discharged. *MR.63, SHS.3.254.*

POOLEY, THOMAS, Roy Stewart's (Edinburgh) Regiment. From Perth. Taken at Carlisle. Died? *MR207.*

POOR, THOMAS, Manchester Regiment. Imprisoned in York Castle. "Taken in actual rebellion." There is no further reference to him. *MR198, SHS.3.254.*

PORTEOUS, ANDREW, of Burnfoot, Falkirk. Merchant in Dalkeith. Balmerino's Life Guards. Imprisoned 30 April 1746 Perth, 10 August 1746 Canongate, Carlisle. Pardoned on condition of enlistment 22 July 1748. At his trial on 19 September 1746 he pleaded guilty and was sentenced to death, but he was reprieved. The Court Records state that "he appeared a lame miserable object on crutches." If this was so it is doubtful whether he was taken for the army. Testimonials were received on his behalf. *SHS.8.138, SHS.3.254.*

PORTEUS, SAMUEL, salt watchman from Prestonpans. Continued in the exercise of his office and uplifted the dutie for the rebels. Now at home. *SHS.8.138.*

PORTUOS, WILLIAM, from Bridgetown, French officer's servant, Irish Piquets. Imprisoned 10 May 1746 Dundee. Discharged 14 March 1747. *MR137, SHS.3.256.*

POTIERE, RIERE, French Service. From France. Imprisoned Edinburgh Castle, Carlisle, 8 August 1746 Penrith. Discharged. *SHS.3.256*.

POTTER, CHRISTOPHER, aged 19 from Richmond, Yorkshire. Imprisoned Inverness June 1746, *Wallsgrave* Tilbury Port. "A Yorkshire husbandman on suspicion." There is no further reference to him. *SHS.3.256*.

POTTER, RICHARD, conveyed from Penrith to Brough, Westmoreland in the company of 19 other Jacobites. *CQS.354*.

POUSSIN, JEAN, Lally's French Service, from Dieppe, France. Taken at capture of Carlisle 30 December 1745, imprisoned Carlisle, Marshalsea. Discharged. *SHS.3.256*.

POWER, ROBERT, Bulkeley's French Service. Taken *Louis XV* Berwick, imprisoned February 1746 Hull. Discharged. *SHS.3.256*.

POWSTIE, JOHN, from Edinburgh. Imprisoned Hul and York. Transported. *SHS.3.256*.

POWSTIE or POUSTIE, JOHN, tailor from Edinburgh, Roy Stuart's Regiment. Imprisoned 3 October 1745 Livingston's Yards, Edinburgh Castle, 15 January 1746 Edinburgh, Carlisle. Transported 9 November 1748. On suspicion. Pleaded guilty at his trial on 19 September 1746 and was sentenced to death, but this was commuted to transportation. He tried to escape the day before his transportation. Married to Elizabeth Yeaman. *SHS.3.256, MR207*.

PRICE, BENJAMIN, from Worcester. Deserter from Guise's Regiment. Imprisoned Gartmore, 28 February 1746

Perth, 12 May 1746 Stirling Castle. No further reference to him is to be found. He was probably handed over to the military authorities. *SHS.3.258.*

PRICE, RALPH, a miller, born 1713 Lancashire. Captured near Penrith, imprisoned for high treason in the House of Correction, Whitehaven from 15 January 1745. Petitioned unsuccessfully against transportation. Transported 25 February 1747 from Liverpool to Virginia in *Gildart*, arriving Port North Potomac, Maryland, 5 August 1747. *PRO.T1.328, SHS.3.258, CQS.346, CQS.359.*

PRIESTMAN, JOHN, jail in Whitehaven. *CQS.359.*

PRIESTMAN, JONATHAN, born Carlisle. Imprisoned in House of Correction, Whitehaven from 15 January 1745 for high treason. Was committed on suspicion by Sir Everard Fawkener, secretary to the Duke of Cumberland. A Jonathan Priestman, of Bolton, was bound in his own recognizance of £40 and two others of £20 each to appear at the next (Christmas) sessions, charged with drinking the pretender's health. *CQS.346.*

PRIDMORE, ..., soldier, Lord John Drummond's French Royal Scots Cavalry. From France. Taken in Perth 18 February 1746. "Taken north by the Duke of Cumberland's army" after they occupied Perth. He may have died, or he may have been treated as a prisoner of war and discharged to France with other French prisoners. *MR.63, SHS.3.258.*

PRIMROSE, Sir ARCHIBALD, of Dunipace, Stirlingshire, had a commission amongst Baggot's Hussars. Imprisoned July 1746 Aberdeen, Canongate, 8 August 1746 Carlisle. Executed Carlisle 15 November 1746. Son of George Foulis of the Ravelston family, who, on inheriting Dunipace from his grandfather, assumed the surname of

Primrose. He was captured near Aboyne in July 1746, was tried at York, pleaded guilty, and when tried he pleaded guilty, was sentenced to death, and executed at Carlisle on 15 November 1746. He was buried in St Cuthbert's Carlise. Sir Archibald's wife was his kinswoman, Lady Mary Primrose, daughter of the 1st Earl of Rosebery. By her he had ten daughters and one son. Mrs Janet Cuningham claimed upon the forfeited estate for an annuity of 1000 merks due to her, as widow of George Primrose of Dunipace. Her claim is dated 30 May 1746, and she is then described as "now spouse to William Innes, writer to the Signet." *SHS.3.258, SHS.8.58, SHS.8.373.*

PRIMROSE, JANET, wife of John Primrose, late Officer of Excise, Dalkeith. Closs attended her husband the rebels and uplifted £1. 6. 5. Of Excise from two Compounders in this district. At Dalkeith. *SHS.8.138.*

PROCTOR, RICHARD, Manchester Regiment. "A sprightly lad" aged 20, from Lancashire. Taken at capture of Carlisle. Imprisoned 30 December 1745 Carlisle, Lancaster. Transported 8 May 1747 to Antigua. *SHS.3.258, MR198.*

PROCTOR, ROBERT, Kilmarnock's Horse, cooper from Wharton Lancasshire. Imprisoned Macclesfield, Chester Castle. Said to have served in Hamilton's Dragoons. His fate is not traceable. He may have been handed over to the military authorities as a deserter. *SHS.3.258.*

PROUTON, ANTHONY, aged 19, French Service, Irish Piquets. Imprisoned Inverness, *Pamela* Tilbury. His name appears only in the *Pamela* list of 9 August 1746. He probably died in that ship. *MR137, SHS.3.258.*

PUNTON, JOHN, porter in Leith, Midlothian. Was in the rebellion and served as Carter to the rebels. Now in Leith. Evidence from his fellow porters. *SHS.8.254, SHS.8.340.*

PURDON, GILBERT, soldier, Lord John Drummond's French Royal Scots Cavalry. From Ballyclogh, Cork, Ireland. Imprisoned Inverness, September 1746 *Pamela* Tilbury. "This man Mons. Carpentier applies for as a subject of France and represents that he cannot speak English; yet the man has signed an acknowledgement that he was born as here reported, that he is a subject of the King's pleasure , and speaks as good English as can be expected from an Irish papist." Transported 1747. *SHS.3.258, MR.63.*

QUIGLEY, JAMES, Bulkeley's French Service. Taken at sea *Louis XV*, imprisoned 28 November Hull. Discharged. From France. *SHS.3.260.*

QUIRHIN, ANDRE, Berwick's French Service. From France. Taken at sea *Louis XV*, 28 November 1745 Berwick, February 1746 Hull. Discharged. *SHS.3.260.*

RALPHO or RAPHO, NICHOLAS, wigmaker from Provence, France. Soldier, Lord John Drummond's French Royal Scots Cavalry. From France. Imprisoned 1 February 1746 Stirling, 7 February 1746 Stirling Castle, Canongate 5 September 1746. Discharged. *MR.63, SHS.3.262.*

RAMBOUS or RAMBOUR, ROBERT, Berwick's French Service. From France. Taken at sea *Louis XV*, imprisoned Berwick, Hull. Discharged. *SHS.3.260.*

RAMSAY, ANDREW, from Edinburgh. Imprisoned 10 August 1746 Canongate. Released under General Pardon,1747. *SHS.3.260.*

RAMSAY, CHRISTOPHER, labourer from Seton. Went with the rebels to England and continued with them till dispersed. Fled the country. *SHS.8.138.*

RANDALL or RANALD, ROBERT, Excise Officer from Edinburgh, Quartermaster, Rebel Service. Imprisoned Nov 1745 Coldstream, Edinburgh Castle, 15 January 1746 Edinburgh, 8 August 1746 Carlisle. Pardoned on condition of enlistment 22 July 1748. He pleaded guilty on being arraigned, and was sentenced to death. He was, however, reprieved. *SHS.3.262.*

RANNIE, WILLIAM, salt watchman from Prestonpans. Continued in the exercise of his office for the rebels. Now at home. *SHS.8.140.*

RATCLIFFE, or RADCLIFFE, CHARLES, The Hon (*de jure* 4th Earl of Derwentwater), Captain, Dillon's French Service. From France. Imprisoned November 1745 *Esperance,* Tower of London. Executed Tower Hill 8 December 1746. He was brother of the James, 3rd Earl of Derwentwater, who was executed on 24 February 1716 for his share in the Rising of 1715. Charles Ratcliffe was also captured and condemned, but escaped from Newgate and went to France, where he settled and had a pension from James VIII. While in France he assumed the attainted title of his brother. In November 1745 he was again captured on board the *Esperance* on his way to Scotland with other French officers and, after identification, was imprisoned, along with his son, in the Tower. He was brought before the Court of King's Bench and condemned to suffer the sentence previously passed on him in 1716. This was carried out on 8 December 1746. *SHS.3.262.*

RATCLIFFE or RADCLIFFE, JAMES BARTHOLOMEW, The Hon (afterwards titular 3rd Earl of Newburgh), Captain, Dillon's French Service. Aged 21, son of Charles

Ratcliffe. Imprisoned November 1745 *Esperance*, Tower of London. Released 28 February 1746. Taken prisoner with his father, but released. *SHS.3.262.*

RATCLIFFE, JOHN, Manchester Regiment. Weaver from Lancashire. Taken at capture of Carlisle 30 December 1745, imprisoned Lancaster Castle. Tried at Carlisle, September 1746, and sentenced to death, but recommended to mercy by the Jury. Died in prison November 1747. *MR198, SHS.3.264.*

RATTRAY, JOHN, surgeon to the Prince, from Edinburgh, "Surgeon in Prince's Army". Imprisoned 16 April 1746 Culloden, Inverness, 28 May 1746 Edinburgh, London (Messenger's house). Liberated May 1746, again liberated 7 January 1747. Brother of James Rattray of Craighall. He was put in a church along with his friend Dr Lauder, among a crowd of prisoners; but their instruments were removed. He was captured on the field of Culloden while administering help. At Lord President Forbes' request to Cumberland he was released after a short detention. On arriving in Edinburgh he was again taken prisoner and sent to London by Cumberland's orders, to act as witness. He was finally released 7 January 1747. *SHS.3.264.*

REDPATH, THOMAS, salt officer from Prestonpans. Continued in the exercise of his office and uplifted the duty for the rebels, now employed as formerly and at home. *SHS.8.138.*

REID, …….., wife of John Skeen, Crail, Fife. Gave fire, coals and tar to burn one of the King's boats that was lost in time of the rebellion. Said the two men that extinguished the flames ought to have had ropes about their necks and is always exclaiming against the present government. Now at home. Evidence from John, James and Thomas Watson, etc in Crail. *SHS.8.68, SHS.8.352.*

REID, ALEXANDER, journeyman goldsmith, Edinburgh, Midlothian. Carried arms in the rebel army. Whereabouts not known. Evidence from William Ayton and Robert Low, goldsmiths, Edinburgh. *SHS.8.254, SHS.8.340.*

REID, JAMES, innkeeper from Leith, Midothian. Had a commission from the rebels as provisor for their horses. Riffled the Old Stage Coach lofts of corn and hay for their use, and managed and directed their waggons, etc. Now at home and appearing publicly. Evidence from Mr Balfour of the old Stage Coach Office. *SHS.8.254, SHS.8.340.*

REID, JAMES, salt watchman from Cockenzie. Continued in the exercise of his office for the rebels. Now at home. *SHS.8.140.*

REID, JOHN, French Service, from France. Imprisoned Marshalsea. Captured at sea in the *Soleil* privateer while going to Scotland. "Prays not to be sent back to France." It is not clear whether his petition was granted. *SHS.3.268.*

REID, JOSEPH, born Carlisle. Imprisoned for high treason in House of Correction at Whitehaven since 15 January 1745. Committed on suspicion by Sir Everard Fawkener, secretary to the Duke of Cumberland. *CQS.346, CQS.359.*

REILLY or RILEY, EDMUND or EDWARD, Lieutenant, Dillon's French Service. Captured at sea on the way to Montrose in *Esperance* (late *Soleil*), brought into Deal, 25

November 1745 Deal, Marshalsea. Discharged. *SHS.3.268.*

REILLY or RILEY, JOHN, French Service, from Ireland. Captured at sea on *Esperance*, 25 November 1745 Deal, Marshalsea. Pardoned on condition of permanent banishment 2 July 1747. *SHS.3.270.*

REILLY, PETER, Dillon's French Service. From Ireland. Captured at sea on *Esperance*, 25 November 1745 imprisoned in Deal, Marshalsea. Pardoned on condition of permanent banishment 2 July 1747.

RELF, THOMAS, conveyed from Penrith to Brough, Westmoreland in the company of 19 other Jacobites. *CQS.354.*

RENALLY, THOMAS, Lieutenant, Lally's French Service. Captured at sea on *Esperance*, 25 November 1745, Deal. Discharged. *SHS.3.270.*

REYNOLDS, LUKE, Lieutenant French Royal Scots Cavalry. Taken 15 January 1746. Banished. *MR.62.*

RICE, JOHN, Clare's French Service. Taken at sea *Louis XV*, 28 November 1745 Berwick, February 1746 Hull. Discharged. *SHS.3.270.*

RIDDLE, ADOLPHUS, glazier from Leith, Midlothian. Assisted in taking and carrying provisions to the rebel horses and driving their waggons, etc. Now about Leith. Evidence from Mr Balfour of the old Stage Coach Office. *SHS.8.254, SHS.8.340.*

RIDDLE, JOHN, of Grange in Fife, from Inverask. Joined in the Pretender's son's Life Guards before Preston battle and continued in the service to the end. Whereabouts not known. *SHS.8.138.*

RIDDOCH or RUDDOCK, PATRICK or PETER, aged 26, slater from Doune, Stirlingshire, Kilmarnock's Regiment. Imprisoned Doune 25 May 1746, Stirling Castle, 8 August 1746 Carlisle. Transported 22 April 1747 from Liverpol to Virginia in *Johnson*, arriving Port Oxford, Maryland 5 August 1747. Evidence from John Christy, multerer in Doune Miln, John Mitchel, merchant there, Alexander Campbell, gunsmith there, James Kemp, innkeeper there and James and William Taylors both innkeepers there. *SHS.3.392, SHS.8.318, SHS.3.272, MR45, PRO.T1.328.*

RIDING, RICHARD, Manchester Regiment. Aged 24, weaver from Lancashire. Taken at capture of Carlisle 30 December 1745, imprisoned Lancaster. Transported 1747. *SHS.3.272, MR198.*

RIGHLEY, THOMAS, Manchester Regiment. From Lancashire. Taken at capture of Carlisle 30 December 1745. No further information available. *MR198, SHS.3.272.*

RITCHIE, JOHN, of Sinks, St Ninians parish, Stirlingshire. Hath carried arms in the rebel army from November 1745 till defeat at Culloden. Whereabouts not known. *SHS.8.58.*

RITCHIE, JOHN, soldier, Lord John Drummond's French Royal Scots Cavalry. From Kirkcaldy. Deserter from Col McKay's Dutch Regiment. He asked not to be sent back to France and was transported. Imprisoned Huntingtower 29 February 1746 Perth, 12 May 1746 Stirling Castle, 8 August 1746 Carlisle. Transported 1747. *SHS.3.274, MR.63.*

ROBERTS, WILLIAM, from Bolton in the Water, Gloucestershire. Imprisoned Coventry, Stafford. Was wounded and captured at Prestonpans - said he escaped but was taken at Carlisle. "Soldier in Col Lascelles Regiment" and therefore a deserter. Committed on suspicion. He was probably handed over to the military authorities. *SHS.3.274.*

ROBERTSON, JAMES, weaver in Bannockburn, St Ninians parish, Stirlingshire. Did drink the Pretender's son's health as Prince of Wales, and spoke many things most indecently, scandalously and maliciously of his Prent. Majesty. Evidence from Margaret Logan, spouse to John Logan, brewer in Bannockburn, Robert Davidson, weaver in Glasgow and Henry Corbet, Officer of Excise in Airth. *SHS.8.60, SHS.8.316.*

ROBERTSON, JAMES, servant to the Laird of Houstoun, Houstoun. Engaged and went as groom with Lord George Murray into the rebellion. Whereabouts not known. *SHS.8.266.*

ROBERTSON, JOSEPH, non jurant Minister from Haddington. Aided and assisted the rebels and influenced people to join them, particularly George Anderson and Joseph Forbes his own nephew before mentioned. He also sollicted the Pretender's son's the Monday after Preston battle for an order to preach in Haddington kirk, who replied "that was going on too fast." *SHS.8.138.*

ROBERTSON, ROBERT, brewer from Ormiston, East Lothian. Imprisoned on suspicion 2 May 1746 Ormiston, 3 June 1746 Edinburgh Jail, Canongate. Discharged 27 February 1747. "The day of Preston battle drank the Pretender's and his son's health, by the names of King James and Prince of Wales, and Success to their Arms, expressing his Attachment to their interest in the strongest manner, and went several times out with the rebels, and assisted in robbing the Country of horses." *SHS.3.278, SHS.8.138.*

ROBERTSON, THOMAS, servant to Peter Spalding, goldsmith, Edinburgh, Midlothian. Carried arms in the rebel army. Now in the City Guard. Evidence from William Ayton and Peter Spalding, goldsmiths. *SHS.8.256, SHS.8.340.*

ROBERTSON, THOMAS, journeyman barber from Glasgow. Enlisted in the rebel army and continued to the end. Imprisoned July 1746 Canongate. No further reference to him. Evidence from Thomas Breakenrig, barber, William Currie, innkeeper, and Thomas Robins, founder, all in Gorbals at Glasgow. *SHS.3.280, SHS.8.274, SHS.8.346.*

ROBINSON, CHARLES, Roy Stewart's (Edinburgh) Regiment. Aged 40, labourer from Dullater, Perthshire. Taken at Carlisle. Pardoned on enlistment. *MR207.*

ROBINSON, JAMES, Clare's French Service. Taken at sea *Louis XV*, 28 November 1745 Berwick, February 1746 Hull. Discharged. *SHS.3.282.*

RODGER or ROGERS, CHARLES, from Dumbarton-shire, servant to Sir Archibald Primrose. Imprisoned 10 July 1746 Glentanar, Aberdeen, 2 August 1746 Canongate. Discharged 26 March 1747. "Declares he was sent by Sir Archibald's Lady in July last in quest of him; that he found him near Abergeldy, and was taken prisoner about four days later." *SHS.3.282.*

ROE or ROW, DAVID, from Fife. Imprisoned York Castle. Executed York 8 November 1746. "Once an officer of the Customs." "Taken in actual rebellion." He pleaded guilty at his trial at York and was sentenced to death 2 October 1746. *SHS.3.282.*

ROGERS, JOHN, Captain, Berwick's French Service. Imprisoned 24 March 1746 *Prince Charles* (late *Hazard*), HMS *Sheerness*, Berwick. Pardoned on condition of permanent banishment 2 July 1747. *SHS.3.284.*

ROGERS, JOSEPH, Lance-Corporal, Berwick's French Service. Taken at sea 24 March 1746 Berwick. Discharged. *SHS.3.284.*

ROLLAND, ELIZABETH, see *Elizabeth Crawford.*

ROLLO, DAVID, son to the Laird of Powis, St Ninians parish, Stirlingshire. Carried arms in the rebel army till the defeat at Culloden. Lurking. Evidence from John Baad, merchant in Airth, Christ. Davidson, spouse to William Logan, brewer there, and the Excise officer. *SHS.8.58, SHS.8.316.*

ROLLO, JAMES, of Rowhouse, St Ninians, Stirlingshire. Imprisoned 23 May 1745 Edinburgh Castle, Edinburgh Tolbooth. Liberated 28 May 1746. The Scots Magazine reported that, shortly after the Prince's landing, he was imprisoned in Edinburgh by warrant of the Lord Advocate on suspicion. His two sons, David and James, served through the campaign but escaped the consequences. *SHS.3.284.*

ROLLO, JAMES, son to the Laird of Powis, St Ninians parish, Stirlingshire. Carried arms in the rebel army till the defeat at Culloden. Lurking. Evidence from John Baad, merchant in Airth, Christ. Davidson, spouse to William Logan, brewer there, and the Excise officer. *SHS.8.58, SHS.8.316.*

ROOTH, …….., Colonel, Rooth's Picquet, French Service. Captured off Ostend 21 February 1746 *Bourbon*, imprisoned Marshalsea. Discharged. *SHS.3.284.*

ROPER, EDWARD, Sergeant, Manchester Regiment. Weaver from Lancashire. Taken at capture of Carlisle 30 December 1745, imprisoned Lancaster Castle. Executed at Carlisle on 18 November 1746. *SHS.1.150, MR198. SHS.3.284.*

ROSCOE, ROBERT, Englishman. Captured at the surrender of Carlisle. Was tried at Carlisle 19-16 September 1746 and acquitted. *SHS.3.284.*

ROSS, DANIEL, Roy Stewart's (Edinburgh) Regiment. Aged 26, from Inverness. Taken. *MR207.*

ROSS, DONALD, Roy Stewart's (Edinburgh) Regiment. Servant to Stewart of Cromar, aged 24. Taken and transported 20 March 1747 from Tilbury. *MR207, SHS.3.288.*

ROSS, JAMES, aged 20, carpenter from Edinburgh, Duke of Perth's Regiment. Imprisoned York Castle, Lincoln Castle. Transported Antigua 8 May 1747, from Liverpool to Leeward Islands, arriving Martinique June 1747. *SHS.3.288, MR75, PRO.SP36.102.*

ROSS, PATRICK, weaver in Edinburgh. Imprisoned 13 January 1746 Linlithgow, 20 January 1746 Leith. Discharged on bail 7 February 1746. *SHS.3.290.*

ROUN, ..., Father, Almoner from France. Taken at sea on *Bourbon*. Banished. *SHS.3.292.*

ROW or RUE, DAVID, from Anstruther, Fife, Lochgarry's Regiment. Imprisoned Carlisle, September 1746 York. Executed York 8 November 1746. Gentleman. Customs officer. "Joined the rebels at the first and carried Arms with them into England. Prisoner at Carlisle." He was probably captured at the surrender of the town on 30 December 1745. He was at the battle of Prestonpans. He pleaded guilty at his trial at York, on October, and was sentenced to death. *SHS.3.290.*

ROWBOTHAM, JOHN, Sergeant, Manchester Regiment. From Lancashire. Taken at capture of Carlisle 30 December 1745. Imprisoned Carlisle, Lancaster Castle. Executed at Penrith, 28 October 1746. He pleaded guilty at his trial at Carlisle, 9 September 1746, and was sentenced to death. *MR.196, SHS.1.151, SHS.3.292.*

ROWE, JAMES, Bulkeley's French Service. Taken on *Louis XV* Berwick, imprisoned Feb 1746 Hull. Discharged. *SHS.3.292.*

ROY, WILLIAM, aged 24, from Lanark. Imprisoned June 1746, *Jane of Alloway*, Tilbury. No further reference to him. He may have died. *SHS.3.292, MR207.*

ROYSTON, HENRY, tailor from Staffordshire. Imprisoned Stirling. Released under General Pardon, 1747. *SHS.3.292.*

RUE, DAVID, gentleman from Anstruther, Fife. Joined the rebels at the first and carried arms with them into England. Now prisoner at Carlisle. Described also as an officer of customs. He was brought before the judges at York in October 1746, and having pleaded guilty, was executed there on 8 November. *SHS.8.68, SHS.8.374.*

RUFFO, NICHOLAS, French Service. A French man. In hospital 3 February 1746 with broken leg. Imprisoned Stirling Castle. Discharged. *SHS.3.292.*

RUSSELL, ALEXANDER, cordwainer from Edinburgh, Duke of Perth's Regiment. Imprisoned 30 December 1745

Carlisle, Chester Castle, London. Discharged. Taken at capture of Carlisle. Turned King's Evidence against the officers of the Carlisle garrison. *SHS.3.294.*

RUSSELL, ROBERT, merchant in St Ninians. Imprisoned 26 July 1746 St Ninians, 28 July 1746 Stirling. Released under General Pardon, 1747. "Subsisted himself in prison." *SHS.3.294.*

RUSTON, RONALD, Pitsligo's Regiment. Riding servant to Squire Hackston, from Lancashire. Imprisoned 1 February 1745/6 Stirling, 6 February 1745/6 Edinburgh Castle. Released under General Pardon, 1747. *SHS.3.294.*

RUTHERFORD, JAMES, journeyman goldsmith from Edinburgh, Midlothian. Carried arms in the rebel army. Now at home. Evidence from William Ayton and Robert Low, goldsmiths, Edinburgh. *SHS.8.256, SHS.8.340.*

RUTHERFORD, ROBERT, shoemaker, Potterow, Edinburgh, Midlothian. Carried arms as a volunteer in the rebel army. Now lurking about Edinburgh. *SHS.8.254.*

RYAN, JOHN, Lieutenant, Bulkeley's Regiment. Captured at sea off Montrose *Louis XV*, 28 November 1745 imprisoned Edinburgh Castle, 26 December 1745 Berwick, February 1746 Hull. Pardoned on condition of permanent banishment 2 July 1747. *SHS.3.294.*

RYAN, LAWRENCE, Bulkeley's French Service. Taken at sea, *Louis XV*, imprisoned 28 November 1745 Berwick, February 1746 Hull. Discharged. *SHS.3.296.*

RYAN, LUKE, , Bulkeley's French Service. Taken at sea, *Louis XV*, imprisoned 28 November 1745 Berwick, February 1746 Hull. Discharged. *SHS.3.296.*

RYAN, THOMAS, , Bulkeley's French Service. Taken at sea, 28 November 1745, Hull. Discharged. *SHS.3.296.*

RYLEY, RICHARD, Clare's French Service. Taken at sea, *Louis XV*, imprisoned 28 November 1745 Berwick, February 1746 Hull. Discharged. *SHS.3.296.*

ST CLAIR, FRANCISCO, Captain, Irish Grenadiers, Spanish Service. Taken at sea *Louis* XV 28 November 1745, February 1746 imprisoned Berwick, Hull. Pardoned on condition of permanent banishment 2 July 1747. *SHS.3.296.*

ST JOHN, ..., imprisoned Messenger's house, London. He was presumably a French prisoner, but the only reference to him is a decision that he was "to find bail or be committed." *SHS.3.296.*

ST JOHN, JOHN (JEAN), Captain, Lord John Drummond's Royal Scots. From France. Imprisoned 17 April 1746 Inverness, Marshalsea. Discharged. *SHS.3.296.*

ST.LEGER, JEAN, Paymaster, French Royal Scots Cavalry. Taken at Culloden, discharged. *MR.61.*

ST LOUIS, PETER ALCHEAR, Bulkeley's French Service. Taken at sea *Louis XV* 28 November 1745, imprisoned Berwick, February 1746 Hull. Discharged. From France. *SHS.3.296.*

SALBOLD, ..., Captain of *Prince Charles* (late HMS *Hazard*). Taken 24 March 1746 *Prince Charles* (late HMS *Hazard*), imprisoned HMS *Sheerness*, Berwick. Discharged. From France. *SHS.3.296.*

SALMON, GEORGE, from Edinburgh, Artillery. Imprisoned 30 December 1745 Carlisle, York Castle. Taken at capture of Carlisle. There is no further reference to him. He may have died, as he does not appear on the transportation lists. *SHS.3.298.*

SAMUEL, GEORGE, aged 18, book binder from Edinburgh, Duke of Perth's Regiment. Imprisoned Carlisle, Lincoln Castle. Transported Antigua 8 May 1747, from Liverpool to Leeward Islands in *Veteran*, arriving Martinique June 1747. *SHS.3.298, MR76, PRO.SP36.102.*

SANDERS, MICHAEL, French Service, from France. Imprisoned Hull. Discharged. *SHS.3.298.*

SANDERSON, JOHN, "Rebel Service" from Newcastle. Imprisoned Gardmore, 29 February 1746 Perth, 12 May 1746 Stirling Castle. On the Jail return he is shown as of "General Guise's Regiment." He was therefore a deserter. This may have been the man who was tried at Carlisle in September 1746 and sentenced to death. *SHS.3.298.*

SARSFIELD, PATRICK, French Service, from Ireland. Imprisoned Berwick. Pardoned on condition of permanent banishment 2 July 1747. *SHS.3.300.*

SAUNDERSON or SANDERSON, JOHN, Captain, Manchester Regiment. Colliery overseer from Northumberland. Imprisoned 30 December 1745 Carlisle, Lancaster Castle, June 1746 London (Southwark), August 1746 in messenger's hands. Pardoned on condition of banishment in perpetuity, September 1748. He was captured at the fall of Carlisle. When tried in London he pleaded guilty and was sentenced to death. He was, however, reprieved, and in August 1746 placed in the hands of a messenger, where he still was in June 1748. In September 1748 he had a pardon conditional on going abroad and never returning. *SHS.3.298, MR.195.*

SAUNDERSON, JOHN, Manchester Regiment. Labourer from Lancashire. Taken at capture of Carlisle and pardoned on enlistment 22 July 1748. Imprisoned 30 December 1745 Carlisle. *MR198, SHS.3.300.*

SCOT, ANDREW, Roy Stewart's (Edinburgh) Regiment. Taken at Carlisle. Died? *MR207.*

SCOT, CHARLES, brother to Gordonberry, Teviotdale. Was sometime Chamberlain to Buccleugh, joined the rebel army. Whereabouts not known. *SHS.8.280.*

SCOT, FRANCIS, barber from Hawick. Carried arms with the rebels and was active in robbing the country. Now lurking. *SHS.8.280.*

SCOT, WATER, conveyed from Penrith to Brough, Westmoreland in the company of 19 other Jacobites. *CQS.354.*

SCOTT, GEORGE, porter from Leith, Midlothian. Assisted in taking and carrying provisions to the rebels' horses and driving their carts. Now at home. Evidence from Mr Balfour. *SHS.8.256, SHS.8.342.*

SCOTT, JOHN, Roy Stewart's (Edinburgh) Regiment. Aged 17, herd from Athole. Taken at Carlisle. Pardoned on enlistment. *MR207.*

SCOTT, ROBERT, baker from Leith, Midlothian. Carried arms and prompted the rebels to pillage the Customhouse of Leith. Now at home. Evidence from the neighbourhood and Henry Morrison, Excise Officer. *SHS.8.256, SHS.8.342.*

SCOTT, THOMAS, Volunteer, Bulkeley's Regiment, Irish Piquets. Taken at Culloden, IMPRISONED 17 April 1746 Inverness. Discharged. *MR136, SHS.3.304.*

SCOTT, WILLIAM, Roy Stewart's (Edinburgh) Regiment. From Perthshire. Taken at Carlisle. Pardoned on enlistment. *MR207.*

SCOTT, WILLIAM, Carrier from Sedbergh, Yorkshire. Imprisoned Coventry "committed on suspicion." This is probably the man who petitioned to be transported instead of being convicted. His fate is not known. *SHS.3.304.*

SEDDEN or SHEDON, CHARLES, aged 70, servant (coalgrieve) from Ayr. "Taken in actual rebellion." Imprisoned York Castle. Transported 1747. *SHS.3.304.*

SEMPLE, JAMES, weaver from Linlithgow, Kilmarnock's Regiment. Imprisoned Inverness. "Carried arms in Kilmarnock's troop and was active in seizing horses." There is no further reference to him, but he never reached London. *SHS.3.304, SHS.8.266.*

SERVANTE, JOHN, Berwick's French Service. From France. Taken at sea 28 November 1745 *Louis XV*, imprisoned Berwick, February 1746 Hull. Discharged. *SHS.3.304.*

SETON, ALEXANDER, merchant from Dubbieside, Fife. Joined the rebels before Preston battle, acted as deputy Collector of Excise under the Earl of Kelly, and on his collection was always attended by a strong party of rebels. Now lurking. *SHS.8.260.*

SETON, ALEXANDER, son to Christopher Seton, Methil, Weems, Fife. Evidence from his receipts to traders in Fife. *SHS.8.344.*

SETON, CHRISTOPHER, merchant from Methil, Weems, Fife. Aided and assisted the rebels and was along with a party searching the Ex: officer's house for himself and books. Now at home. Evidence from Elizabeth Dowie, spouse to David Ramsay, sailor in Leven and Isobell Burns his neice. *SHS.8.260, SHS.8.344.*

SETON, DAVID, salt grieve to the Laird of Lundin, Drumachie, Fife. Assisted the rebels and concealed two of them in his house since their defeat. Now lurking. *SHS.8.260.*

SETON or SEATON, JAMES, aged 15, "apprentice to William Robertson, from Sawmill near Leven, Fife, Cromarty's Regiment. Imprisoned Perth 10 August 1746, Canongate, Carlisle. Acquitted 9 September 1746. Son of George Seton of Cariston. He was wounded in the heel at Culloden. He was captured when escaping and was eventually taken to Carlisle. Through the interest of John, Earl of Crawford, with the Duke of Hesse, he was released and went abroad to Holland. He untimately got a commission in the British Army. Tried and acquitted. *SHS.3.304, SHS.8.260.*

SETON, JAMES, Captain, Rooth's French Service. Captured at sea on the way to Montrose *Esperance* (late *Soleil*) brought into Deal 25 November 1745. January 1747 Tower of London. Pardoned on condition of permanent banishment 2 July 1747. *SHS.3.306.*

SETON, JOHN, baker from Kennoway, Fife. Joined the rebels after Preston battle. Left them in a fortnight and has since followed his business. Now at home. *SHS.8.260.*

SETON, ROBERT, from Edinburgh, Life Guards. Imprisoned Inverness. Discharged. Son of William Seton, WS. "Robert Seton was wounded almost to death making his escape down the country from the field of Culloden." No further reference to him in State Papers, but he was captured and obtained a pardon. *SHS.3.306, SHS.8.256.*

SHABILLARD, ..., French Gens d'Armes. Imprisoned 24 March 1746 *Prince Charles* (late *Hazard*), HMS *Sheerness*, Berwick. Discharged. *SHS.3.306.*

SHADDON, CHARLES, coal grive to Kilmarnock. Carried arms in the rebellion. In York gaol. *SHS.8.266.*

SHADE, WILLIAM, labourer from Queensferry. Imprisoned on suspicion December 1745 Linton, Edinburgh Castle, 15 January 1746 Edinburgh. Released under General Pardon, 1747. *SHS.3.306.*

SHAIRP, JOHN, labourer from Queensferry. Imprisoned December 1745 Linton, Edinburgh Castle, 15 January 1746 Edinburgh. Released under General Pardon, 1747. *SHS.3.306.*

SHARP or SHARPE, WILLIAM, aged 16, gentleman from St Andrews, Ensign, Life Guards. Imprisoned 1 February 1746 Montrose, 10 March 1746 Stirling Castle, Carlisle, September 1746 York, Carlisle. Reprieved November 1746, but escaped from prison August 1747. Son of Sir Alexander Sharp, Bt, of Scotscraig, merchant, and great-grandson of Archibishop Sharp. "A very young man and influenced by bad company." The Professors of St Leonard's College, St Andrews, appealed for mercy for him. When tried at York he pleaded guilty and was sentenced to death, but was reprieved. On 20 August 1747 the Privy Council recommended a free pardon for him. After his reprieve he was left in Carlisle jail till August 1747, when he escaped. He served in the French and Portuguese armies, and became Major-General in the latter. He was pardoned by Royal Warrant, 3 April 1769 and succeeded his father in the baronetcy soon after. *SHS.3.308, SHS.8.68, SHS.8.374.*

SHEA (CREAGH), ROBERT, Captain, Quartermaster, Fitzjames' Horse, French Service. Taken at Culloden April 1746, imprisoned Inverness, June 1746 *Alexander & James*, Tilbury, Marshalsea. Discharged ?1747. He landed with the squadron which arrived at Aberdeen 21 February 1746. He was taken prisoner at Culloden, and was sent to London, and sent back to France subsequently. In 1766 he wrote to the Prince from Metz drawing attention to a sum of 150 guineas he had lent the latter. *MR38, SHS.3.310.*

SHEA or SHEE, LEWIS, Captain, Rooth's French Service. Captured at sea on the way to Montrose on *Esperance* (late *Soleil*) brought into Deal 25 November 1745, November 1745 Deal, February 1746 Customs Smack *Caroline* Greenwich. Discharged. *SHS.3.310.*

SHENHEROW or SHENREW or SHECHREW, CHARLES, soldier, Lord John Drummond's French Royal Scots Regiment. From Normandy. Imprisoned 1 February 1746 Stirling, 7 February 1746 Stirling Castle, Canongate, 5 September 1746 Carlisle, Penrith. Discharged. In hospital with wound to leg. Surgeon's fee, 6s 8d. *SHS.3.310, MR63.*

SHENHURUE, JOHN, from Ireland, Bulkeley's or Clare's French Regiment. Irish Piquets. Taken 10 November 1745 Millport, 6 December 1745 Edinburgh Castle. Says he was a soldier in Lord Clare's French regiment with which he came over to Scotland. Discharged. *MR137, SHS.3.310.*

SHENNAN, ANTONY, Clare's French Service. From France. Imprisoned Marshalsea. Died 1746. *SHS.3.310.*

SHERRIFF, ANDREW, brewer and maltster from Prestonpans. Acted as salt officer and uplifted the duty for the rebels during their stay in Edinburgh. Now in Leith. *SHS.8.140.*

SHERROCK or SHARROCK or SHORROCK, JAMES, aged 21, "a papist." Tailor from Preston, Lancashire. Taken at capture of Carlisle 30 December 1745, imprisoned Lancaster. Transported 1747. *SHS.3.312.*

SHERWOOD, JAMES, aged 63, from Fife, Kilmarnock's Regiment. Imprisoned Inverness, June 1746 prison ship *Thane of Fife*. No further reference to him. May have died. *SHS.3.312.*

SHIMNEY, ANTOINE, French Service, from France. Taken at sea in the *Soleil* privateer going to Scotland. Imprisoned 25 November 1745 Deal, Marshalsea. Discharged. *SHS.3.312.*

SHORROCK, DAVID, Manchester Regiment. Weaver, aged 19 from Lancashire. Imprisoned Carlisle and Lancaster Castle. Transported 1747. *SHS.3.312, MR198.*

SHORROCK, JAMES, Manchester Regiment. Tailor from Preston, Lancashire. Taken and transported 1747. *SHS.3.312, MR198.*

SHUGRUE, JOHN, French Service, Irish Piquets. Taken 9 April 1746, imprisoned Edinburgh Castle, Berwick. Discharged. *SHS.3.312, MR137.*

SIBBALD, CHARLES, gentleman from St Andrews, Fife. Carried arms in the rebel service and was in the company that proclaimed the Pretender at Cupar. Now lurking in Fife. Evidence from David Coupar in Colinsburgh,

Robert Bell, merchant in Cupar, John Arnot, surgeon and David Nicol, stabler there. *SHS.8.68, SHS.8.352.*

SIDE, JOHN, aged 30 from Liddesdale. Imprisoned June 1746 *Wallsgrave* Tilbury. No further reference to him. *SHS.3.312.*

SIMON, FRANCIS, soldier, Lord John Drummond's French Royal Scots Cavalry. From France. Taken and imprisoned 18 February 1746 in Perth, "taken north by the Duke's army", Inverness. Discharged. *MR.63, SHS.3.314.*

SIMPSON, JAMES, writer in Edinburgh, Midlothian. Acted as Clerk to the rebel Artillery. Whereabouts not known. *SHS.8.256.*

SIMPSON, JOHN, brewer and maltster from Falkirk, Stirlingshire. Very active in procuring boats for the rebels to pass to the Forth. At home. Evidence from James Cowan of Powside in the parish of Airth, and Henry Corbet, officer of the Excise there. *SHS.8.60, SHS.8.316.*

SIMPSON, MARGARET, aged 33, from Haddington, East Lothian. "Lady. Captain Hamilton's woman." Imprisoned York Castle. Transported 1747. This entry may mean that she was the wife of Captain G Hamilton who was executed at York Castle, or that she was that lady's maid. *SHS.3.314.*

SINCLAIR, JAMES, tenant, Stobo, Tweedale. About the middle of November 1745 he went after the rebels to England in quest of some horses taken from him by them, and as there is no account of him since it is feared he has been obliged to join them, though (I'm informed) not his inclination. Whereabouts not known. *SHS.8.84.*

SINCLAIR, JAMES, Captain, Rooth's Regiment, Irish Piquets. From France. Taken at Culloden, imprisoned Inverness, August 1746 *Pamela* Tilbury, House of Mr Vincent, Messenger. Wounded and taken prisoner at Culloden. He was handed over to a messenger's custody on 13 August 1746 with orders to bring him before the Duke of Newcastle. The Lord Justice Clerk wrote to the latter on 21 November 1747 about him, and forwarded his memorial showing he had been forced. He appealed to be allowed to remain in Scotland. The decision on this point is uncertain. *MR136, SHS.3.316.*

SINCLAIR, WILLIAM, salt watchman from Prestonpans. Continued in the exercise of his office for the rebels. Now at home. *SHS.8.140.*

SINGLETON, FRANCIS, Manchester Regiment, weaver, aged 17 from Preston. Imprisoned 30 December 1745 after capture of Carlisle, Lancaster Castle. There is no further reference to him, he may have died. *MR198, SHS.3.316.*

SINGLETON, ROBERT, Manchester Regiment. From Lancashire. Taken at capture of Carlisle 30 December 1745, Lancaster Castle. Transported to Antigua 8 May 1747. *MR198, SHS.3.316.*

SKENNELL, ANDREW, from Cork. Imprisoned on suspicion of treason 8 March 1746 Crieff, Stirling Castle, 4 April 1746 Stirling. Released under General Pardon, 1747. SHS.3.318.

SKIRLING, ANDREW, French Service, from France. Taken at sea, imprisoned Berwick. Discharged. *SHS.3.318.*

SMITH, ABRAHAM, French Service, from France. Imprisoned Marshalsea. Discharged. *SHS.3.318.*

SMITH, ALEXANDER, son to Thomas Smith, writer, Linlithgow. Carried arms in the Pretender's son's Life Guards. Now lurking. *SHS.8.266.*

SMITH, ALEXANDER, writer, Edinburgh, Midlothian. Carried arms in the rebel Life Guards and was active in seizing horses. Whereabouts not known. *SHS.8.266.*

SMITH, ANDREW, Roy Stewart's (Edinburgh) Regiment. Weaver from Edinburgh. Born 1729. Taken and transported 24 February 1747 from Liverpol to Virginia in *Gildart*, arriving Port North Potomac, Maryland, 5 August 1747. *SHS.3.320, MR207, PRO.T1.328.*

SMITH, DANIEL, Roy Stewart's (Edinburgh) Regiment. Deserter from Lascelles Regiment. Executed for desertion 17 October 1745. *MR207.*

SMITH, GEORGE, from Edinburgh, servant to Cassie of Kirk House. Imprisoned 1 February 1746 Kersynook, 7 February 1746 Stirling Castle. Released under General Pardon, 1747. *SHS.3.322.*

SMITH, JAMES, "Gentleman" from Linlithgowshire, Lord Elcho's Life Guards. Imprisoned 11 May 1746 King's Park, Edinburgh, 11 May 1746 Edinburgh, Carlisle. Died in prison. A Writer in Edinburgh, son of the late James Smith, writer. At his trial he pleaded guilty and was condemned, but died before execution. *SHS.3.322, SHS.8.380.*

SMITH, JAMES, writer from Edinburgh, Midlothian. Carried arms in the Pretender's son's Life Guards. Now a prisoner in Edinburgh. *SHS.8.256.*

SMITH, JOHN, sailor from Bo'ness. Imprisoned on suspicion 10 May 1746 Perth. Escaped 7 March 1747. "Says the rebels carried him prisoner to the North in February last, denied that he carried arms." *SHS.3.324.*

SMITH, JOHN, aged 21, from Derby (deserter, Guise's Regiment). Irish Piquets. Taken 16 December 1745, imprisoned Stirling Castle, June 1746 *Alexander & James, Liberty & Medway* Tilbury. He had deserted from Guise's Regiment and subsequently again deserted from the Prince's army. Transported 1747. *MR137, SHS.3.324.*

SMITH, JOHN ANDREW, soldier, Lord John Drummond's French Royal Scots Cavalry. From Ireland. Imprisoned 2 May 1746 Moniaive, 2 May 1746 Dumfries. "Handed over to Ensign Carr of Price's Regiment." His disposal indicates that he was a deserter from the British army. *MR.63, SHS.3.324.*

SOLOMON, JEAN, Berwick's French Service. Taken at sea *Prince Charles*, imprisoned Berwick. Discharged. *SHS.3.326.*

SOMERVELL, DAVID, soldier, French Royal Scots Cavalry. From Edinburgh, Lord John Drummond's Regiment. Imprisoned 25 February 1746 Perth. Died 15 August 1746. *MR.63, SHS.3.326.*

SOULANT, DENIS, Berwick's French Service. From France. Taken at sea *Louis XV*, 28 November 1745 Berwick, February 1746 Hull. Discharged. *SHS.3.326.*

SOUTER, DAVID, Roy Stewart's (Edinburgh) Regiment. Highlander. Taken. Died? *MR207.*

SOUTER, DOUGALD, Messenger at Arms, Edinburgh, Midlothian. Carried arms in the rebel army. Whereabouts not known. Evidence from George

Robertson and Francis Paterson, Excise Officers. *SHS.8.256, SHS.8.340.*

SOUTTAR, ARCHIBALD, from Dunbar, Artillery. Imprisoned 30 December 1745 Carlisle. Taken at capture of Carlisle. No further reference to him. *SHS.3.326.*

SPARK, WILLIAM, porter from Leith, Midlothian. Assisted in taking and carrying provisions to the rebels' horses and driving their carts. Now at home. Evidence from Mr Balfour. *SHS.8.256, SHS.8.342.*

SPARKS, JAMES, Manchester Regiment. Framework knitter from Derby. Imprisoned Carlisle, Derby, York. Executed 1 November 1746. The charge against him was that he went out a mile to meet the Prince's army and led them to quarters at Derby. He was tried at York, 2 ocrtober 1746, found guilty and sentenced to death. *MR198, SHS.3.328.*

SPEATSON, WILLIAM, soldier, Lord John Drummond's French Royal Scots Cavalry. From France. Imprisoned 1 February 1746 Stirling, Canongate, 5 September 1746 Carlisle. Discharged. *MR.63, SHS.3.328.*

SPENCER, WILLIAM, Manchester Regiment. From Lancashire. Imprisoned 30 December 1745 taken at capture of Carlisle, Lancaster Castle. No further reference to him, may have died. *MR198, SHS.3.328.*

SPITTS, FREDERICQUE, Berwick's French Service. From France. Taken at sea *Prince Charles*, Berwick. Discharged. *SHS.3.328.*

SPREWL or SPRUEL or SPRULE, ANDREW, aged 55, writer from Gaudbridge, ?Glasgow district, Captain (?Volunteer), Pitsligo's Horse. Imprisoned 16 April 1746 Culloden,

Inverness. In June 1746 boarded prison ship *Wallsgrave* Tilbury, London (Southwark). Acquitted 17 December 1746. "Was Captain in the Rebel Foot till their dispersion, he used to practise his business at Edinburgh." When tried he was acquitted "by consent of the Attorney General, without entering into the evidence for the Crown." The reason probably was that a witness showed that he had prevented an attack on the house of Sir Michael Bruce in revenge for the latter having raised men for the government. Evidence from John Rob and John Johnston, Town Officers in Glasgow, Alexander Dick, maltman there and James Buchanan, stabler there. *SHS.3.330, SHS.8.278, SHS.8.346, SHS.8.381.*

SQUAIR, JOHN, weaver from Bridgend, Stirlingshire. Evidence from John Christy, multerer in Doune Miln, John Mitchel, merchant there, Alexander Campbell, gunsmith there, James Kemp, innkeeper there and James and William Taylors both innkeepers there. *SHS.8.318.*

SQUARE, SAMUEL, aged 33, from Suffolk. Deserter from Ligonier's Regiment. Imprisoned Inverness June 1746 *Alexander & James,* Tilbury. Nothing known of his disposal, may have died. *SHS.3.330.*

STACK, ROBERT, Captain, Lally's French Service. Imprisoned 17 April 1746 Inverness, Carlisle, Berwick. Pardoned on condition of permanent banishment 2 July 1747. He was still in Carlisle in June 1748, where he was hostage for the debts of the French officer prisoners. *SHS.3.330.*

STAFFORD, FRANCIS, French Service. From France. Imprisoned Berwick. Pardoned on condition of permanent banishment 2 July 1747. *SHS.3.330.*

STAPLETON, NICHOLAS, Cornet, Fitjames'. From France. Taken at sea, 21 February 1746 *Bourbon*, imprsoned Edinburgh Castle, Berwick, February 1746 Hull. Pardoned and banished. *SHS.3.330.*

STAPLETON, NICHOLAS, Berwick's French Service. From France. Taken at sea *Louis XV*, 28 November 1745 Hull. Pardoned and banished. *SHS.3.330.*

STAPLETON, WALTER, Lieutenant Colonel and Brigadier-General, Berwick's Regiment, Irish Piquets. From France. Landed 22 November 1745 with Lord John Drummond. He commanded the Irish Picquets and took command of the siege of Fort Augustus. On the entry of Cumberland into Inverness after Culloden Stapleton sent a message offering to surrender and asking quarter. He was wounded at Culloden and died of his wounds, April 1746. Imprisoned Inverness. *MR136, SHS.3.330.*

STEVEN, ALEXANDER, porter from Leith. Evidence from Henry Morrison, Excise Officer. Evidence from George Robinson and Kathleen Reid, late servants to Mrs Rolland in Anstruther Wester. *SHS.8.342, SHS.8.352.*

STEVEN, ANDREW, farmer from Ferrytown, Clackmannan. Evidence from James Cowan of Powside in Airth parish and James Buchan, merchant in Borrowstounesss. *SHS.8.316.*

STEVENS, ALEXANDER, soldier, Lord John Drummond's French Royal Scots Cavalry. From Ireland. Imprisoned 1 May 1746 Moniaive, 2 May 1746 Dumfries, Berwick. Released under General Pardon, 1747. *MR.63, SHS.3.334.*

STEVENSON, ALEXANDER, servant, journey wright, from Edinburgh. Imprisoned 25 February 1746 Perth, 10

August 1746 Canongate, Carlisle. Executed Carlisle 15 November 1746. Was in charge of the baggage at Prestonpans. He pleaded guilty at his trial on 19 September and was sentenced to death. Evidence from Robert Brown, Excise Officer and Alexander Jackson, shoemaker, Edinburgh. *SHS.3.334, SHS.8.340.*

STEVENSON, THOMAS, French (Irish) Piquets. Deserted, taken 16 December 1745, imprisoned in Stirling Castle. It is not known how he was disposed of. *MR137, SHS.3.334.*

STEWART, ALLAN, of Innerhadden, half brother to Strathgarry. Captain, Roy Stewart's (Edinburgh) Regiment. *MR205.*

STEWART, ANGUS, Ensign, Roy Stewart's (Edinburgh) Regiment. Farmer from Park Begg. *MR205.*

STEWART, ARCHIBALD, from Edinburgh. Imprisoned 30 October 1745 Edinburgh, Tower of London. Acquitted 31 October 1747. Lord Provost of Edinburgh. Cousin of Sir James Stewart of Goodtrees. The Scots Magazine reported his arrest on suspicion on 30 October 1745, and imprisonment. He was allowed out on bail on 23 January 1747, six gentlemen being bound in large recognizances for his appearance before the High Court of Justiciary, Edinburgh. His name appears on the list of those who were specially excepted from the General Pardon of June 1747. Criminal letters were signeted against him on 17 June 1747. He was charged with negligence in regard to the holding of Edinburgh against the rebels. He ws tried 13 July 1747 but the diet was deserted, the Lord Advocate reserving power to insist against him afterwards. At his retrial on 26 October 1747 which lasted until 31 October 1747 he was found not guilty and was discharged. Commenting to the Duke of Newcastle on the result the

Lord Justice said, "the behaviour of the Jacobites has been most insolent." *SHS.3.338, SRO. JC26/135/2355, SRO.RH9/14/121-122.*

STEWART, CHARLES, wright, Cannongate, Edinburgh. Evidence from Jonathan and James Aitkin, wrights in Cannongate, Edinburgh and Thomas Wallace, smith in Cannongate, Edinburgh. *SHS.8.340.*

STEWART, DANIEL, Roy Stewart's (Edinburgh) Regiment. Farmer from Drumore, Perthshire. Taken at Carlisle. Died? *MR207, SHS.3.338.*

STEWART, DUNCAN, Roy Stewart's (Edinburgh) Regiment. Cattle herd, Breadalbane, Perthshire. Taken and transported 1747. *MR207, SHS.3.340.*

STEWART, DUNCAN, Roy Stewart's (Edinburgh) Regiment. Tailor from Strathbrand. Taken at Carlisle. Pardoned on enlistment. *MR207.*

STEWART, JAMES, soldier, French Royal Scots Cavalry. From Borland, Glentanar. *MR.63.*

STEWART, JAMES, Roy Stewart's (Edinburgh) Regiment. From Banff. Taken at Carlisle. Died? *MR207.*

STEWART, JOHN, Volunteer, Roy Stewart's (Edinburgh) Regiment. Bailie, Inverness, cousin to John Roy. *MR206.*

STEWART, JOHN, Roy Stewart's (Edinburgh) Regiment. Aged 18, from Perthshire. Taken at Carlisle. Transported 5 May 1747 from Liverpool to Leeward Islands in *Veteran*, arriving Martinique June 1747. *SHS.3.346, MR207, PRO.SP36.102.*

STEWART, JOHN ROY, Colone, Roy Stuart's (Edinburgh) Regiment, former Dragoon Officer. Escaped. *MR205.*

STEWART, LUDOVIC, Captain, Roy Stewart's (Edinburgh) Regiment. From Glenlivet. *MR205.*

STEWART, PATRICK, Major, Roy Stewart's (Edinburgh) Regiment. (? of Kininder, Banff). *MR205.*

STEWART, PETER, soldier, French Royal Scots Cavalry. From Borland Glentanar. *MR.63.*

STEWART, ROBERT, Captain, Roy Stewart's (Edinburgh) Regiment. From Glenlivet. Wounded at Keith. Pardoned. *MR205.*

STEWART, WILLIAM, Captain, Roy Stewart's (Edinburgh) Regiment. From Breagach, Banff. *MR205.*

STEWART, WILLIAM, Lieutenant, Roy Stewart's (Edinburgh) Regiment. From Clashmore, Banff. Taken at Carlisle. Acquitted. *MR205.*

STEWART, WILLIAM, in jail in Whitehaven. *CQS.359.*

STIRLING (of Keir), CHARLES, Mr, from Stirlingshire. Imprisoned 11 May 1746 Dumbarton. Released under General pardon, 1747. Although in the Return he is described as son of James Stirling of Keir, this cannot have been so. The entry "of Keir" is probably incorrect. *SHS.3.348.*

STIRLING, (of Keir), HUGH, younger, Gentleman, from Calder near Glasgow, Lanark, in Elcho's Life Guards. Imprisoned 8 May 1746 Port Glasgow, on a Dutch tobacco ship, 11 May 1746 Dumbarton. Escaped 20 May 1746. "Son to the Laird of Keir." "Joined the rebels at or immediately after the battle of Preston, was one of the party which came with Hay to raise the first contribution at Glasgow, being 4500 lib. He came South on the defeat at Culloden and was apprehended and imprisoned in Dumbarton Castle from thence he made his escape and is now said to be in Isle of Man, prisoner. Evidence from Robert Tennent, vintner in Glasgow, David Dunn his drawer, William Cunningham, his gardener and William Anderson, hostler to said Tennent. *SHS.8.346, SHS.3.350, SHS.8.276.*

STIRLING, (of Keir), JAMES, Mr, from Calder, near Glasgow. Imprisoned 8 May 1746 Port Glasgow, on board a Dutch tobacco ship, 11 May 1746 Dumbarton. Released 29 January 1747. James Stirling had been out in the '15 and was in hiding for some years. He took no active part in the '45, being 66 years old, but was "a zealous friend for the Pretender's interest; was in the rebellion of the 1715 and influenced his two sons to join them now by going to Edinburgh and presenting them to the Pretender's son; he was also close with the Rebels at Glasgow and prompted them to vex and oppress the inhabitants. On news of the defeat he fled his house." He was apprehended at Largo on board a Dutch ship in May 1746 along with his son Hugh, trying to escape to Rotterdam. According to family papers he was discharged because he developed dropsy. Evidence from Robert Rea of Littlegovan near Glasgow, John Hamilton, innkeeper in Glasgow, Alexander Dick, maltman there and James Buchanan, stabler there. *SHS.3.350, SHS.8.276, SHS.8.346.*

STIRLING, JAMES, of Craigbarnet, Burrie, Campsie, Lanark, Life Guards. Imprisoned 8 May 1746 Port Glasgow, 11 May 1746 Dumbarton. Escaped 20 May 1746. "Carried arms in the Rebel Life Guards, was wounded at the battle of Preston and it's said he shot a soldier there, when the poor man was begging quarter; he committed many outrages in the parish of Campsie and escaped with Hugh Stirling (as above). He's possest of an estate of 500 merks yearly." He was "apprehended on board a Dutch ship," but escaped from Dumbarton Castle. His name was on the list of those who were specially excepted from the Act of Pardon of June 1747. Evidence from Archibald Graham, Jonathan Muir, William Muir and Jonathan Calder, portioners in Burdstone in the parish of Campsie and many others in that parish. *SHS.3.350, SHS.8.276, SHS.8.346.*

STIRLING, JAMES, son to the Laird of Northside, Glasgow. Influenced by his father joined early in the rebellion, was of the Command that came to Glasgow for money, he was a volunteer in a British Regiment at the battle of Dettingen. Whereabouts not known. Evidence from Robert Tennent, vintner in Glasgow, David Dunn his drawer, William Cunningham, his gardener and William Anderson, hostler to said Tennent. *SHS.8.278, SHS.8.346.*

STIRLING, JAMES, at the house of Erskine, and the parish of that name, and Renfrew County. Evidence from magistrates of Renfrew. *SHS.8.326.*

STIRLING, WILLIAM, son to the Laird of Keir, Calder, near Glasgow, Lanark. Employed by the rebels as his brother above and made his escape from Culloden. Whereabouts not known. Evidence from Robert Tennent, vintner in Glasgow, David Dunn his drawer, William Cunningham, his gardener and William Anderson, hostler to said Tennent. *SHS.8.346, SHS.8.276.*

STIVEN, ALEXANDER, trone man from Leith, South Leith parish, Midlothian. Carried a barrel of gunpowder to the Pretender's son and wore a white cockade. Whereabouts not known. *SHS.8.68, SHS.8.256.*

STIVEN, ANDREW, farmer in Ferrytoun, Clackmannan parish, Clackmannanshire. Carried off two Dragoon horses from the battle of Preston. At home. *SHS.8.60.*

STIVENSON, ALEXANDER, journeyman wright, Cowgate of Edinburgh, Midlothian. Carried arms in the rebel army and was wright to the Artillary carriages. Whereabouts not known. *SHS.8.256.*

St LEGER, MATHIEU, Captain, Artillery. Irish Piquets. Killed at Culloden. *MR136.*

STRATTON, ARCHIBALD, watchmaker from Edinburgh, Midlothian. Seen dismounting Dragoons on their flight from Preston and seizing their horses, etc. Now at home. Evidence from Mark Sprott, skinner and George Areskine, chandler, Edinburgh and Excise Officers. *SHS.8.256, SHS.8.340.*

STRATTON or STATTON, JAMES, from Berwickshire, surgeon to the Garrison. Imprisoned 30 December 1745 Carlisle, London. Acquitted and discharged 2 August 1746. Taken at the capitulation of Carlisle. He was brought up for trial in London on 2 August 1746, but as there was no evidence that he bore arms, and as it appeared he was forced, he was acquitted, in spite of the fact that the Chief Justice pointed out that although he carried no arms the prisoner, as a surgeon, was a party to levying war. *SHS.3.356.*

STRETCH, JOHN, Berwick's French Service. Taken at sea, imprisoned Berwick. Discharged. *SHS.3.356.*

STRICKLAND, FRANCIS (or ROGER), Colonel. From Ireland. Imprisoned 30 December 1745 Carlisle. Died January 1746. He was probably a member of the Jacobite family of Sizergh in Westmorland. He was one of the small party who accompanied the Prince from France to Scotland. He was left behind at Carlisle when the Prince's army retired north, and was captured along with the whole garrison. At the time he was very ill, and died there three or four days later. *SHS.3.356.*

STUART, CHARLES, Bewick's French Service. From France. Taken at sea *Louis XV*, 28 November 1745 Berwick, February 1746 Hull. Discharged. *SHS.3.338.*

STUART, CHARLES, wright from Canongate, Edinburgh, Midlothian. Was a Lieutenant in the rebel army and as such mounted Guard in the Canongate. Whereabouts not known. *SHS.8.256.*

STUART, DAVID, of Ballahallan, Callander parish, Perthshire. Had a commission in the rebel army and collected his Majesty's revenue for them. Lurking. This is most probably Major Stewart, brother to the laird of Ardvorlich, who, along with six other rebels, was surprised in a hut on the Braes of Leny, where they were in hiding after Culloden. Their assailants were a party of the Perth volunteers, who, after a touch conflict, overpowered Stewart and his comrades, and carried them to Stirling, where the Major died of his wounds. The others taken with him were Captain Malcolm Macgregor of Cornour, Captain Donald MacLaren, Sergeant King, alias Macree, later of Lord Murray's regiment, and three privates. It is related of Captain MacLaren that when being carried towards Carlisle, strapped to a dragoon, he cut the strap, threw himself over a cliff, and escaped. *SHS.8.60, SHS.8.373.*

STUART, JOHN, of Glat, Callander parish, Perthshire. Carried arms in the rebel army. Whereabouts not known. *SHS.8.60.*

STUART, JOHN, resident of Kirkcaldy, Fife. Joined the rebels and continued with them to the end. Escaped to England. *SHS.8.260.*

STUART, JOHN, brewer of Collingtowngill, Callander parish, Stirlingshire. Went along with the rebel army. Whereabouts not known. *SHS.8.60.*

STUART, PATRICK, servant to the late Coll Stuart, from Hamilton, Lanarkshire. Carried arms in the rebel Life Guards and was active in seizing horses. Whereabouts not known. *SHS.8.278.*

STUART, PETER. Evidence from James Cousland, servant to Thomas Borland in Udston in Blantyre parish, Jonathan Borthwick, servant to Major Robertson in Emock near Hamilton and James Scott, servant to Jonathan Henderson in Emock hill in said parish. *SHS.8.346.*

STUART, WALTER, servant to Craigbarnet, Burry, Campsie. Carried arms in the rebel army, went to England with them and returned again. Whereabouts not known. Evidence from Malcolm Cowbrugh's sen, and jun, in Campsie parish and James Reid, gardener in Herriot's Work. *SHS.8.278,* Evidence from Robert Tennent, vintner in Glasgow, David Dunn his drawer, William Cunningham, his gardener and William Anderson, hostler to said Tennent. *SHS.8.278, SHS.8.346.*

SULLIVAN, CORNELIUS, Clare's French Service. From France. Taken at sea *Louis XV*, 28 November 1745 Berwick, February 1746 Hull. Discharged. *SHS.3.356.*

SULLIVAN, DANIEL, Berwick's French Service. From France. Taken at sea *Louis XV* 28 November 1745, imprisoned Berwick, February 1746 Hull. Discharged. *SHS.3.354.*

SULLIVAN, JEREMY, Lord John Drummond's Regiment. Aged 20, from Cork. Imprisoned Crieff, 2 May 1746 Perth, 12 May 1746 Stirling Castle, 8 August 1746 Carlisle. Transported 1747. *SHS.3.358, MR.63.*

SULLIVAN, OWEN, Clare's French Service, from Ireland. Taken at sea *Louis XV*, 28 November 1745 Berwick, February 1746 Hull. Discharged. *SHS.3.358.*

SUTHERLAND, JOHN, aged 24, French Service. Imprisoned Carlisle. Transported 1747. He asked not to be sent back to France and was transported instead. *SHS.3.360.*

SWAN, ANDREW, shoemaker from Canongatehead, Edinburgh, Sergeant, Manchester Regiment. Imprisoned Canongate, Carlisle. Executed at Penrith 28 October 1746. "Carried arms as a volunteer in the rebel army." Pleaded guilty at his trial and was sentenced to death. *SHS.3.360, SHS.8.256, SHS.8.380, MR.196.*

SWEENY, BRYAN, Bulkeley's French Service. From France. Taken at sea *Louis XV* 28 November 1745 Berwick, February 1746 Hull. Discharged. *SHS.3.362.*

SWINNEY, MYLES, aged 30, from Flanders. Lieutenant, Lally's French Service. Imprisoned Inverness June 1746 *Thane of Fife*, Southwark, Marshalsea. Pardoned and banished. *SHS.3.362.*

SYDALL, THOMAS, Adjutant, Manchester Regiment. Barber, son of a blacksmith who was taken prisoner in the 1715 and executed. He joined the Prince and was appointed Adjutant of the Manchester regiment, and was captured at the surrender of Carlisle 30 December 1745. In his speech before execution he regretted the "scandalous surrender of Carlisle, to which he had been opposed."

Imprisoned 30 December 1745 Carlisle, Southwark, London. Executed at Kennington Common on 30 July 1746. *MR.195, SHS.1.151, SHS.3.362.*

SYMERS, ANDREW, bookseller from Edinburgh, Midlothian. Carried arms as a volunteer in the rebel army. Whereabouts not known. *SHS.8.256.*

TAAFE, PETER, Lieutenant, Rooth's French Service. Imprisoned 17 April 1746 Inverness, Marshalsea. From France. Discharged. *SHS.3.362.*

TAIT, ADAM, goldsmith from Edinburgh, Midlothian. Carried arms as a rebel Hussar. Whereabouts not known. Evidence from Charles Blair and Robert Low, goldsmiths in Edinburgh. *SHS.8.256, SHS.8.340.*

TALBOT, GEORGE ANTHONY, "Capitaine de Fregate," French Service. Commanded *Le Prince Charles* (ex *Hazard)* when that ship was driven ashire by English cruisers at Tongue on 25 March 1746. He petitioned for the release of two pilots, Bligh and Leslie, and for them to be treated as prisoners of war instead of as ordinary Jacobite prisoners. Taken at sea and imprisoned in Berwick. Pardoned on condition of permanent banishment 2 July 1747. *SHS.3.362.*

TASKER, ALEXANDER, servant ot Mrs Brand, Kinghorn, Fife. Left his service and joined the rebel army. Whereabouts not known. *SHS.8.260.*

TAYLOR, ALEXANDER, aged 38, labourer from Edinburgh. Imprisoned 28 November 1745 Edinburgh, 28 November 1745 Edinburgh Tolbooth, 8 August 1746 Carlisle. Transported 22 April 1747 from Liverpool to Virginia in *Johnson,* arriving Port Oxford, Maryland, 5 August 1747. *SHS.3.362, PRO.T1.328.*

TAYLOR, CHRISTOPHER, Ensign, Manchester Regiment. From Wigan, Lancashire. Imprisoned 30 December 1745 Carlisle, London, House of Mr Dick, the messenger. Educated in France, and had just come home when the '45 broke out; taken at capture of Carlisle. He pleaded guilty at his trial, 16 July 1746; was sentenced to death, but reprieved. Kept in the house of a messenger until he was transported. Transported 21 July 1748. *MR.195, SHS.3.364.*

TAYLOR, JOHN, boatman from Newport, Glasgow, Duke of Perth's Regiment. Imprisoned Inverness. "Was seized by the rebels on his way to Edinburgh, forced into their service and carried to England. It is thought this man was by accident and against his will forced into the rebel service." There is no reference to his further disposal. He is not in the lists at Tilbury. *SHS.3.366.*

TAYLOR, JOHN, farmer from St Ninians, Baggot's Hussars. Imprisoned Feb 1746 Denny, 25 February 1746 Stirling, Canongate, 8 August 1746 Carlisle, York Castle. Released. "Servant to one Duchart, officer of the Rebel Hussars." In hospital in Edinburgh with jaundice. Surgeon's fee, 8s. "Several witnesses say he was with the rebels and marched in arms wearing the White cockade." This man turned King's Evidence at the York trials. He was probably released as an Evidence though his name is in the transportation list. *SHS.3.366.*

TAYLOR, OLIVER, Manchester Regiment. From Lancashire. Taken at capture of Carlisle 30 December 1745, Lancaster Castle. Fate unknown. No further reference to him. Died? *MR198, SHS.3.366.*

TAYLOR, PETER, Manchester Regiment. Joiner from Lancashire. He was captured at the fall of Carlisle 30

December 1745 and sent to Lancaster 2 February 1746. He refused to sign the petition for mercy and was sent for trial to Carlisle 1 August 1746. Here he escaped from the Castle but was recaptured at Kendal. He was in due course tried and sentenced to death. Executed Brampton, 21 October 1746. *SHS.1.151, MR198, SHS.3.366.*

TAYLOR, ROBERT, aged 30, shoemaker from Edinburgh, Captain, Duke of Perth's Regiment. Imprisoned Edinburgh, January 1746 Edinburgh Castle, 15 January 1746 Edinburgh Tolbooth, 8 August 1746 Carlisle, Oct 1746 York, Carlisle. Released October 1747. He was captured outside Edinburgh Castle a few days after joining the Prince. Albemarle says he raised "a company of militia" and promised to capture the Castle. When he was tried for his life at Carlisle in September 1746 he was sentenced to death, but was recommended for mercy for having helped the wounded English at Prestonpans, and was reprieved on condition that he enlisted. He refused to do this, and was one of the ringleaders who tried to dissuade other prisoners from enlisting. The Duke of Newcastle ordered him to be sent back to Carlisle and executed. This sentence was not carried out, and he was released in Oct 1747. Albemarle, writing on 15 Nov 1746 to Newcastle, described him as of so infamous a character that he regretted his reprieve. *SHS.3.268.*

TAYSPELL, DANIEL, from Essex. Imprisoned Craiganet 30 April 1746, Stirling Castle. Against his name is the word "Prince's." This reference to "Prince's" regiment indicates that he was a deserter. He was probably handed over to the military authorities. *SHS.3.368.*

TEAFE, PETER, Lieutenant, Rooth's Regiment, Irish Piquets. Taken at Culloden. Discharged. *MR136.*

TELMONE, FRANCOISE, French service. From France. Taken at sea in the *Soleil* privateer or *Esperance* going to Scotland, imprisoned Marshalsea. Discharged. *SHS.3.368.*

THOIRS or THORES, JAMES, weaver's apprentice from Edinburgh. Imprisoned Edinburgh Castle, 15 February 1746 Edinburgh Jail. Liberated 9 May 1746. "Decrepit." "In the rebellion." "Was a Volunteer in the Rebel Army." On suspicion. *SHS.3.370.*

THOIRS, JAMES, from Edinburgh. Imprisoned Carlisle. Acquitted 26 September 1746. Son of Gilbert Thoirs, Writer. Gentleman. Was tried 12 September 1746 at Carlisle, and acquitted. *SHS.3.370.*

THOMAS, JOHN EDWARD from Shropshire. Irish Piquets. Imprisoned Crieff, 25 February 1746 Perth, 12 May 1746 Stirling Castle, 8 August 1746 Carlisle. "Deserter in the rebel service." Soldier in Genereal Guise's Regiment. The Carlisle list shows that he was a French soldier. He asked not to be sent back to France, and was transported 1747. *MR137, SHS.3.370.*

THOMSON, ANGUS, Roy Stewart's (Edinburgh) Regiment. From Argyll, (deserter). Deserted. Taken. Pardoned. *MR207.*

THOMSON, HECTOR, salt watchman from Edmonston pans. Did salt officer's duty and uplifted the money for the rebels while they continued there. Now at home. *SHS.8.140.*

THOMSON, JAMES, brewer and maltster from Dalkeith. Went from Dalkeith with the rebels in their way to England with a white cockade and tartan plaid. Pretends he went in quest of a cart and horses which went off with the rebel baggage two days before, but notwithstanding he assumed the authority of one of their officers and with a party extorted victuals for himself and horses without payment, particularly at the Laird of Kirkeat's and other places in Gallow water, where and at Ginglekirk he assisted the rebels in taking horses, but deserted before they entered England. At home ever since. *SHS.8.140.*

THOMSON, JOSEPH, conveyed from Penrith to Brough, Westmoreland in the company of 19 other Jacobites. *CQS.354.*

THOMSON, ROBERT, Roy Stewart's (Edinburgh) Regiment. From Dublin. Taken at Carlisle. Imprisoned 30 December 1745 Carlisle, Lincoln Castle. Transported 22 April 1747. *MR207, SHS.3.372.*

THOMSON, THOMAS, Manchester Regiment. From Lancashire. Taken at capture of Carlisle 30 December 1745. Conveyed from Penrith to Brough, Westmoreland in the company of 19 other Jacobites. Nothing more is know of him. Died? *MR198, SHS.3.372, CQS.354.*

THOMSON, WILLIAM, boatman from Pittenweem, Fife. Twice demanded parties from the rebels to break the Customhouse and carry off the goods seized for his Majesty's behoof, but was often refused. This proceeded from his affection towards the smugglers to whom he is serviceable both by sea and land and is himself remarkably disaffected to the present government. Now at home. Evidence from John Skinner, Compt of the Customs at Anstruther, and John Fullen, excise officer there. *SHS.8.68, SHS.8.352.*

THOMSON, WILLIAM, aged 17, tailor from Glasgow. Imprisoned 2 May 1746 Perth, 10 August 1746 Canongate, Carlisle. Transported 24 February 1747 from Liverpool to

Virginia in *Gildart*, arriving Port North Potomac, Maryland, 5 August 1747. *SHS.3.372, PRO.T1.328.*

THORES, JAMES, weaver from Edinburgh, Midlothian. Was a volunteer in the rebel army. Whereabouts not known. *SHS.8.256.*

TICKHALL, WILLIAM, Manchester Regiment. Tailor from Lancashire, aged 30. A papist. Taken at capture of Carlisle 30 December 1745, imprisoned Lancaster Castle. Transported 21 February 1747. *SHS.3.374, MR198.*

TIERCON, SAMUEL, Manchester Regiment. From Chester. Taken at capture of Carlisle 30 December 1745. No further reference to him. Died? *MR198, SHS.3.374.*

TINSLEY, ROBERT, Manchester Regiment. Weaver from Wigan. Taken at capture of Carlisle 30 December 1745, imprisoned Lancaster Castle. Tried at Carlisle September 1746 and sentenced to death, but reprieved. Pardoned on condition of enlistment. *MR199, SHS.3.374.*

TODD, ARCHIBALD, weaver from Mussleburgh. Joined the Pretender's son's Life Guards before they went for England and continued with them till dispersed. Imprisoned Edinburgh. Released under General Pardon, 1747. *SHS.8.140, SHS.3.374.*

TODD, THOMAS, town clerk of Mussleburgh. Collected the excise in Mussleburgh and Fisheraw to the extent of £66.16s.11d and applied it in part payment of $250 imposed by the rebels on these places as a contribution all at his own hand without any authority. Now at home. *SHS.8.140.*

TODD, WALTER, tanner from Edinburgh, Midlothian.
Carried arms in the rebel army during the whole rebellion.
Now lurking about Edinburgh. *SHS.8.256.*

TOUTSAINT, THOMAS, Berwick's French Service. Taken at sea imprisoned *Sheerness*, Berwick. Discharged. *SHS.3.376.*

TOWNLEY, FRANCIS, Colonel, Commander Manchester Regiment. Formally commissioned in the French Service, and joined the Prince in Preston. Imprisoned 30 December 1745 Carlisle, London (Southwark). Aged 36, an English Roman Catholic from Lancashire. Son of Charles Towneley of Towneley Hall, Lancashire. He was born 1709 and when 19 years old entered the French army. He served abroad for some years, and then returned to England and settled in Wales. The French King sent him a Colonel's commission in 1744. When the Prince reached Manchester and a regiment was raised there on 30 November 1745, Towneley was put in command of it. When the Prince's army retired to Scotland he was left Governor of the town of Carlisle. When the town was summoned by Cumberland he wished to hold out and quarrelled with Hamiton, governor of the Castle, who wished or was forced to surrender. Towneley was tried at Southwark in July 1746 and claimed to be treated as a prisoner of war, owing to his holding a French commission. This plea was repelled, and he was executed on Kennington Common on 30 July 1746. *MR.195, SHS.1.151, SHS.3.376.*

TRAPONT, GREGORY, Corporal, Clare's French Service. From France. Taken at sea *Louis XV* 28 November 1745 Berwick, February 1746 Hull. Discharged. *SHS.3.376.*

TRAQUAIR, Earl of, CHARLES STUART. Imprisoned 29 July 1746, Great Stoughton, Huntingdon, 9 August 1746

Tower of London. Released on bail 9 February 1748, released Oct 1748. The fifth Earl succeeded his father in 1741. He was a keen Jacobite and belonged to the King's rather than the Prince's party. He was opposed to the Prince's coming to Scotland without French aid, and himself took no part in the operations of the '45. Murray of Broughton was bitterly opposed to him, and, in consequence of evidence Murray brought against him at Lord Lovat's trial, Traquair was thrown into the Tower of London about August 1746. He was specially excluded from the Act of Pardon. Here he was kept until February 1748, when he was released on bail and finally discharged in October 1748. In one of the Privy Council Minutes of 20 August 1747 permission was given him to "walk in the Tower, attended by an officer." He returned to Scotland and died in Edinburgh 24 April 1764. *SHS.3.376.*

TROUP, JOHN THOMAS, aged 20, gardener from Stirling, "Matross" Artillery. Imprisoned 30 December 1745 Carlisle, Lincoln Castle. Taken at capture of Carlisle. Transported 5 May 1747, from Liverpool to Leeward Islands in *Veteran*, arriving Martinique June 1747. *SHS.3.378, MR132, PRO.SP36.102.*

TURNER, ANDREW, hosteler in Linlithgow. Imprisoned 13 January 1746 Linlithgow, 20 January 1746 Leith, 7 February 1746 Edinburgh. Released under General Pardon, 1747. *SHS.3.380.*

TURNER, THOMAS, Manchester Regiment. Shoemaker from Bury, Lancashire. Taken at capture of Carlisle 30 December 1745, imprisoned Lancaster Castle. Tried at Carlisle in September 1746 and sentenced to death. The jury recommended percy, and he was reprieved. Pardoned on condition of enlistment 22 July 1748. *MR199, SHS.3.380.*

TURNER, THOMAS, Manchester Regiment. Weaver from Walcot, Lancashire. Taken at capture of Carlisle 30 December 1745, imprisoned Lancaster Castle. Tried at Carlisle, September 1746 and sentenced to death, but recommended to mercy by the jury. Pardoned on condition of enlistment 22 July 1748. *MR199, SHS.3.380.*

TURON LA GARQUE, HIPPOLYTE, Lieutenant, French Service, Irish Piquets. From France. Imprisoned Inverness, and banished. *MR136, SHS.3.380.*

TYDIEMAN, JOHN, servant to Lord Elcho, Fife. Attended said master in the rebellion. Whereabouts not known. *SHS.8.260.*

TYRIE, JOHN, Carter's servant from Leith, Midlothian. Assisted in taking and carrying provisions to the rebels' horses and driving their carts. Now at home. *SHS.8.256.*

TYRRELL, JOSEPH, Berwick's French Service. From France. Taken at sea *Louis XV*, 28 November 1745 imprisoned Berwick, February 1746 Hull. Discharged. *SHS.3.380.*

URQUHART, ADAM, Lieutenant, Lord John Drummond's. Captured at sea *Esperance* 25 November 1745 Deal, imprisoned February 1746 Custom's Smack *Caroline* Greenwich, Marshalsea. Pardoned on condition of permanent banishment 2 July 1747. *SHS.3.382.*

URQUHART, JAMES, coppermsith from Stirling, Stirlingshire. Acted as Commissary for the rebel army. Whereabouts not known. *SHS.8.60.*

URQUHART, JOHN, from Edinburgh, Glenbucket's Regiment. Imprisoned Carlisle, Chester, London (messenger's house). Released after June 1748. He turned King's Evidence at the trials in Southwark, against Aeneas

Macdonald and others. His name is on the list of those in custody of Carrington, the messenger, June 1748. *SHS.3.382.*

USHER, ROBERT, from Aberdour, Fife. "Engaged himself in the rebellion." Servant to John Stones, carrier. There is no other evidence as to where he was imprisoned or what happened to him. He was probably taken "on suspicion" and released. *SHS.3.382.*

USHET, ROBERT, servant to Jonathan Stones, Carrier, Aberdour, Fife. Engaged himself in the rebellion. Now a prisoner. *SHS.8.260.*

VALENTINE, JEAN, Lance-Corporal, Lord John Drummond's Regiment. Taken at sea, imprisoned Berwick. Discharged. *SHS.3.382.*

VALIVA, EDWARD, soldier, Lord John Drummond's French Royal Scots Cavalry. Aged 28, from Dunkirk, France. Imprisoned Buchlyvie, 25 April 1746 Stirling Castle, Carlisle. Transported 1747. *MR.63, SHS.3.382.*

VALLANCE, ROBERT, merchant, from Cupar, Fife. Imprisoned 25 April 1746 Dundee. Discharged 16 March 1747. *SHS.3.382.*

VAN DE BOIS, GODEN, Berwick's French Service. From France. Taken at sea, imprisoned Berwick. Discharged. *SHS.3.382.*

VEITCH, PATRICK, carter from Elphingtoun. Voluntarily engaged with the rebels to drive their carriages when they went to England and continued with them till their defeat at Culloden. Now lurking. *SHS.8.140.*

VERLY, WILLIAM, carpenter, Alloa. Was of great use to the rebels in passing the Forth at Alloa; was overseer to the workmen who built them a boat and assisted in providing victualls etc for them. Absconded. *SHS.8.148.*

VEZAZI, MICHAEL, Italian. Imprisoned 16 June 1746 Dumbarton Castle, 31 August 1746 Edinburgh Tolbooth. Released on parole 15 September 1746. "Long in the Pretender's service." *Lyon* styles him Vizozi Michael. Young Ranald McDonald, son of Borradale, says that he met him on the ship which brought the Prince over to Scotland, and had known him in Rome and Paris eight years before. *SHS.3.382.*

VIARE, JOSEPH, Berwick's French Service. From France. Taken at sea *Louis XV*, 28 November 1745 imprisoned Berwick, February 1746 Hull. Discharged. *SHS.3.384.*

VICKMAN, PIERRE, Lally's French Service, from Dieppe, France. Taken at capture of Carlisle 30 December 1745, imprisoned Marshalsea. Discharged. *SHS.3.384.*

VICKMAN, PEIERRE GUILLAUME, French Service, a servant. From France. Taken at sea, imprisoned Marshalsea. Discharged. *SHS.3.384.*

VINTER, HENRY, Berwick's French Service. From France. Taken at sea, imprisoned *Sheerness*, Berwick. Discharged. *SHS.3.384.*

VITCHER, JOHN, French Service. From France. Imprisoned Marshalsea. Discharged. *SHS.3.384.*

WADDELL, JOHN, ship master from Prestonpans. Acted as salt officer and uplifted the duty for the rebels during their stay at Prestonpans. Now at home. *SHS.8.140.*

WADDELL, JOHN, from Perthshire, Irish Piquets. Deserted. Taken 13 December 1745. Discharged. *MR137.*

WADESON, JAMES, from Bolton, Yorkshire. Imprisoned Chester Castle. Committed to the Asizes "for declaring that if the Pretender came he would be his man; and that he thought King James had been wronged of the Crown and everybody ought to have his own right." No further reference to him. He was probably discharged. *SHS.3.384.*

WALKER, DANIEL, Clare's French Service. From France. Taken at sea *Louis XV*, imprisoned 28 November 1745 Berwick, February 1746 Hull. Discharged. *SHS.3.386.*

WALKER, JAMES, journeyman candlemaker, Canongate, Midlothian. Carried arms, was at Preston battle and wore a white cockade. Now at home. Evidence from John Izate, candlemaker in Cannongate and Francis Paterson, Excise Officer. *SHS.8.258, SHS.8.340.*

WALKER, JOHN, Manchester Regiment. Aged 20, labourer from Lancashire. Imprisoned Carlisle, York Castle. Pardoned on condition of enlistment 22 July 1748. "Taken in actual rebellion." He was tried at York 2 October 1746, pleaded guilty, was sentenced to death, but reprieved. *SHS.3.386.*

WALKINSHAW, JOHN, from London. Was taken into custody on suspicion. The War Office reported to the Duke of Newcastle that he was in "the rebellion of 1715, a noted Jacobite, and was on the scaffold with Lord Balmerino, whose wife now lives with him." He was a relative of Miss Clementina Walkinshaw. *SHS.3.386.*

WALLACE or WALLAS, JOHN, miller from Linlithgowshire. Imprisoned Canongate, House of Correction Whitehaven from 15 January 1745, 8 August 1746 Carlisle. Accused of high treason. Executed Carlisle 15 November 1746. Was captured outside Carlisle. At his trial at Carlisle on 19-26 September, he pleaded guilty and was sentenced to death. According to his petition, was taken up by a party locally, and forced in. He "could not be prevailed upon to carry arms, so was left in the Castle at Carlisle" on the journey southwards. He "found means to make his escape, both out of the Castle and city by the Irish gate" in the company of William Lackey (from Perth), but both were apprehended at some distance from the city and carried to Whitehaven. *SHS.3.386, CQS.344.*

WALMSLEY, JOHN, Manchester Regiment. From Lancashire. Imprisoned 30 December 1745 Carlisle, Lancaster. Taken at capture of Carlisle. There is no reference to his disposal. *MR199, SHS.3.388.*

WALSH, EDWARD, soldier, Lord John Drummond's French Royal Scots Cavalry. Taken at Carlisle. He begged not to be sent back to France and was transported. *MR.63, SHS.3.388.*

WALTER, ABRAHAM, tea merchant from London. Imprisoned Newgate. Pardoned 1747. Taken prisoner on charge of running tea and carrying firearms. The only reference to this man is in regard to his pardon. *SHS.3.388.*

WARD, HENRY, Berwick's French Service. Taken at sea, imprisoned Berwick. Discharged. *SHS.3.388.*

WARD, MAURICE, soldier from Ireland. "Came over with the Irish Piquets to Scotland." Bulkeley's Regiment. Imprisoned 10 November 1745 Milfort, 6 December 1745 Edinburgh Castle. Discharged. *MR137, SHS.3.388.*

WARDLAW, HENRY, son to John Wardlaw, factor to the late Earl of Wigtown, near Falkirk. Served in the rebel Life Guards and assisted in seizing horses for that Regiment. Whereabouts not known. *SHS.8.266.*

WARING, GEORGE, Manchester Regiment. Weaver from Lancashire. Taken at capture of Carlisle 30 December 1745, imprisoned Lancaster Castle. Pardoned on condition of enlistment 22 July 1748. Tried Carlisle, September 1746 and sentenced to death, but reprieved. *MR199, SHS.3.388.*

WARING, MATTHEW, Manchester Regiment. Weaver from Lancashire. Taken and pardoned on enlistment. *MR199.*

WARREN, JAMES, Manchester Regiment. Taken at fall of Carlisle. Turned King's Evidence and was discharged. *MR199, SHS.390.*

WARREN, JOHN, carpenter from Clitheroe, Lancashire. Imprisoned Culloden, Inverness, HMS *Greyhound*, September 1746 *Pamela*, Tilbury. When a prisoner on board the *Greyhound* after the battle of Culloden, when she was engaged with a French man-of-war off Loch Moidart, he worked hard and was of great service, many of the crew being sick. He was accordingly recommended for mercy. He appealed against transportation, but this was refused. Transported 31 March 1747. *MR.47, SHS.3.390.*

WARREN, RICHARD, Captain, Clare's Regiment (ADC to Perth). Irish Piquets. Escaped. *MR136.*

WARRINGTON, THOMAS, Manchester Regiment. Chairmaker from Macclesfield. Taken at capture of Carlisle 30 December 1745, imprisoned Lancaster Castle.

Tried at Carlisle, 19 September 1746 and acquitted 26 September 1746. *MR199, SHS.3.390.*

WARSHOTT, JAMES, from London. Lord Lewis Gordon's Regiment. Taken at capture of Carlisle 30 December 1745. No further reference to him. *SHS.3.390.*

WATSON, JAMES, Quartermaster, Roy Stewart's (Edinburgh) Regiment. Merchant from Keith. Killed at Culloden. *MR205.*

WATSON, JOHN, mason from Edinburgh. Imprisoned 13 January 1746 Linlithgow, 20 January 1746 Leith. Discharged 7 February 1746. *SHS.3.392.*

WATT, ANDREW, slater in Doune, Stirlingshire. Evidence from Thomas Gibson, wright in Doune. *SHS.8.318.*

WATT, ROBERT, slater from Doune, Stirlingshire. Imprisoned "on suspicion" 18 May 1746 Johnshaven, 5 July 1746 Montrose. Released 21 July 1746. Evidence from John Christy, multerer in Doune Miln, John Mitchel, merchant there, Alexander Campbell, gunsmith there, James Kemp, innkeeper there and James and William Taylors both innkeepers there. *SHS.3.392, SHS.8.318.*

WEAVER, SAMUEL, from Worcester. "In Rebel service," deserter from General Guise's Regiment. He was probably handed over to the military authorities. *SHS.3.394.*

WEBSTER, CHARLES, Manchester Regiment. From Derby. Imprisoned Derby and York. At his trial in York 2 October 1746 it was shown that he had been found straying about armed. He said he had been forced out, and had deserted. As there was no evidence produced against him he was acquitted. *SHS.3.394, MR199.*

WEBSTER, JAMES, from London. Ogilvy's Regiment. Imprisoned 22 May 1746 Forfar, 24 May 1746 Montrose. Released under General Pardon, 1747. *SHS.3.396.*

WEEMS, DAVID, surgeon from Cupar, Fife. Carried arms in the rebel army, was also in the rebellion of 1715. Now lurking at home. *SHS.8.70.*

WEEMS, DAVID, resident of St Andrews, Fife. This is the man who promulgate the Pretender's manifesto and had the assurance to go to a minister of the established church with ... Now at home. Evidence from Robert Bell, merchant in Cupar, John Arnot, surgeon there, David Nicol, stabler there and Mr Halket, schoolmaster there, etc. *SHS.8.70, SHS.8.352.*

WEIR, JOHN, coal hewer from Cathcart, Lanarkshire. Joined and went along with the rebels and continued till the last. Now lurking. *SHS.8.292.*

WEIR, WILLIAM, coalier at Cathcart. Evidence from Thomas Bowes and Gavin Lawson and many others in Cathcart. *SHS.8.326.*

WELCH, DAVID, French Service, from Ireland. Captured at sea *Louis XV*, 28 November 1745 imprisoned Edinburgh. He was found to be a deserter from Pulteney's regiment and was hanged 24 January 1746. *SHS.398.*

WELSH, CHARLES, Sergeant, Bulkeley's French Service. Taken at sea *Louis XV*, imprisoned 28 November 1745 Berwick, Hull. Discharged. *SHS.3.398.*

WELSH, PETER, Bulkeley's French Service. Taken at sea 28 November 1745 *Louis XV*, imprisoned February 1746 in Hull. Discharged. *SHS.3.398.*

WENCTANLEY (or WINSTANLEY or WYNSTANLEY), WILLIAM, born near Wigan, Lancashire. Weaver. Manchester Regiment. Taken near Carlisle and imprisoned in House of Correction, Whitehaven from 15 January 1745 for high treason. He was tried, and pleaded "not guilty," but was convicted 22 September 1745 and probably transported, but may have died. According to Muster Roll he was transported 1747. *CQS.346, MR.198, CQS.359.*

WHIGGAM or WHYGGAM, JOHN, from Leadhills, Ensign of Baggot's Hussars. Imprisoned 26 April 1746 Dunfermline. Escaped 18 March 1747. *SHS.3.398.*

WHITAKER, JOHN, yr of Brokercross, Macclesfield. Yeoman. Committed to assizes "for assiting the rebels in search of arms." Imprisoned 24 July 1746 Chester Castle. Discharged. *SHS.3.398.*

WHITE, JOHN, labourer from Liberton, Midlothian, Duke of Perth's Regiment. Imprisoned 30 December 1745 Carlisle, Chester Castle, London. Discharged. He turned King's Evidence at the Southwark trials. He was in the custody of Carrington, the messenger, in July 1747. *SHS.3.400.*

WHITE, ROBERT, aged 28, painter from Glasgow, parents James White and Jane Selkrig. Duke of Perth's Regiment. Imprisoned Canongate, Carlisle. "Carried arms amongst the Atholl men." Transported 1747. Evidence from Jonathan Borland, William Tennent and Robert Kerr, all painters in Glasgow. *SHS.3.400, SHS.8.278, SHS.8.346.*

WHITE, ROBERT, gardener from Linktoun of Arnot, Fife. Artillery. Imprisoned 30 December 1745 Carlisle. Taken at capture of Carlisle. Transported 1747. *SHS.3.400*, *MR133*. *SHS.8.260*.

WHITE, WILLIAM, Dillon's French Service, aged 28 from Dublin. Imprisoned Drummond of Lennoch, 25 April 1746 Stirling Castle, Carlisle. Discharged. *SHS.3.400*, *MR138*.

WHITE, WILLIAM, innkeeper from Edinburgh, Midlothian. Served in the rebel train of Artillery. Whereabouts not known. *SHS.8.258*.

WHITE, WILLIAM, servant to Traquhair, Tweedale. Joined the rebels at first on their way from the north. Whereabouts not known. *SHS.8.84*.

WIGHTMAN, CHARLES, merchant from Anstruther, Fife. Went with his wife and waited on the Pretender's son. Entertained the rebels, had a man in pay in their service at his own expense, is said to be factor for the Earl of Kelly, collected the Excise for him, had the assurance to ask the Excise Officer how he lived under his government and has always been known for a disaffected person. Now at home. *SHS.8.68*.

WILCOCK, EDWARD, Manchester Regiment. From Lancashire. Taken at capture of Carlisle 30 December 1745, imprisoned Lancaster Castle. No further reference to him. *MR199, SHS.3.400*.

WILDING, JAMES, Lieutenant, Manchester Regiment. Dyer. Pardoned. *MR.195*.

WILDING, JAMES, Ensign, Manchester Regiment. Aged 15 from Manchester, Lancashire. "Gentleman, scarlet dyer." Apprentice to his father. Taken at capture of Carlisle 30 December 1745 and imprisoned in London. Tried 18 July

1746 and sentenced to death. He appealed for mercy, but was sentenced to be transported. This sentence was also not carried out, and in August 1748 he appealed for release on the ground that confinement was having fatal effects. He was released. Pardoned 21 July 1748. *SHS.3.400.*

WILL, JANE or JEAN, from France. Lord John Drummond's Regiment. Imprisoned Perth 18 February 1746. "Taken north by the Duke of Cumberland's army." It is not known whether he was treated as a French prisoner of war. *SHS.3.402, MR63.*

WILLIAM, JOHN, sailor from Chester, Fitzjames' Horse French Service. Taken and pardoned. *MR38.*

WILLIAMS, HENRY, soldier, Lord John Drummond's French Royal Scots Cavalry. From Hereford. Taken Crieff, imprisoned 25 March 1746 Perth, 12 May 1746 Stirling Castle. "Soap boiler." Released under General Pardon, 1747. *MR.63, SHS.3.402.*

WILLIAMS, HENRY, French Picquet. Imprisoned 16 December 1745 Stirling Castle. Released. "Deserted from the rebels." *SHS.3.402.*

WILLIAMS, HENRY, Irish Piquets. Deserted. Taken 16 December 1745. Discharged. *MR138.*

WILLIAMS, JOHN, Fitzjames's Horse, sailor from Chester. Imprisoned 1 May 1746 Stirling Castle. Released under General Pardon, 1747.

WILLIAMS, OWEN, Manchester Regiment. From Wales. Taken at capture of Carlisle 30 December 1745. Nothing more known about him. *MR199, SHS.3.402.*

WILLIAMSON, JOHN, Manchester Regiment. From Ireland. Taken at capture of Carlisle 30 December 1745, imprisoned London. Turned King's Evidence. He was taken to London and was in custody of Carrington, the messenger, in June 1747 as a witness. Discharged. *MR199, SHS.3.402.*

WILLIAMSON, THOMAS, Manchester Regiment. From Manchester. Taken at capture of Carlisle 30 December 1745, imprisoned Lancaster Castle. Was tried at Carlisle, 19 September 1746 and acquitted on proving that he had surrendered by the appointed date. *SHS.3.404.*

WILLIAMSON, THOMAS, aged 24, from Edinburgh, Elcho's Life Guards. Imprisoned Inverness, September 1746 prison ship *Pamela*, Tilbury. "Clerk to Adam Fairholme. At Elgin he acted as clerk to patullo, the rebel Commissary General." Transported 31 March 1747 from London to Jamaica in *St George or Carteret*, arriving Jamaica 1747. *SHS.3.404, MR9, PRO.CO137.58, BHMS.85.*

WILLIAMSON, THOMAS, Manchester Regiment. From Manchester. Taken and acquitted. *MR199.*

WILLYSON, JOHN or JAMES, from Edinburgh, Duke of Perth's Regiment. Imprisoned 20 June 1746 Haddington, Edinburgh Royal Infirmary. Discharged 28 April 1747. Appealed on 27 December 1746 saying he had been pressed into rebel service but left and enlisted in the "Scots Royal," but when drunk made certain "unguarded exprisions" for which he was imprisoned. Evidence from William Begg and Charles Campbell, Excise Officers. *SHS.3.404, SHS.8.342.*

WILSON, ……., innkeeper from Edinburgh, Midlothian. Enlisted man for the Pretender's service. Whereabouts not known. *SHS.8.256.*

WILSON, DAVID, Berwick's French Service. Taken at sea, imprisoned Berwick. Discharged. *SHS.3.404.*

WILSON, JOHN, barber, Cannongate, Edinburgh. Carried arms in the rebel Life Guards. Whereabouts not known. Evidence from George Porteous, Excise Officer and Francis Montgomery, barber, Cannongate, Edinburgh. *SHS.8.258, SHS.8.340.*

WILSON, WILLIAM, turner from Edinburgh, Artillery. Evidence from David Morrison, brewer and Jonathan Davidson, wright, both in the Abbey. Imprisoned 30 December 1745 Carlisle, York Castle, London. Discharged. Taken at capture of Carlisle. Became King's Evidence, and was in custody of Carrington, the messenger, in June 1747. *SHS.3.406.*

WINRAM, JAMES, son to Mr Windrum of Eyemouth, from Abbayhill, South Leith, Midlothian. From Cannongate, Edinburgh. Carried arms in the Pretender's son's Life Guards. Whereabouts not known. Evidence from George Robertson, Ninian Trotter and Francis Pringle, Excise Officers. *SHS.8.258, SHS.8.340.*

WINSTANLEY, WILLIAM, Manchester Regiment. Weaver from Wigan. Captured near Carlisle. Imprisoned Carlisle and Whitehaven. Was tried and pleaded not guilty, but was convicted 22 September 1746. He was probably transported or he may have died. *MR199, SHS.3.406.*

WISE, NINIAN, attended his master in the rebellion. Whereabouts not known. *SHS.8.266.*

WISEMAN, JAMES, conveyed from Penrith to Brough, Westmoreland in the company of 19 other Jacobites. *CQS.354.*

WOOD, ANDREW, aged 21, from Glasgow, Captain, Roy Stuart's (Edinburgh) Regiment. Imprisoned 16 April 1746 Culloden, Inverness. In June 1746 boarded the prison ship *Thane of Fife*, London. Executed Kensington Common 28 November 1746. "Gentleman," also shown as "shoemaker." He appears to have joined the Prince in England. In the speech he made before his execution he says he was made a captain and "raised a company out of my own pocket." He was probably captured after Culloden and sent to London. Before his death he was received into the Church of England. He was stated to have made shoes for the Prince's men. He himself pleaded that he had saved nine men who had been captured by the Jacobite army, and this was sworn to by various persons before the Lord Provost of Glasgow. Evidence from James McKettrick, Excise Officer and his son, both Glasgow. *SHS.3.408, SHS.8.272, SHS.8.346, SHS.8.381, MR205.*

WOOD, SAMUEL, servant to Kilbrachmant, junior, Kilbrachmant, Fife. Attended his said master at Preston battle. Now at home. *SHS.8.260.*

WOODHOUSE, JEREMY, Fitzjames' French Service. From Norfolk. Deserter from Col Palquet's Regiment at Portmahon. Imprisoned 10 May 1746 Perth, 12 May 1746 Stirling Castle. Was probably handed over to the military authorities. *SHS.3.410, MR38.*

WORDIE, WILLIAM, merchant from Leven, Fife. Joined the rebel army before Preston in the Pretender's son's Life Guards. Whereabouts not known. *SHS.8.260.*

WRIGHT, DUNCAN, carrier from Doune, Stirlingshire. Evidence from Robert and John Mitchel, merchants in Doune and Marjory Paton, spouse to Robert Balfour there. *SHS.8.318.*

WRIGHT, DUNCAN, Roy Stewart's (Edinburgh) Regiment. Aged 40, farmer from Appin, Argyll. Taken and transported 31 March 1747 from London to Jamaica in *St George or Carteret*, arriving Jamaica 1747. *SHS.3.410, PRO.CO137.58, MR207.*

WRIGHT, JOHN, surgeon from Foodie, Dairsie parish, Fife. Joined the rebel army after the battle of Preston and carried arms with them. Whereabouts not known. Evidence from Robert Bell, merchant in Cupar, John Arnot, surgeon there, David Nicol, stabler there and Mr Halket, schoolmaster there, etc. *SHS.8.70, SHS.8.352.*

WRIGHT, ROBERT, from Edinburgh. Imprisoned 10 August 1746 Canongate, Carlisle. Escaped August 1747. "Gentleman." "A volunteer in the rebel service." Son of James Wright, Writer in Edinburgh, who had been out in the 1715. He was tried 19 September 1746 and sentenced to death, but recommended to mercy by the jury. In August 1747 he escaped from Carlisle along with William Sharp. Just previously the Privy Council had decided to pardon him on his giving security that he did not return to Scotland. *SHS.3.410, SHS.8.258.*

WYCE, NINIAN, gardener from Falkirk. Kilmarnock's Regiment. Imprisoned Kippin, 27 May 1746 Stirling Castle. Released under General Pardon, 1747. *SHS.3.410.*

WYER, or WYRE, DOMINIQUE, Lieutenant, French Royal Scots, French Service. Taken at sea *Prince Charles*,

Berwick. Pardoned on condition of permanent banishment 2 July 1747. *SHS.3.410.*

WYMES, DAVID, Lord Elcho. Eldest son of James, fourth Earl of Wemyss, was aged about 24 when he joined the Rebellion. He is thus referred to in the *Mercury* of 30 September 1745. "There is now forming and pretty well advanced a body of Horse Life-Guards for his royal highness the Prince, commanded by the Right Hon. The Lord Elcho; their uniform is blue trimmed with red, and laced waistcoats; they are to consist of four squadrons of gentlemen of character." In the *Scots Magazine* the troops commanded by Lord Elcho and Lord Kilmarnock are said to have numbered 160 men. After Culloden he escaped to the Continent, and, having been attainted, was debarred from the succession. On his death in 1787 his younger brother Francis became Earl of Wemyss. Was a Colonel of the rebel Life Guards during the whole rebellion. Now in France. *SHS.8.258, SHS.8.381.*

YOUNG, ALEXANDER, Berwick's French Regiment, Irish Piquets. Taken at Culloden 16 April 1746. There is no further reference to him. He may have died, or he may have been transferred to Berwick as a French prisoner. *MR138, SHS.3.412.*

YOUNG, CHARLES, French Service. Taken at sea, imprisoned Berwick, February 1746 Hull. Pardoned on enlistment in Brigadier Fowlkes' Regiment at Gibraltar 24 September 1746. *SHS.3.412.*

YOUNG, JOHN, from Edinburgh. Imprisoned Aberdeen. Discharged. "Confesses he served as a waggoner in the Rebels." *SHS.3.412.*

YOUNG, ROBERT, Physician from Tipperary, Irish Piquets. Imprisoned 11 May 1746 Perth, 12 May 1746 Stirling

Castle. His name appears in the Carlisle transportation lists in October 1746. Transported 1747. *MR136, SHS.3.412.*

www.ingramcontent.com/pod-product-compliance
Lightning Source LLC
Chambersburg PA
CBHW051634230426
43669CB00013B/2301